CHURCHILL'S CHALLENGES
~ 1918–1940 ~
VOLUME 1 OF 2
❖

OTHER BOOKS BY THE AUTHOR

The Race for the Atom Bomb
Churchill's Enemies
The Greatest Spy
The Passionate Spies
How Churchill Saved Civilization
Churchill the Young Warrior

PRAISE FOR JOHN HARTE
HOW CHURCHILL SAVED CIVILIZATION

"Harte minces no words in presenting Churchill as the central figure and driving force in the West's resistance to Nazi Germany – resistance that was by no means a given. Harte describes Churchill as unique in being alert to danger, perceptive in analyzing it, and decisive in responding to it. Churchill's failures and shortcomings were penumbras of his ability and insight. Nor, in the context of his times, was he a blinkered imperialist nor a destructive racist. Unabashed and unapologetic, this is a controversial and useful addition to the literature."

– Dennis Showalter, PhD, author of *Patton and Rommel, Hitler's Panzers.*

THE RACE FOR THE ATOM BOMB

"This is the detailed backstory of a covert race during World War II to build the world's first atomic bomb. Robert Oppenheimer, teamed with American and British physicists, toil in the New Mexico desert while the Soviet Union works to better their timeline. Journalist John Harte's detailed research provides an excellent resource for future historians who wish to understand the espionage, experiments, challenges, and conspiracies revolving around the first atomic weapon deployment in 1945."

– Stephen L. Moore, author of *Patton's Payback.*

CHURCHILL'S CHALLENGES

~ 1918–1940 ~

VOLUME 1 OF 2
❖

JOHN HARTE

Pen & Sword
MILITARY
AN IMPRINT OF PEN & SWORD BOOKS LTD.
YORKSHIRE - PHILADELPHIA

First published in Great Britain in 2024 by
PEN AND SWORD MILITARY
An imprint of
Pen & Sword Books Limited
Yorkshire – Philadelphia

Copyright © John Harte, 2024

ISBN 978 1 03610 036 0

The right of John Harte to be identified as Author of this work has been asserted by him in accordance with the Copyright, Designs and Patents Act 1988.

All rights reserved. No part of this book may be reproduced, stored in a retrieval system or transmitted, in any form or by any means, without the written permission of the author.

Typeset in Times New Roman 10/12 by
SJmagic DESIGN SERVICES, India.
Printed and bound in the UK by CPI Group (UK) Ltd.

Pen & Sword Books Limited incorporates the imprints of Atlas, Archaeology, Aviation, Discovery, Family History, Fiction, History, Maritime, Military, Military Classics, Politics, Select, Transport, True Crime, Air World, Frontline Publishing, Leo Cooper, Remember When, Seaforth Publishing, The Praetorian Press, Wharncliffe Local History, Wharncliffe Transport, Wharncliffe True Crime and White Owl.

For a complete list of Pen & Sword titles please contact
PEN & SWORD BOOKS LIMITED
George House, Units 12 & 13, Beevor Street, Off Pontefract Road,
Barnsley, South Yorkshire, S71 1HN, England
E-mail: enquiries@pen-and-sword.co.uk
Website: www.pen-and-sword.co.uk

or

PEN AND SWORD BOOKS
1950 Lawrence Rd, Havertown, PA 19083, USA
E-mail: uspen-and-sword@casematepublishers.com
Website: www.penandswordbooks.com

Contents

Preface		vii
Introduction		x

I: THE MIDDLE EAST CRISIS

Chapter 1	Clementine (1908)	2
Chapter 2	Pressures of Events (1919)	7
Chapter 3	The World Crisis	15
Chapter 4	The Bolshevik Power-Grab	19
Chapter 5	The Russian Civil War (1920)	23
Chapter 6	The Warlords	27
Chapter 7	Justice for All	31
Chapter 8	The Soul of Nations	35
Chapter 9	Churchill's Obsession (1920)	40
Chapter 10	The Middle East Upheaval (1921)	45
Chapter 11	The Kingmakers (1921–22)	52
Chapter 12	Feisal's Reward	59
Chapter 13	Gertrude of Arabia (1921–22)	66
Chapter 14	Churchill's Middle East Ambition (1921–23)	76

II: THE RUSSIAN CRISIS

Chapter 15	The Enemy on the Left (1920–23)	84
Chapter 16	Realities and Illusions	90
Chapter 17	Political Rivals	96
Chapter 18	The Most Terrible Event (1922–23)	100
Chapter 19	Troublemakers (1923)	110
Chapter 20	Chartwell	114
Chapter 21	Social Reengineering	120

III: BAD NEWS FROM GERMANY

Chapter 22	Hunting Down the Idle Rich (1924)	125
Chapter 23	Churchill in the Roaring Twenties	129
Chapter 24	A Brilliant Creature	129

CHURCHILL'S CHALLENGES, 1918–1940

Chapter 25	Bad News from Germany	133
Chapter 26	Collective Security (1925)	138
Chapter 27	A Liberal at Heart	144
Chapter 28	Winston, a Star Turn (1925–26)	149
Chapter 29	The Enemy on the Right	154
Chapter 30	Balancing the Budget (1925–26)	158
Chapter 31	Living Space	162
Chapter 32	Consolidating Power (1926–27)	165
Chapter 33	Clash of Cultures	171
Notes		176
Index		189

Dates beside chapter headings are intended only as guidelines, which cannot be completely accurate in a tapestry of moving events.

Author's Note

This account of Winston Churchill's life and times during the period between two World Wars (1918-1940) is described in two volumes entitled *Churchill's Challenges: 1918-1927*, and *Churchill's Enemies: 1927-1940*. The first title represents Part 1 of the narrative, while the second title forms Part 2. Part 2 will be published later in the year. It describes what led to World War 2 and the Holocaust.

Preface

Young Winston Churchill freely admitted that he was devoured by egotism. Nevertheless, he adored his beautiful American mother Jennie, and possessed an enduring love for Clementine, the adopted daughter of Colonel Henry Hozier, whom he married. His gifts and flaws as an individual with endless drive and initiative, as a gallant soldier, a freelance war correspondent without fear or favour, and as a Member of Parliament and a Cabinet minister, are described against a background of one world crisis after another. His positive and pro-active attitude towards all problems was motivated by his and Clementine's love of Great Britain.

He was Secretary for War, and became Home Secretary when the communist revolution in October 1917 and civil war (1920-1923) spilled over Soviet Russia's borders, and there were threats of revolution in England. He was appointed Colonial Secretary when the entire Middle East was in peril. The Nazis were taking over Germany when he was out of office in a government reshuffle and was almost helpless to act. And the women in Winston's life – including his old girlfriend Violet Asquith, daughter of the Prime Minister – were united by a common purpose to make Winston Prime Minister. It was his first major challenge, from which other momentous challenges would follow. He was thrown into all sorts of other national crises with their own particular problems when he rose in stature from Member of Parliament to being appointed as a Minister of the Crown.

This is the author's fourth book about Winston Churchill. It is a true story. All the characters in it are historic figures. And yet, at the foundation of most cultures there has been a temptation to invent fictional legends of a heroic character compelled to undertake demanding challenges against heavy odds. All have a similarity that has come to symbolise the individual story of each of us as we face our own challenges and respond in ways that become milestones in our passage from birth to death.

Perhaps the most enduring legend describes the adventures of Odysseus, which is thought to have been written by a blind poet named Homer. Biblical heroes abound in the Old Testament, like the shepherd boy David defeating the giant Goliath. All are stories of how a hero arises at a crucial moment to overcome one challenge after another and triumph as a consequence of his or her courage and wisdom or cunning. The legend of St George killing an evil dragon is commemorated in several different countries. Many are symbolic works of fiction that form the seeds of a nation's culture or its mission. The difference is that Winston Churchill's odyssey is true and part of Great Britain's more modern and factual history, as opposed to a historical romance.

CHURCHILL'S CHALLENGES, 1918–1940

Churchill was confronted by a considerable number and variety of dramatic challenges soon after the post-war Peace Conference at Versailles in 1918. One was to write an enduring account of the first industrialised war, which he called *The World Crisis*. If we search through all the hurdles he had to overcome during the first half of his career, to separate his major challenges from more typical and minor ones, we immediately find three that had global consequences, before being reminded of two others that were more localised but lingered in the national agenda for over a century.

When he was Secretary for War and Air in Prime Minister Lloyd George's post-war coalition government, Churchill attempted to prevent communism from spilling over the Soviet Russian border to contaminate the British Isles and cause a revolution that had been eagerly encouraged by Marx and Engels. Lenin had become firmly entrenched in power when Trotsky's brutal Red Army won major victories over the patriotic Imperial Russian army in the civil war. At the same time, Secret Police Chief Felix Dzerzhinsky led the CHEKA in a ruthless campaign of terror to subdue all internal opposition. That was when Churchill's battle against the Soviet Russian regime began. It would continue to his death.

As Secretary of State for the Colonies in 1921–22, his next great challenge was to fill the leadership vacuum in the Middle East after Britain had defeated the Turkish Empire in 1918. It required redrawing national frontiers and crowning two Arab kings; Feisal and Abdullah, of Iraq and Transjordan. King Ibn Saud of Saudi Arabia crowned himself after defeating his enemies in battle with the help of British gold and weaponry, and the Secret Intelligence Service. Churchill achieved the goals set for him by Prime Minister David Lloyd George at a time when there was still a threat of Soviet Russia invading the Middle East and of the Turkish Army returning to fill the vacuum before Britain could achieve its mandate of self-determination according to the terms of the League of Nations.[1]

Churchill's third great challenge in a row was to resist threats from Nazi Germany to invade the whole of Europe. That episode is described in Volume 2, entitled *Churchill's Enemies*. It would represent the greatest challenge of his career, because he would have to be appointed Prime Minister to achieve it.

Perhaps more difficult for a new generation to remember were the years that Churchill spent pacifying Indian nationalists to prevent Muslims and Hindus from slaughtering each other, and dissuading Hindu nationalists from encouraging the carnage. He was drawn into a similar situation in Ireland between Catholics and Protestants.

Britain's greatest national hero has almost become a figure of legend as new and younger generations apparently have no idea who he was. In a recent poll, 20 per cent of respondents thought Churchill was a fictional figure in a strip cartoon.[2]

Fictions invented about his life on cinema and TV screens have not helped his image. Nor have the continual lies invented by his three main adversaries to tarnish his reputation: Marxists, Fascists, and Islamist fanatics. Truth is not only stranger than those fictions, but far more multi-layered and, of course, authentic. This description of the first half of Winston's career is an attempt to pin down the

PREFACE

real man on the following pages by describing his personality and attributes, and his odyssey. Even so, there is no way to avoid the magnitude of his heroic status that set him apart from everyone else. The significance of Churchill's odyssey was that it resulted in his status as a legendary figure pitting his wits against injustices and the forces of evil. That future situation did not escape Professor John Lukacs when he wrote his *Four Days in London: May 1940*. He described the newly appointed Prime Minister Churchill as representing the forces of light in a personal duel against Hitler, who represented the forces of darkness.

Far more readers today choose novels to read rather than non-fiction. Whether they are romances, fantasies, science fiction, or contrived crime stories, they are popular because each tells the same story of challenges that have to be overcome by a hero or a heroine. The familiarity of those stories adds to the reader's ability to identify with the main protagonist, because the events in their journeys reveal what it is to be human.

Hero myths have persisted over the centuries. According to the theories of psychologist Otto Rank, myths expand universal themes. His studies of mythical heroes reveal the hero to be the embodiment of our individual struggle for independence and the development of our individuality.[3] Young Winston differed in that he was a hero who continually overcame real historic challenges on a similar monumental scale as those myths portray. But Winston Churchill – for all his extraordinary talents – was no myth. He retained his authenticity throughout his life as a highly moral individual dedicated to common decency. It was not without careful thought that George Orwell named the hero of his famous novel, *Nineteen Eighty-Four,* after Winston, as the moral conscience of the world in his confrontations with the sadistic 'Big Brother' who watched everyone from the other side of the TV screen.

Winston Churchill was a sentimental and romantic individual who frequently wept at the miseries and cruelties the world imposed on humanity. He was also practical and realistic, like most legendary heroes, and courageous enough to take enormous risks to overcome considerable dangers. He survived at least twenty assassination attempts by gunmen from the IRA, Indian nationalists, Arab fanatics, and German Nazis, which were often thwarted by his plainclothes bodyguard from Scotland Yard.

Introduction

This narrative combines a social and cultural history of the times with an unusual biography of Winston Churchill, to reveal how he responded to his society and time and how he influenced it.

In his 1929 memoir, he wrote, 'When I survey this work as a whole, I find I have drawn a picture of a vanished age. The character of society, the foundations of politics, the methods of war, the outlook of youth, are all changed …'

His own character would be transformed just as dramatically from the eager and ambitious youth with an impish sense of humour that he liked to recall while writing his memoir of the early years that shaped him, to the shrewd and successful politician he had already become. Even more important to the following description of his endeavours is that both he and the world in which he grew up would become so altered since his death in 1965 that it is almost unrecognisable to those who view it from the perspective of the twenty-first century. All the sweeping changes that took place have left today's generation with a sense of dislocation and disappointment when they attempt to understand what life was like in Churchill's time before, during, and after the Second World War. Most are unable to evaluate other people's attitudes or virtues, or his particular world view, since they are now shared by so few people in this century.

Journalists and film-makers in particular tend to rearrange the past to suit the wishful thinking of today's readers and audiences. Most choices made by cinema-goers and TV addicts reveal that the greater majority want to escape from reality into impossible fantasies. They want to imagine history like a historical romance instead of how it really was. Consequently, they are unaware of the lessons and warning signals that are lost to them because of their blind inventions and rearrangements.

Hopefully, this account of the first half of Winston Churchill's life will help readers to focus more sharply on how the world developed as a consequence of his influence in the ministerial positions he filled. Similarly, the changes in Churchill came about as a consequence of his experiences of the changing world in all its richness, and its descriptions by other great writers and leaders who lived before him. Later impatient young generations experienced none of it. Nor did many realise how history could enrich their lives. Moreover, in understanding – or failing to understand – what drove Winston Churchill, they cannot conceive that his entire life was deeply involved in solving one bleak problem after another in a cynical and perilous world. His primary motivation was always to protect the British Isles from its adversaries.

INTRODUCTION

In attempting to describe what that far-off world was really like, my own panoramic views of events benefited from being born in 1925 when much of what he saw was happening around me, too.

Anyone growing up with a sharply inquiring mind at that time would soon have discovered that historians, economists, journalists and politicians, were still perplexed at what had caused the First World War. They had plenty of theories, but their evidence was uncertain and inconclusive. The most likely cause was problematic, because it amounted to a deluded German state of mind that feared its country might be encircled by France, Russia, and a British army, although there was no evidence for it. I sought to untangle that puzzle at the same time as I observed the postwar rise to power of the Nazi Party in Germany and the menacing military buildup to World War 2. It would take Winston Churchill to write several volumes between 1923 and 1931 about the crisis that had caused the war and all its irrationalities, as well as its brutalities – such as the cost to kill every German soldier was the lives of two or three Allied infantrymen.[1]

Writing about critical episodes in history that one has lived through is vastly different from a detached account written long after the events by an academic who cannot feel or know the attitudes or customs of those times, or the nuances that separate people today from their fathers and grandmothers. Having been there enabled me to convey the realities of the times to anyone who cares to read and think about Winston Churchill, his society, and the national and global challenges that were thrust on him in great rapidity because of the variety of problems he faced in the very different ministerial positions he held.

This is the story of a unique leader whose character and skills were so exceptional that it is useless to seek comparisons. The Duke of Wellington, Napoleon, Alexander the Great, even Churchill's distinguished ancestor the 1st Duke of Marlborough, were unique. So was Winston Churchill. He knew from the earliest age that he was destined to lead the nation he loved and admired. Few people today would have the self-confidence or audacity to dream of such a future. How did he manage to achieve all he did? And from where and what did he acquire the sheer impudence to feel entitled to the privileges of high office?

Churchill grew up in the Victorian era, when everything in Britain appeared to have been carved in stone for eternity. Everyone knew how to behave in their particular station. Queen Victoria and her Prince Consort proclaimed with confidence that this was how life should be lived, how people should behave according to the highest standards in the world. Winston had watched his country transformed from a rural and agricultural society into an industrial one, where country squires and their wives, and villagers, no longer travelled long distances on foot, or longer journeys on horseback, and even longer ones by stagecoach, as a consequence of the new network of iron bridges and railways that stretched up and across the British Isles.

City folk took the train into the countryside for the first time out of curiosity, to see how the other half had lived their entire lives in tiny villages or hamlets in previously remote rural areas and green valleys. We cannot imagine the culture shock when very different people confronted each other for the first time. Even romantic novelist Thomas Hardy, who chose to write about rural life in the nineteenth century, could not conceive that moment, or he would have described the confrontation in one of his novels. Industrialisation changed everything.

If the country people felt less sure of themselves after contact with city folk arriving as tourists to patronise them, the Victorians in their stovepipe hats, with their ladies in crinolines, were convinced they were the masters and mistresses, not only of their own personal realms of influence, but of the known world. Winston inherited that supreme self-confidence of the Victorian age, with the audacity of its explorers and pioneers of flight and speed, and the study of the human mind. All conceived and brought about the modern age.

Winston Churchill is generally known today as a dedicated and visionary statesman, orator, Member of Parliament, Prime Minister, fine author and, in particular, the leader of the victorious Allies who defeated the biggest, best-trained and equipped, and most efficient armies in the Second World War. Since his earliest desire was to lead Great Britain and protect the British Isles, that audacious motivation seems to have been passed on to him as a historic prerogative of the previous leading families.

Most nations are desperate for dynamic leaders today, and here was a man who knew from the earliest age that he was destined to lead the nation he loved and of which he was proud. If we respect successful and charismatic leaders and want to know how they are shaped, we need answers to those critical questions about how young Winston leapt from being a junior army officer at the age of twenty to a successful journalist and a Member of Parliament with several important ministerial portfolios.

The purpose of writing this story of young Winston and the history of his time between the end of the First World War and the beginning of the next, is to prevent it from being forgotten, or distorted beyond the clearly defined reality of those desperate and tragic years. But it has become distorted by the biggest influence on the largest audiences, which are commercial TV and cinema depictions whose main goal was to amuse a public comprised largely of teenagers. While it was commendable to entertain mass audiences, the lure of box office revenues evidently enticed producers and script writers to follow the lead of Hollywood's successful formula for fiction, instead of attempting to mirror the reality of the world.

Despite that, most readers are likely to know that Churchill achieved his aims and ambitions against personal and political resistance by his opponents, and threats of disorder from the discontented classes and subversives who planned to seize Europe, Great Britain, and the world.

The tapestry of events in the grim twentieth century reveals a complacent and defensive political atmosphere in Britain and America after the First World War, because most people were tired of war and confused by a new and dire situation that confronted them. After a brief sigh of relief at being on the winning side, they wanted to return to living a normal life.

The losing side faced a very different problem – chaos and a gathering whirlwind on the continent of Europe, which provided opportunities for popular dictators to

INTRODUCTION

take control of leaderless and divided nations by promising to impose law and order by force. The goal of the extreme political left and the extreme right was to isolate Great Britain by destroying its allies, then seek to acquire or destroy the British Empire. It is astonishing what envy and jealousy empires created. A great many nations envied Britain's success and wanted empires themselves.

Churchill anticipated those events from his profound knowledge of history. When undertaking his responsibilities as Home Secretary at the age of thirty-six in 1910, he experienced at first-hand the effectiveness of subversives of all types who aimed to undermine Great Britain from the inside and destroy its social and political foundations. He also experienced the rising mood of aggression on the continent of Europe through personal contacts with its ambitious leaders.

The following true acount is intended to describe and preserve Churchill's unique and extraordinary personal attributes and attitudes; also his thoughts and actions and character, as they really were, and to correct the erroneous caricatures that frequently distorted his life.

If we wish to understand how Winston Churchill influenced and even dominated our history during his lifetime, we have to examine the scrawny little twenty-year-old second lieutenant who suddenly realised that he needed to educate himself for the tasks he envisioned ahead of him. We also need to keep in mind that young Winston was the embodiment of the older statesman who would eventually become what Professor John Lukacs called 'the incarnation of the reaction to Hitler, the incarnation of the resistance of an old world, of old freedoms, of old standards ...'

> His aim was to galvanize the free world against a brutal and alarmingly efficient military force which was obsessed with delusions of conquest or death, and highly motivated, trained and armed to slaughter all opposition. And yet, Churchill was 'Shunned and distrusted by the majority of his own political party, the ruling party in Britain ... people in Britain thought Churchill to be impulsive, erratic, wordy, unduly combative, a maverick, perhaps a publicity hound, in one word, unsteady ...'[2] His telephone calls were tapped by the prime minister's lackeys as a consequence.[3]

When reflecting on young Winston's past and the future Prime Minister and world leader he would become, we find ourselves in a 'then and now' situation.

Where and when did the seeds of global greatness ripen and open up to reveal the nature of the man inside? It is a puzzle. Was it in the heart and mind of the as-yet unformed junior army officer when he realised he had never been properly educated at his prep school or at Harrow, and he had better do something about educating himself?

'As with most great historians, Churchill was self-taught and self-trained. Certainly he had no formal education for a career as historian – indeed it is accurate to say that he had no formal education for anything except soldiering.'[4]

Winston complained in his memoir of his early years at how disappointed he had been with the poor teaching at his prep school and Harrow, where – like most other British public schools at that time and later – they were more intent on thrashing little boys in their care than educating them. Since they could not get him to Oxford, he would have to teach himself. He would also have to make his own way in life because his widowed mother Jennie, whom he adored, was a beautiful and vain spendthrift who soon ran out of her inheritance from Lord Randolph Churchill's estate.

There he was, grooming or saddling his horse in the stables at Sandhurst Military Academy, while brooding on the realisation that he had got himself into a rut that he saw as a dead end. Somehow he had to take charge of his life.

'All through the long, glistening, middle hours of the Indian day,' he wrote, 'from when we quitted stables to when the evening shadows proclaimed the hour of Polo, I devoured Gibbon.' He also studied other famous historians like Macaulay and Lecky, Plato and Aristotle. He approached *The Rise and Fall of the Roman Empire* 'with an empty, hungry mind ...'

Reading history left its mark on him forever. Among the history books he devoured so eagerly was Wynwood Reade's *The Martyrdom of Man*. Its importance in moulding his attitudes towards individuals and nations – whom he would view with compassion because of their helplessness in the face of world affairs – and also towards the world in which civilisations rose and fell, appears to have been lost to most historians. What was the cause of the collapse of empires for which there had been no remedy? He discovered there were many; like the plague that spread across Ancient Greece at its most heroic moment under the leadership of Pericles, causing it to be overrun by Roman legions. Rome's end too was precipitated by a bacterial or viral infection, but civil war appeared to be the most destructive cause of its collapse.

Churchill began to realise the causes of military or cultural failures that crippled civilisations like his own. Sometimes it was an irrational leader or a mindless one, military rebellions or uprisings, inept administrators who held back progress, and might even have caused entire nations to starve to death, or crumble into chaos and vanish from history.

Instead of being disheartened by the idea that nothing lasts whatever you do to hold on to it – so that nothing mattered – Winston's mind was engaged by the strengths and weaknesses of human nature and different cultures and different types of leaders who had to overcome all the problems of impermanence by exchanging ideas, as well as the flows of goods and services in the marketplace. It was a widely read and influential book that, on the other hand, encouraged ambitious predators like Cecil Rhodes to steal other people's land in Africa.

Ancestral Voices

A transformation from soldier to politician came about as Winston reshaped his thinking by studying those crucial books that he had asked his mother to send him. The wish to improve himself had very likely been initiated by vivid memories of growing up in the ancestral mansion of the 1st Duke of Marlborough, where he had played on the floor with hundreds of little lead soldiers as a child, and was constantly reminded of history by the paintings and books about his illustrious ancestor, General John Churchill.

INTRODUCTION

Blenheim Palace had been a gift from Queen Anne and a thankful nation for saving Great Britain from defeat when his ancestor had been Commander in Chief of the English forces in the War of Spanish Succession. John Churchill had been the greatest general in the whole of Britain's history. He had never lost a single battle. Winston was justifiably proud to have descended from a military leader who had achieved victory over a long line of French field marshals at the Battles of Blenheim, Ramillies, Oudenarde and Malplaquet. Not only was John Churchill Britain's greatest general, but also an astute politician. His cavalry charge with 50,000 horsemen at the Battle of Ramillies had changed the power structure in Europe from the tyranny of the 'Sun King', Louis XIV, to leadership by Great Britain.

Reading with awe his ancestor's exploits was a stimulus to young Winston's romantic nature. It heartened him, because as he wrote each volume of his book about his ancestor in the 1920s and '30s, he was constantly reminded of the parallel between what had occurred then and what was happening now with the rise of another tyrant who wanted to dominate Britain, Europe, and the world. It is even possible that Churchill saw how to defeat Nazi Germany while he researched history and wrote *Marlborough, His Life and Times* during the rise of Hitler and his Nazi Party.

John Churchill had received his first commission as colonel in 1711. The family history was preserved in a splendid library at Blenheim Palace, which young Winston would use for his own research in 1929 when ancestral voices would urge him to research and write a biography of his brilliant and colourful ancestor. It would take him ten years, and it was published when Winston Churchill was fifty-nine years old. What took him so long would be revealed in four huge volumes in 1934, 1936 and 1938. The first volume consists of 557 pages of vivid historical accounts and commentaries on Marlborough's character and attributes, which could not help but fascinate readers. Winston appears to have been mesmerised into identifying himself closely with Marlborough.

His map of Europe showed his intimacy with the locations of all the important battles and peace treaties. Winston differed from most of his English contemporaries in knowing Europe intimately, whereas most British politicians in Churchill's time did not. Europe was a nuisance to Great Britain. Most British politicians were not soldiers, whereas Winston – even when young – possessed what the great military strategist von Clausewitz called 'a sense of location', with which an experienced general can examine the terrain before battle and visualise the impending clash of arms taking place on the soil, through the woods, across the river, or in the marshland, and foresee the ideal battlefield for his intended victory.

In the 1968 introduction to *Marlborough,* American historian Henry Steele Commager described Winston Churchill as 'beyond all doubt, that statesman who became the greatest historian, and that historian who became the greatest statesman, in the long annals of England'. And he added, 'Doubtless Churchill preferred making history to writing it.'

Winston planned to write his father's biography when he was still that skinny little soldier who had written little else but first-hand accounts of battles. He had been only twenty when his father, Lord Randolph, had died horribly, strapped in a straitjacket, in 1895. *Lord Randolph Churchill* was published in two volumes in 1906.

In spite of young Winston having been treated so abominably by his arrogant and pompous father, he understood Lord Randolph's potential greatness and his tragic failure. Failure was not an option for Winston and never would be. He possessed an extraordinary sense of loyalty to his father, to his ancestor, to Great Britain and the Empire; to the working classes in Britain, and even to the comfortably-off middle classes; but not to the insular and separate English upper crust of the time. It was why he fell out with the Conservative Party who represented them. He was a rebel, and had been one from as far back as his prep school days.

Churchill would write thirty-two volumes of history and biography, and twenty volumes of his speeches. The first twelve reveal his character and outlook during the early stages of his life. What he aspired to in his idealistic historical novel *Savrola* in 1899, he would attempt to become when appointed Undersecretary of State for the Colonies in the Liberal government in 1905.

Young Winston was never too shy to offer advice to Prime Ministers when off the battlefield. The first of his published books when a seasoned officer in the army at the age of twenty-four was aimed at doing exactly that. The final book on that shortlist describes the stepping stones that led up to the Second World War, where this narrative ends.

1898: *The Story of the Malakand Field Force.* (Longmans Green, London).
1899: *The River War.* (Longmans Green, London).
1899: *Savrola.* (Longmans Green, New York).
1900: *London to Ladysmith via Pretoria.* (Longmans Green, London).
1900: *Ian Hamilton's March.* (Longmans Green, London).
1906. *Lord Randolph Churchill* (Macmillan, London).
1908: *My African Journey.* (Hodder and Stoughton, London).
1923–31: *The World Crisis.* (In five volumes. Scibner, New York).

Those books represented his literary output before the 1929 crash of the New York Stock Exchange, in which he lost all his savings. From then on, his added incentive for writing new books of history was to shore up his finances to stave off bankruptcy. He would write four more books before the Second World War diverted all his time and skills to defeating Nazi Germany. After the war was over, 'Churchill deeply wished to be remembered as a peacemaker ...'[5] *

Churchill the Politician

Although young Winston was depicted by the Conservative Party as a political turncoat who betrayed his class, he was more interested in individuals than people who slavishly followed a doctrine of one political party, and did not attach much

---

* He would be nominated as one of the candidates for the Nobel Peace Prize in 1945, but it would go to American Secretary of State Cordell Hull instead.

INTRODUCTION

importance to social class – whereas the Conservatives represented the upper crust. Winston thought like an individual who was mindful of his own experiences and those of the greatest leaders. He scorned insincerity and mediocrity.

He knew how misleadingly vague and deceptive political labels were, and how meaningless were personal political attachments and prejudices. He appears not to have noticed if people's skins were coloured or not. He was only interested in people who managed to achieve success by merit. He would join any political party that could get his reforms passed by Parliament. If he was fixated on any ideology at all it was what he called English Democracy.

Although his first offer of a seat in the House of Commons came from the Conservatives, he soon realised that they only represented the ruling class at that time, and moved swiftly to the Liberal benches instead. When English Liberalism declined as an influential force, he felt obliged to serve a more liberal and enlightened Conservative Party. And yet, he would be able to work in a professional relationship and a genuine personal friendship with the leader of the Labour Party in the wartime coalition in 1940. He knew he could rely on Clement Attlee as his deputy, largely because Churchill sympathised with many of the more humane beliefs of people like Attlee, who possessed a genuine social conscience, as he himself did. Attlee respected and deferred to him.

He knew that human nature oscillated from authoritarianism to liberty and back again, and wrote of Burke the philosopher and politician: 'On the one hand he is revealed as a foremost apostle of Liberty, on the other as the redoubtable champion of Authority.'

But, 'His soul revolted against tyranny, whether it appeared in the aspect of a domineering Monarch and a corrupt Court and Parliamentary system, or whether … it towered up against him in the dictation of a brutal mob and wicked sect. No one can read the Burke of Liberty and the Burke of Authority without feeling that here was the same man pursuing the same ends, seeking the same ideals of society and Government, and defending them from assaults, now from one perspective, now from the other.'[6]

The same thing could be said of Winston Churchill. He did whatever he could to find opportunities for peace and solve problems without deferring to party dogma. He was always his own man.

Tired Old Men

Although still a young man in his thirties during subsequent episodes in his life, young Winston would become the victorious opponent of Hitler as a consequence of his experiences as a soldier and a politician during his formative years.

In his first volume of *The World Crisis*, published in 1923, he pointed out how it was felt that the British Empire had reached a peak of confidence and prosperity in 'the palmy days' of Queen Victoria's reign, when Britain, the inventor of the Industrial Revolution, was still its main beneficiary. To Britons, it looked like 'the end of the story' of its centuries of struggle for wealth and power. It had won the race against all other nations. How much further could any civilised nation go with its standards of material comfort, education, science and industry, and health? Most importantly, England was no longer only for the very few who were at the top of the social and economic pyramid, as most civilisations had been until then.[7]

Nevertheless, just as with the Roman Empire at the peak of its power, there were always the evil eyes of envy from other nations who wanted a share of the wealth, and were determined to obtain it by coercion or force. 'Man is a wolf to man' when competing for resources or power.[8]

Upholding liberty and parliamentary democracy against those wolves forming themselves into packs on the continent of Europe in the 1920s and '30s, was what Winston Churchill described as the weakest governments in Britain's history. Prime Ministers Ramsay MacDonald and Stanley Baldwin had no idea what they were destined to face, and were completely unprepared for what was about to happen.

Mussolini observed that Britain's leaders were not the same men who had made the British Empire – just the last in a line of tired old men whose virility was hopelessly sapped. France was defeatist before the French even began to defend themselves against their enemies. It was an opportunity for their adversaries to unite and become even more powerful. Italy and Soviet Russia allied themselves to Germany instead of to Great Britain. Although Germany was powerful on its own and did not need allies, Britain was too small and powerless to stand alone. Stalin lost confidence in the British because of their hesitant leaders who were out of touch with reality at a time of world crisis.

Britons had previously been pressed to involve themselves in bloody and irrational conflicts in Europe on three occasions since the reign of Queen Elizabeth I, each time on their own (except for the Battle of Waterloo) against far more powerful enemies. Britain had achieved victory each time after the most ruinous engagements. How many more times must Britain spend its manpower, its finances, and its weaponry, to save Europe? It was inconceivable that a fourth occasion would arise, but it did; this time to defend freedom in Europe against the German Kaiser's enlarged army and modernised fleet of warships.

The Industrial Revolution

Germany and Japan copied the English Industrial Revolution to concentrate their production on arming their military and naval forces, while Britain and the United States had focused on raising the living standards of their populations by producing industrial and consumer goods and raising more of the working classes into the comfortable middle classes. By focusing on the well-being of their people, they had allowed the Kaiser's Germany to recruit, arm and train the most powerful military and naval forces on the continent of Europe. Industrial assembly lines had developed a life of their own in producing more and more weapons of greater

INTRODUCTION

and greater powers of destruction in an arms race between nations to achieve naval superiority and, ultimately, even dominate the skies.

'Every morning when the world woke up, some new machinery had started running. Every night while the world had supper, it was running still. It ran on while all men slept.'[9]

Although the troops marched to their deaths with exemplary dignity and courage, what the government and the military had not envisaged was the extraordinary growth of Germany's population. It was now double the size of Britain's. Each generation of its soldiers could easily be replaced in the convulsions of the battlefields by even more troops who went bravely to their deaths until 1918.

Unfortunately, as Churchill would write, 'There is always more error than design in human affairs.'[10] An industrial war was something new and without precedence. And nothing went right from the beginning.

Such flaws and errors persisted not only in Great Britain, but also in France, Russia, the Austro-Hungarian Empire, and particularly in Germany. So that their investments in military materials and resources prior to the Great War allowed the general standard of living of Britain's population to rise above any other economy in Europe. The choice had been whether to use funds from the Treasury to raise living standards or raise armed forces to protect the British Isles. While Britain chose the former option, its enemies chose the latter.

Young Winston Churchill knew most of the political, diplomatic, and military leading players on the international scene personally. He had attended German military manoeuvres as an observer in 1906, when he was a young officer of thirty-two in the Territorial Army. He found the Prussians were still old-fashioned. But the enormous growth of German industries like Krupp would very soon transform the pageantry on horseback into a huge and relentless mechanised killing machine.

Glancing back fourteen years later, he would write; 'Ah! Foolish-diligent Germans, working so hard, thinking so deeply, marching and counter-marching on the parade grounds of the Fatherland, poring over long calculations, fuming in new-found prosperity, discontented amid the splendour of mundane success, how many bulwarks to your peace and glory did you not, with your own hands, successively tear down!'[11]

Britain's navy was critically important to the British Isles, since the very reason for Britain's need to 'rule the waves', and the importance of keeping its fleet competitive and dominant, was to connect an overseas empire containing 23 per cent of the world population.[12] Battleships could be sent to any trouble spot on the globe. Not only could they land fighting marines, but also bring much-needed supplies, or escort merchant ships that brought essential goods to its colonies. Their primary importance was to protect the British Isles from attack or invasion, and prevent Britain from being blockaded by enemies who might cut off its food supplies and other essential resources. It was therefore necessary to know the intentions of the enemy beforehand.

There was also the matter of trade, which seafaring captains were well aware of even before Admiral Nelson. At the time of Queen Elizabeth I, Sir Walter

Raleigh had proclaimed, 'Whosoever commands the sea, commands the trade, whosoever commands the trade of the world, commands the riches of the world – and consequently, the world itself.'

Churchill was in charge of Britain's naval affairs as First Lord of the Admiralty at the end of August 1914, when a German light cruiser named *Magdeburg* was wrecked in the Baltic Sea. The Russians managed to pick up the body of a drowned German officer soon afterwards. Clutched in his rigid arms were 'the cipher and signed books of the German Navy and the minutely squared maps of the North Sea and the Heligoland Bight'.

An Imperial Russian Naval Attaché visited Winston Churchill about a week later, on 6 September. He explained that he had been informed of the situation by Petrograd. Russia's Admiralty had managed to decode parts of German naval messages by using the cipher and signal books. As Britain's ally, they felt that the British Admiralty should have these sea-stained and priceless books and charts.

Analysis and study of Germany's wireless, and translation of its messages, were placed in the hands of Britain's Director of Naval Intelligence, Sir Alfred Ewing. It took until the beginning of November to make sense of portions of some of the messages. A careful collection of some of those scraps produced a body of information that revealed the enemy's plans 'with a fair degree of accuracy'.[13]

British Intelligence had already begun setting up directional wireless stations in the previous month. 'Our Intelligence service,' wrote Churchill, 'has won and deserved world-wide fame. More than perhaps any other Power, we were successful in the war in penetrating the intentions of the enemy. Again and again the forecasts both of the military and the Naval Intelligence Staffs were vindicated to the wonder of friends and the chagrin of foes.'

Churchill was justified in boasting about Britain's Secret Intelligence Service and its agents, since he'd had a hand in inventing and developing the SIS when he had been Home Secretary in 1911, and was closely in touch with it. He used the intelligence reports of its agents more than any other minister of the Crown, since he understood their value in predicting enemy intentions. In general, however, he was circumspect in wrapping most of their activities and his close connection with them in mystery, in order to continue to deceive Britain's enemies, both within the British Isles and overseas.

This deception by Germany would make him particularly aware of how vulnerable the coastal towns of the British Isles were to any enemy on the far side of the English Channel – particularly when Germany widened and deepened the Kiel Canal to provide an outlet into the North Sea for the Kaiser's modern navy, making all of Britain's east coast vulnerable to attacks.

Enemies Within and Without

Churchill was curious to know the answer to a particular question when he was responsible for the security of the realm against subversives, like the Irish Fenian forerunners of the IRA, anarchists from Poland and Italy, and Spain, and Russian Bolsheviks, members of Tsarist Russia's secret police (the *Okhrana*), and socialists

INTRODUCTION

risking destroying Britain's economy by launching unreasonable strikes that created mass unemployment. The puzzling question that had previously occupied the ancient world, as well as Machiavelli in the Italian Renaissance, and intelligence services right up to the present time was: 'What makes people, whether teachers or ordinary citizens, act in ways that corrupt the political orders they inhabit?'[14]

Churchill explained that the worst difficulties did not come from without but from within: not from wage-earners or home-owners, but from 'a peculiar type of brainy people always found in our country, who, if they add something to its culture, take much from its strength'.[15] He claimed that they followed defeatist doctrines that tainted and weakened our politicians.

No doubt he meant Marx in London and Engels in Manchester, among other political activists who corrupted socialists and the working classes with propaganda designed to incite a revolution; so that threats to Britain emerged almost simultaneously from within and without.

It took more than two months for an opportunity to arise to test the fortuitous Russian discovery and the usefulness of the German ciphers in the hands of Britain's Admiralty. It was 14 December when Admiral Sir Arthur Wilson suddenly initiated a meeting with Churchill when First Sea Lord, and the Chief of Staff. He informed them that his examination of the available intelligence about the enemy movements showed a probability of an impending invasion of Britain's coastal towns in East Anglia, which he thought would be made from German battlecruisers.

Although highly speculative at that early stage, 'Orders were therefore given immediately for the battle-cruisers and the 2nd Battle Squadron, with a light-cruiser squadron and a flotilla of destroyers, to raise steam and proceed to sea at such hours and such speeds as to enable them to be in an intercepting position at daylight the next morning.'[16]

Britain's coastal forces were placed on alert, and its Harwich Force would be at sea off Yarmouth. Eight overseas submarines would be in position off Terschelling to guard against a southward raid. Then Churchill and the others waited impatiently for thirty-six hours with considerable curiosity and some small doubt.

At half past eight on the morning of 16 December, Churchill was taking his regular morning bath – he took several throughout each day – when his bathroom door was flung open by an officer with a message from the War Room, which he placed in Winston's dripping hands. It informed him of German battlecruisers bombarding Hartlepool with shells.

Young Winston jumped out of his bath with mixed feelings of delight that the ciphers had worked and sympathy for the residents of Hartlepool, and prepared the Royal Navy to retaliate.

The 3rd Battle Squadron was instructed to prevent the enemy from escaping. Here was an opportunity to destroy the German Fleet. So Britain's Grand Fleet was ordered out and Commodore Keyes was told to bring out his two destroyers and his submarines from Terschelling, into the Heligoland Bight, to intercept the enemy on their return home.

The very idea of an enemy bombarding Britain's coastal towns was something new until the Great War. Effective bomber aircraft had not yet been invented.

Britons had not realised then that major cities like London and coastal towns were vulnerable to attacks by enemy battleships. They had been protected so far by the English Channel. Now the wolf packs closed in, and shells began to destroy private homes in Hartlepool and Scarborough.

Admiral Warrender soon had the enemy battleships within a distance of 7,000 yards, and Admiral Beatty within only 6,000. Then mists descended and curtained off the English coast from the North Sea. Britain's Fleet was evidently closing in on the enemy warships, but visibility was now only up to 2,000 yards. Two and a half hours before dawn, at the very centre of the North Sea, British destroyers engaged in battle with German warships.

Shelling began and several British vessels were hit. Then the German ships retreated.

They turned out to be three squadrons of the advancing German High Seas Fleet in full force. But the Kaiser was too proud of his new navy to let it be destroyed in a battle with the British Fleet, and had given a 'muzzling order' to prevent it from happening. 'The [German] Fleet must be held back and avoid actions which might lead to heavy losses.'[17]

Imagining the havoc that British torpedoes could do to his ships in the dark, Admiral von Ingenohl hastily turned the entire German Fleet around and steamed off, heading for home waters. He left the German Second Squadron under the command of Admiral Scheer. Having now ceased bombarding Britain's coastal towns, Germany's raiding cruisers sought to return home at maximum speed. The British Fleet headed after them from about 100 miles away at over 40mph. They were only 25 miles apart at one point when a heavy mist descended again, and 'the sea ran high'.

All that the British people knew of this complicated game of chess played out on the high seas by the Kaiser with his new modernised navy, was that Hartlepool, Whitby, and Scarborough had been shelled by a German force of cruisers, and that the Germans had retired at full speed on sighting the British Fleet, and escaped into the deepening mist.

Nearly five hundred British civilians were killed by the German shelling. But at least the Admiralty now knew that they possessed reliable German ciphers that could be decoded to give forewarning of any future German attacks by sea.

The chess game ended in a stalemate, because now that the Kiel Canal was widened and its lock capacity significantly increased, it would provide a corridor for Dreadnought-sized battleships to travel from the Baltic Sea and emerge into the North Sea without having to go around Denmark. Britain's coastal towns would remain under threat from the enemy throughout the First World War.

Sharing the World with Germany

'How strange it is that the past is so little understood and so quickly forgotten,' Churchill remarked, after he had completed writing *The World Crisis* in 1931. 'We

INTRODUCTION

live in the most thoughtless of ages. Every day headlines and short views. I have tried to drag history up a little nearer to our own times in case it should be helpful in the present difficulties.'[18]

So has the author of this book, by describing the world's follies beyond 1916 and during those dysfunctional two decades that resulted in the Second World War.

After Churchill was chosen as Prime Minister in 1940, the question everyone wanted answered was, 'Would Britain come to an agreement with Hitler to divide the world between them, or would Britain go to war with Nazi Germany instead?'

Britain was one of the last progressive strongholds of liberty and the pursuit of happiness, which had fought for freedom and human rights for centuries. Now it was under siege. This is the story of what led to Winston Churchill's vow to members of his War Cabinet that each of them, together with the British people, would be better off to choke in their own blood while resisting the Nazis, than continue to appease them, as Britain's previous governments had done.

It may surprise some readers to be catapulted from one world war to the next in only two or three paragraphs, when they have been accustomed to regard each war as a separate entity. In reality, the second was a continuation of the first after an interval of only two decades. Germany's military caste had argued against the armistice that halted the Great War, by insisting they had not lost it, but had only run out of war materials. Their priority was to buy time to keep Germany's military power intact for another onslaught when they had replenished their squandered weaponry and would be able to provide another generation of fresh young men to continue the battle.

American General John Pershing, who was in command of all United States troops on the Western Front in 1917, had no doubts about Germany's intention to start another war as soon as they were ready. He opposed the armistice, and was determined to continue the war and crush the German military caste for all time, but was ordered by US President Wilson not to meddle in politics.

The Next World War

Britain's War Cabinet's unanimous decision to fight Germany in the Second World War was largely a consequence of the stubborn spirit of defiance and rebellion of one man who was prepared to hold on to the last shreds of liberty, independence, and sanity, in order to fight to remain free. No one else possessed Winston Churchill's determination to challenge the biggest and most powerful, well-trained, and well-armed military machine in the world, which was already mobilised for war, and was eager to engage in it. Hitler had already seduced the gullible German nation with lies to follow him blindly in a delusion of glory that would lead to their graves.

Whatever was learned by the previous generation passed away with them, leaving gaps in our knowledge of what really happened, what led up to it, and why. The most important items lost in the fog of time were all the signposts that warned previous generations of threats and dangers and their imminent peril; so that each generation had to learn them all over again at the last moment when they were on the edge of extinction.

As for our future, written history is the only way to hold the past in our hands and examine it, to discover the keys to wise judgments and read the finger-posts pointing to possible disasters. As historian Carlyle wrote, 'Men are mostly fools.' History is a record of their follies. Without it for reference points, our children and grandchildren are likely to be confused and baffled about what really happened, and in jeopardy from the whims of more powerful, or more irresponsible, and even the most cautious of nations.

History is also filled with apparent contradictions and paradoxes that historians need to view from a realistic perspective. We are fortunate to have a wealth of deep insights about that period from Winston Churchill, which helps us to understand what really happened in both world wars.

Curiosity about what happened in the past drove the eminent American historian Barbara W. Tuchman, to investigate customs and behaviour in fourteenth-century France and England for her 600-page book, which she called *A Distant Mirror*; because, when she looked into it, she saw a reflection of our own mindless and irrational behaviour. Regardless of different political or religious beliefs, and despite the very different surroundings and circumstances of that time, she found that people behaved in the same ways as in the twentieth century: foolishly.

What she found was 'economic chaos, social unrest, high prices, profiteering, depraved morals, lack of production, industrial indolence, frenetic gaiety, wild expenditure, luxury, debauchery, social and religious hysteria, greed, avarice, maladministration, decay of manners'.[19] Violence was always present. So was an obsession with sex.

In both centuries there was also a constant expectation of invasion and attack by enemy armies. Swiss historian de Sismondi described that century as 'a bad time for humanity'.

Fifty million died of the plague in Europe. Trotsky, who wrote a detailed account of the Russian Revolution, called the twentieth century 'a bad time to be born in,' when over 108 million were killed in two world wars, of which more than 60 million were deliberately put to death by totalitarian regimes of the extreme right and the political left, after their property was stolen from them.

The Man in Full

Despite the grim challenges that young Winston Churchill faced seriously and with resolve, the news media and the rest of the entertainment industry continued to depict him as a chubby and comic figure. It was entirely misleading, and failed to represent the real man in full; particularly as he admitted to loving war. He was a young, eager and energetic, unconventional individual: a modern man consumed

INTRODUCTION

by curiosity about the world and the bizarre behaviour of other people and other nations, as well as his own.

Young Winston was actually a narrow-shouldered and narrow-chested, scrawny man of only 5ft 6in, as photos of him in his twenties and thirties show very clearly. But he contained an unusual intelligence and imagination and drive. And, most important of all, an abundance of courage, character and charisma, so that he was impressive and imposing, and appeared to be larger than life.

Winston Churchill's endless curiosity and his inquiring mind, which analysed life's motivations, drove him, as a soldier in his twenties, to study the influence of Social Darwinism on the survival of the human species. As well as reading historians like Macaulay and Herodotus on Ancient Greek and Roman cultures, he studied French and English history. He read Plato on ideal forms of government, Reade on the miserable lives of men and women in Africa and other continents; Malthus on the competition for limited resources; and Schopenhauer's *On the Sufferings of the World*.

When he realised at the age of twenty-two that he had not been taught a number of important subjects for a leader of men and women, like ethics and economics, he asked his mother to send him those precious books that engaged him and sharpened his mind. We know he read Plato's *Republic* and Winwood Reade's *The Martyrdom of Man*, Hallam's *Constitutional History*, and Adam Smith's *The Wealth of Nations*. He read Schopenhauer on 'Pessimism', economist Malthus on 'Population', and Darwin's *The Origin of Species*.

When working as Under-Secretary at the Colonial Office in 1906, he took a short trip to Paris and wrote to his Private Secretary Eddie Marsh in London on 23 August, 'I have bought a lot of nice French books.' As Marsh recorded, they were the complete works of Maupassant, Balzac, Musset, Voltaire, Lamartine. Chateaubriand, Michelet, Sevigné, the *Correspondence of Louis XVI and Marie Antoinette,* and *Manon Lescaut* by Prévost: 267 volumes in all.

It would become clear from his own future authorship that he learned a great deal from them. He did not passively absorb what was on the printed page, but realised how history often hinges on misplaced attitudes and beliefs. The first lesson as a young soldier was that: 'The story of the human race is war.' It was how he became a war leader, like Marlborough, Wolfe, Clive, Washington and Lee. The importance of leadership was evident in every history he read. History, he maintained, was made 'by those exceptional human beings whose thoughts, actions, qualities, virtues, triumphs, weaknesses and crimes have dominated the fortunes of the race'.[20]

What also emerged from his readings were the virtues of the heroic figures in history and the accomplishments of Roman law, government and empire. He admired the 'Roman virtues of order, justice, fortitude, resoluteness, and magnanimity'.[21]

He also took heart in the poetic justice that those who flouted those Romano–British virtues were 'doomed to decay and dissolution'.

Churchill could not help but realise from his readings that how life turns out depends very largely on how we deal, not only with chance and discontinuity, but also with problems that appear to be unreal, like the typical delusions of the human condition. He had read about dysfunctional leaders in history and knew several of them himself. His world view, as a consequence, revealed a very different individual than the traditional conservative elder statesman of typical biographies of politicians.

The Young Rebel

Churchill was a young rebel from the start. He rebelled against the unrealistic and incompetent English public school system. Just as many students do today, he rebelled against the limitations and conformity of a university education. He rebelled against the old-fashioned and inept army traditions, which he claimed were twenty-five years out of date. He rebelled against the Conservative Party of his day, because it ignored the welfare of the majority of the population. He would not accept outdated and inefficient traditions, policies, or military tactics and training. And he harassed the opposition parties in the House of Commons for their inability to lead or cooperate, or produce effective results to create an equable and just society. Instead, they wasted everyone's time and energy in attacking the party in power and each other.

Whenever appointed to head a Ministry, Churchill immediately set to work to improve and modernise it. When appointed to the Home Office he rebelled against the injustices of the prison system and reorganised it.

What many left-wing politicians who were born between the 1890s and 1918 shared was a 'late nineteenth century mix of cultural self-confidence informed by a duty to engage in public improvement'.[22] Among left-wing intellectuals, but not of their set, was young Winston Churchill – always overlooked in this category because he was not an intellectual mesmerised by artificial, romantic and unrealistic ideologies, like socialism or Marxism, but of the more moderate left. Like Léon Blum in France, he was motivated to protect and guarantee reasonable working-class conditions.[23] He was a Liberal in politics and a lifetime learner dedicated to self-improvement and progressive improvement of the government and the welfare of the British people.

He was not a frequenter of cafés or bistros or salons where left-wing intellectuals met to exchange Marxist or socialist, fascist, or other theoretical ideas, and who influenced each other in a narrow and introverted world of their own making that had little to do with the realities of human nature or the world. Although a sentimentalist with high principles, he was also a realist.

He differed from most other Edwardians of his social set in that he had no time for socialising or frivolity, because he was an introvert, dedicated to hard thought and the stimulating challenges of continuous work and constant improvement. His friendships were deeply connected to responsible political or military purposes and mostly involved active and adventurous and original thinkers and doers like

INTRODUCTION

himself. He was impatient, and did not waste time with dreamers or theorists who had nothing to offer but their questionable personal opinions.

Nevertheless, he was persuaded to attend a soiree where he met young Clementine Hozier for the first time and was speechless at her unusual beauty and poise and intelligence. They were married in 1908. Their correspondence in subsequent years provides an opportunity to learn their reactions to the world crisis and the upcoming world war. Extracts from their personal letters they continued to write to each other show their enduring love, and their reactions to contemporary events.

Churchill was aware of how fleetingly time passed and how opportunities never returned. It made him an obsessive-compulsive, driven to learn whatever he could about people and their motives, their passions, their irrational behaviour and failings; and why previous cultures had declined and collapsed. It spurred him to warn Parliament in 1935 of 'the endless repetitions of history', which were never far from his mind, because they held the keys to how the future was likely to unroll.

Most readers are unaware how he confronted the Russian Revolution and Civil War or its aftermath as Britain's Secretary of State for War; or what he did to rearrange the Middle East when he was Colonial Secretary, or how he was limited to warning the government about the rise of a militant Germany when he was out of office and could only continue to warn the House of Commons as a Member of Parliament.

This account of his life from the beginning of the twentieth century to 1940 is intended to describe what the authentic Winston Churchill was like, what he had to contend with, and how he met the challenges of the two self-destructive totalitarian regimes of the extreme political left and right, which were the enemies of freedom.

I have not included young Winston's previous experiences as a cavalry officer in India and the Sudan, or as a war correspondent in South Africa in the Boer War; nor the episode when he was taken prisoner of war by Afrikaner guerrilla fighters. All of that occurred prior to his marriage to Clementine Hozier in 1908, when this account begins.

~ I ~
THE MIDDLE EAST CRISIS

1

Clementine
London 1908

As a young man who had mixed most of the time with other men in uniform at one battlefront after another, Winston in his twenties knew he was clumsy at flirting with young women, so he rarely tried. His work took up most of his time. At one of his earliest encounters when seated beside Prime Minister Asquith's pretty twenty-one-year-old daughter Violet at a dinner party, he could find little to talk about to put her at ease but himself. All he could think of saying was, 'I know we are all worms, but I do think I am a glow-worm.'

Despite being gauche with young women and his inability to ask about *them*, Violet not only fell in love with him because she was so passionate about politics, she became obsessed with him. It was a man's world, in which the only way that most women could share in its excitement was through men.

When Winston appointed Eddie Marsh as his Private Secretary to help him at the Colonial Office, they became firm friends. Eddie was a cheerful and witty social butterfly with plenty of male and female friends who adored him. He was tall and handsome with broad shoulders and untidy blond hair. His voice was high pitched and occasionally impeded by a slight stammer that many people found endearing. Eddie attempted to coax Winston away from his work after hours by telling him that 'London is g-getting quite amusing.'

Unlike Winston, Eddie loved light-hearted entertainment with the Smart Set, dancing after hours to all the modern steps, like the Turkey Trot and the Charleston.

'Everyone is very p-pretty this year,' he informed Winston.

Winston knew that *Hullo Ragtime* was playing successfully at a London theatre, and began to wonder what he was missing in the social scene. Affairs of state were often discussed and even decided at soirees such as the one to which he had been invited, as well as at gentleman's private clubs. He had finally relented.

Apparently his mother Jennie had arranged for Eddie to bring him along, since Winston did not enjoy dances or salons and preferred to absorb himself in his work. Not so Eddie Marsh: the social life of Edwardian London was 'the main delight of his leisure hours'. He loved to dance the popular Charleston, which had become suddenly fashionable with the advent of the Edwardian era and the gramophone, now that the staid and pompously formal Victorian age had already faded into the past. It was 1904. Eddie now lived a life of contrasts between his chief's solemn affairs of state and his own light-hearted entertainment with the Smart Set.

As Eddie described what had happened afterwards to a close friend, he had decided to play a game to amuse Winston, in which they would consider the poet Marlowe's quotation about the legendary kidnapping of Helen of Troy because of her famous beauty: 'Was this the face that launched a thousand ships ... ?'

They would decide which of the young ladies at the soiree they considered worth sending a thousand ships to bring her back home. Glancing around the dance floor, their eyes had alighted on only two. There was the famous society beauty, Lady Diana Manners, and Colonel Sir Henry Hozier's adopted daughter, Clementine.[1]

In the parlance of Eddie Marsh's set, everything was 'too wonderful!'

Winston did not know that he had been invited by his mother particularly to meet Clementine. Lady Randolph had decided it was time for him to marry, and Clementine would make him a suitable wife. He was now twenty-nine. But when he was introduced to this glamorous nineteen-year-old redhead at dinner, he had gazed at the tall, slender, and elegant young woman with dazzling blue eyes, and was struck dumb, perhaps for the first time in his life. She was taller than him. Evidently he thought better of talking about himself to this intimidating young woman, and found himself speechless. Not surprisingly in the circumstances, she thought the young man was dull.

What he did not know about this stylish young woman was that her carefully contrived facade of self-assurance concealed a shy and lonely girl. She was obliged to make her own clothes because she had no money and her mother, Lady Blanche, was deeply in debt. Clementine came from a broken home.

She had been adopted by Colonel Sir Henry Hozier, a veteran of an impressive array of military campaigns, from which he had received numerous honours and awards. He was the author of *The Seven Weeks War.* But all the press knew about him, other than that, was that he was a businessman associated in some way with the shipping insurance firm Lloyd's of London. He was always travelling somewhere on secret missions for Britain's fledgling intelligence service. Since he had not wanted children, his wife Blanche had deliberately chosen other fathers for each of her children, regardless of scandal. She was said 'to have juggled up to ten lovers at once'.[2]

'Clementine's life is a success story in and of itself. Born to aristocratic parents, her early life was lonely and marked by rumour and scandal. Clementine's parents, Lady Blanche Hozier and Henry Montague Hozier, despised one another and were so famously unfaithful that associates assumed none of their children was fathered by Henry. He left Blanche when Clementine was six years old, plunging her mother – a notorious gambler – into relative poverty.'[3]

Clementine's neglected and unhappy childhood instilled her with nervous anxiety and a lack of confidence, which was made up for by a determined spirit to overcome problems. Even so, she was hesitant to marry Winston at first for fear of being thrust in the limelight, since her job would be to help create an international statesman. That would require her to encourage him, and also to contain his immense ego to prevent him from tyrannizing everyone around him. She could see for herself what violent reactions he sometimes aroused. Reporting on a recent general election, 'The *Daily Telegraph,* which had never forgiven him for abandoning the Tories for the Liberal Party, reported triumphantly, "We have all been yearning for this to happen ... Winston Churchill is out, Out, OUT."'

She could not help but admire, however, 'the way he habitually picked himself up from defeat, and won another election in Dundee the following month'.

Winston was well aware that he was awkward about courting women. Nevertheless, he had enjoyed a close friendship for the past year with the attractive and intelligent Violet Asquith. Their friendship involved heated arguments about politics. She was still only twenty-one, but could find no common ground with young men of her own age, whom she found dull. According to her stepmother she was, 'alas too brilliant'. However, Winston had not been looking for a political partner or for continual arguments: he was more concerned to plan his future.

After being introduced to Clementine again, he finally asked his cousin Sunny – the present Duke of Marlborough – to invite her to Blenheim Palace.

Clementine was down to her last stylish dress and had no lady's maid of her own. So Jennie sent her own lady's maid to her room at Blenheim. Even so, Clementine had felt shy and awkward. She had already been engaged several times and found that she could not plunge so easily into a marriage in which she might lose her individuality. She had been steered off of Winston because of his notoriety, his powerful ambition, and the heavy demands of his political public life.

Winston offered to show her around the grounds of the Blenheim estate the following day. It had been designed and built by the masterly landscape architect Capability Brown. The weather was warm with intermittent summer showers, one of which propelled them into a small decorative folly of a pseudo-Greek temple for shelter. That was where he asked her to marry him, and she accepted.

'I do not know which of the two is more in love,' wrote Clementine's mother.

Winston's Women

The *Manchester Guardian* had listed Clementine's accomplishments lavishly. They included 'six languages, music and brilliant conversation'.

Violet Asquith had been distressed on hearing the announcement of Winston's engagement, although her father predicted that the marriage would be a disaster. Even so, Violet was not prepared to wait for it to happen. She faked a suicide attempt to obtain sympathy, in the hope of persuading Winston to change his mind. He had to rush up to Scotland, where she was staying near Aberdeen, in an attempt to make peace with her. But she had been inconsolable.

Even after the wedding and in her first pregnancy, Clementine felt she had jealous competition not only from Violet, but also from her new mother-in-law,

CLEMENTINE

Lady Randolph Churchill, for whom Winston had shown such adoration and filial love. He was enchanted by her. When he had been only twenty, he had written possessively to his mother, 'How I wish I could secrete myself in the corner of the envelope and embrace you as soon as you tear it open.'

'Even now,' wrote one biographer, 'Winston often chose to walk arm in arm with his mother, leaving Clementine to feel like an intruder.'

Jennie, as Lady Randolph was more often known, possessed an abundance of influential admirers and social contacts in all sorts of leadership positions who could further Winston's political career, whether in politics, the Church, or the armed forces. They included the King.

The beautiful and fashionable Jennie had always been surrounded by admirers in her youth. She was still as self-absorbed as ever, even though she seemed suddenly to have discovered how interesting her son was, and treated Winston more seriously when he became a celebrity. She became more and more fascinated by him. So much so that, for a while, Clementine had found it difficult to get her mother-in-law out of the house.

Clementine decorated some of their marital home at 33 Eccleston Square in Pimlico, at a time when Art Nouveau was fashionable. They occupied separate rooms to suit their individual lifestyles, as she was an early riser, he a late one after retiring in the early hours of the morning, and often writing or working in bed, as well as anywhere else, since he was an obsessive-compulsive worker and an overachiever.

They established an arrangement of intermittent separations that, for two such strong-willed individuals, gave each of them some relief from the other when needed. A benefit of that lifestyle was that posterity could enjoy vivid descriptions of the times and customs and gossip in their frequent correspondence of 'seventeen hundred letters, telegrams and notes between them that survive today, and a habit of putting their thoughts on paper that persisted even when they were under the same roof'.

Winston wrote to Clementine from France on their first anniversary to say that the bells of the old city of Alsace-Lorraine had reminded him of the chimes that had acclaimed their wedding a year earlier at St Margaret's. He expressed the thought that she had brought him the light of happiness. His thoughts dwelt on their baby daughter, and he wondered what she would grow into. He wished a bright star to shine for her.

Everyone had felt 'curiously pleased at this wedding, but it was Jennie, earthy Jennie, who knew by instinct that her son had found the right woman. No money – she brushed that aside – Winston was an earner. No, it was something else which made her rejoice, the sure sense that behind this gentle loveliness lay qualities of steel – absolute integrity and fortitude that would not snap if things went ill for Winston.'[4]

Clementine wrote to Winston[5] on their first anniversary, 'The year I have lived with you has been far the happiest in my life & even if it had not been it would have been well worth living.'

Winston – who always thought of events as being what they *ought* to be – 'once claimed that after their wedding they had simply "lived happily ever after". That is stretching the truth. There was never a break from the "whirl of haste, excitement and perpetual crisis" that surrounded them.[6] She could not even talk to him in the bathroom without on occasion finding members of the cabinet in there, half-hidden by the steam ... They argued frequently ...'[7]

But however much they disagreed, 'she loved him and revelled in her union with a man so "exciting" and "famous". For his part, he simply doted and depended on her.'[8]

The first three decades of their marriage they were united by a common purpose, which was to make him Prime Minister. Winston's passionate love for all his womenfolk was tied for life to his admiring self-regard, which dominated everything.

2

Pressures of Events
Paris 1919

The First World War finally came to an abrupt end after four and a half years of almost continual slaughter on the battlefields of the Eastern and Western Fronts and in the Middle East. Winston's wartime career had begun as First Lord of the Admiralty. The slowness and failure of the campaign to take Constantinople from the Turks through the Dardanelles had been his own original idea to avoid more bloodshed on the Western Front, and it lost him his position at the Admiralty. After serving in the trenches as a lieutenant colonel, he was appointed Minister of Munitions to ensure that none of the commanders was short of weaponry when needed. Now the desperation to defy the German onslaughts and defeat the enemy was replaced by war weariness and the desire of the victorious Allies to return to their normal lives. It was a romantic notion that turned out to be all but impossible.

First World War Timeline
1914: Austrian Emperor's heir assassinated.
1914: Austria declares war on Serbia in July.
1914. Germany declares war on Britain.
1915: Austria resists Russian advances.
1915: Churchill's failure to end war by attacking Constantinople.
1916: Churchill colonel on Western Front.
1916: Emperor Franz Josef dies. Charles is crowned emperor. Italian resistance.
1917: Germany increases U-boat activities and US declares war on Germany.
1917: Austria wants to end war but her German ally wants to continue.
1917: Charles negotiates peace with France without informing his German ally.
1917: German U-boats attempt to starve Britain into submission.
1917: Churchill Minister of Munitions.
1918: Food shortages in Austria cause famine and starvation.
1918: French President Poincaré admits French tired of war. Troops mutiny.
1918: Austria cannot meet French peace terms including return of Alsace-Lorraine previously lost to Germany.
1918: Charles faces collapse of Habsburg Empire unless he betrays German ally by negotiating peace alone.
1918: Germany takes control of Austria.

CHURCHILL'S CHALLENGES, 1918–1940

1918: Germany and Austria collapse.
1918: Charles exiled and dies. End of Habsburg dynasty and Austrian Empire.
1918: Peace Treaty at Versailles ends war.
1919: Churchill Secretary of War and Air.

The Peace Conference began on January 1919 at Versailles, little more than 26km from Paris. Britain, France, Italy and the United States dominated diplomats from over thirty-two countries. They met day after day for more than six months in order to set the peace terms for the defeated nations, with Winston Churchill occasionally attending as Secretary of State for War, while Europe was starving and disintegrating before their eyes.[1]

> The tasks for the defeated nations were enormous: combating the forces of revolution on the left and militarism on the right, reviving war-ravaged economies, maintaining national morale in the face of the stigma of defeat, the growing burden of 'war guilt', a desire to recover the territories and self-assurances that had been ripped away at the last moment, and a search for scapegoats ...[2]

Former Turkish territory was distributed according to the Mandate, with France taking Syria and Lebanon, and Britain acquiring Iraq and Palestine. Britain was already committed to introducing a Jewish National Home in the western half.

'Millions of refugees were on the move; by 1921, 20,000 refugees a day were pouring through the city of Omsk on the route eastwards. An estimated seven million young orphans wandered through the country. Bandits and other armed groups terrorized the villages and the railways.'[3]

The entire proceedings of the peace talks at Versailles were a chaotic shambles. They were overshadowed by a distracting question that hovered over the delegates like a storm cloud, as the German representatives of the Weimar Republic who had sought an armistice were forced to sign an unworkable agreement. They stubbornly maintained that they had not lost the war, and preferred to believe instead that they were the victims of a conspiracy by the Allies.

The German Kaiser, who had since been forced to flee from Germany to the Netherlands for safety, had claimed as much in the notes he had made on the margin of the original letter that had informed him at the very beginning that Austria, to which Germany was allied by a treaty, had fatally declared war on Serbia. Even now, the German signatories of the armistice still believed they had made the right decision to undertake a pre-emptive strike against France before French forces with their Russian allies could encircle and invade Germany. But there was no evidence that France had planned to do any such thing. The German High Command had acted impetuously out of fear that it *might* happen. It may be a simplification to state that wars arise out of paranoia, but it would be a fair assessment in that case: fear triggered impetuosity.

PRESSURES OF EVENTS

Despite their premeditated plan, Germany had gone to war because its General Staff were still haunted by the spectre of the long-dead French Emperor Napoleon Bonaparte and his *Grand Armée,* which had made war on them and Europe a century earlier.

Even though Napoleon and his armies no longer existed, Germany's leaders and their former Chief of Staff, von Schlieffen, had suffered from a fear-driven obsession that they might be France's victims again if they did not attack the French first. Schlieffen had masterminded a military blueprint to prevent an aggressive France from ever attacking Germany again. His successor, von Moltke, had put the plan into action as soon as Austria declared war on Serbia in revenge for the assassination of the heir to the throne of the Austro-Hungarian Empire. War had come about as a consequence of a chain reaction.

Now that Austria and Germany had lost the war they had waged against the Allies they continued to feel persecuted, sullen and resentful, as if they had been victims in a massive conspiracy to destroy them.

In order to carry out the Schlieffen Plan, the German army had killed over 4 million Allied troops who had gone to the aid of the French. The forces had been evenly matched until Germany had run out of resources to continue the war, and German troops and the German Navy mutinied. The Kaiser and his generals had been forced to request an armistice as a result. One of the Allies' conditions for acceptance was that Germany would pay war reparations for their brutal aggression and destruction.

No-Man's-Land

Twenty-first-century television audiences have become accustomed to watching random battles in far-away places in comfort at home, or on cinema screens, to see much of the action targeted remotely by nuclear missiles or drones, so that it is impossible for them to conceive of the overwhelming force of two equally matched industrial nations relentlessly intent on destroying each other's infantrymen on battlefields under heavy artillery fire, with tanks and machine guns. Their main intention was simply to kill each other and keep on killing young men who faced them in battle, without realising that, as Churchill discovered, it cost the lives of two or three of their own soldiers to kill one of the enemy.

> The wounded died between the lines: the dead mouldered into the soil. Merchant ships and neutral ships and hospital ships were sunk on the sea and all on board left to their fate, or killed as they swam. Every effort was made to starve whole nations into submission without regard to age or sex. Cities and monuments were smashed by artillery. Bombs from the air were cast down indiscriminately. Poison gas in many forms stifled

or seared the soldiers. Liquid fire was projected onto their bodies. Men fell from the air in flames, or were smothered, often slowly, in the dark recesses of the sea.[4]

Now bitter German ex-servicemen who were marginalised and unemployed after the war, perpetrated and began repeating a conspiracy theory that Germany was a victim. But someone had to pay for the destruction and the huge cost of the war, and Germany was bankrupt.

The American General 'Black Jack' Pershing, who had commanded the US troops on the Western Front, had opposed the armistice with Germany on the grounds that even a few more days of fighting would have convinced the Germans that they were licked: 'Had they given us another week, we'd have *taught* them.'

He was angry that his opinion had been swept aside by politicians who allowed the German Army to avoid total defeat by accepting an armistice in 1918. It had also prevented the Allied armies from crossing the Rhine and invading German soil. Consequently, most German combatants refused to believe they had been defeated, and looked around for possible scapegoats to blame for the humiliating terms they were forced to accept at Versailles.

German civilians too imagined they were victims of a conspiracy – just as the German Kaiser imagined he had been manipulated into war by the British. He had even written it all down, as if to justify his actions to posterity by playing a game of 'victim'.

'From the dilemma raised by our fidelity to the old Emperor of Austria we are brought into a situation which offers England the desired pretext for annihilating us under the hypocritical cloak of justice, namely, of helping France on account of the reputed "balance of power in Europe, i.e. playing the card of all the European nations in England's favour against us".'[5]

It was nothing more than the rambling of a guilty leader who realised he had made a huge and costly blunder, and sought someone else to blame for his failure.

It is generally forgotten now that he realized he had made a dreadful mistake in ordering German troops to be mobilized for war, and suddenly imagined the awful consequences. But his Chief of Staff assured him it was too late to call back troops already on the way to Belgium to invade France.

The overwhelming question now was what to do and how to do it, in order to assuage the anger of the French, whose losses were the greatest, with nearly 1.5 million dead and 2 million wounded. Pershing's advice had been to crush Germany's military infrastructure and its irresponsible adventures for all time. But he had been overruled by the politicians.

The American President Wilson had initially dominated the meetings of international delegates at the Peace Conference in Paris, when he had arrived like an avenging dark angel in the black garb of a Puritan elder. But it soon became apparent to wiser heads, like the leading economist John Maynard Keynes, that Wilson's knowledge of Europe and its affairs was limited, since the United States had been isolated from the rest of the world for so long. Keynes left the meeting in despair when he realised that French Prime Minister Clemenceau wanted revenge, instead of helping to organise Europe for a peaceful and prosperous future.

'European civilisation tottered on the brink of collapse.'[6]

Woodrow Wilson had planned to take control of the meeting by imposing his peace formula, which featured 'fourteen points'. But Keynes, who was concerned about Europe's economy, could see that the peace talks would be bound to fail. All that was achieved, according to him, was 'a peace that completed the economic destruction done to Europe by the war'.[7]

The Peacemakers

When Wilson became ill and returned home, the most persuasive leader to dominate the conference was Clemenceau, who was determined to have his own way. Known with good reason as 'the Tiger', he demanded reparations for the German War, and revenge on behalf of the Allies. The problem was how Germany could afford to pay reparations when one of the terms of the Treaty was that its heavy industrial zone in the Ruhr was to be occupied by Allied troops, who would be in control of its factories.

Winston had met Georges Clemenceau on the battlefield of the Western Front when he had been Minister of Munitions, after serving as a lieutenant colonel at the front in Belgium.

They had been driven together towards the front line in their vehicle with German shells bursting all around them, to obtain first-hand opinions from courageous French officers on what would be likely to happen in the anticipated advance of the German Army. The French had been proudly optimistic. Only forty-eight hours later those same officers were dead from the onslaught of the advancing German infantry.

Clemenceau had grown up in the French coastal town of Vendée, where his father admired Voltaire and the French Revolution of 1789. He had studied medicine in Paris in 1861, when living in the Latin Quarter with writers and artists. He had founded a newspaper named *Le Matin*. After completing his studies, he had left for New York during the American Civil War. He would describe himself later as 'a soldier of democracy'.

On returning to France, Clemenceau established a medical practice in his home town. But politics brought him back to Paris, where he became Mayor of Montmartre, and was elected as a Radical Republican Deputy in the National Assembly in 1871. Churchill was born three years later. Despite their difference in ages, they shared many similarities.

Clemenceau founded another newspaper, named *La Justice*, in 1880, and became known as a relentless and merciless critic of republicans, radicals and conservatives – as Winston Churchill would be in England. Clemenceau made many enemies for being outspoken and was attacked in the newspapers – just as Churchill would be attacked to silence him by the Opposition in the House of Commons and by the newspapers. The combined attacks led to Clemenceau being out of office and influence, like Churchill would be, too. And, like Churchill, Clemenceau 'came to be classed among the foremost political writers of his time'.[8]

He was described as 'a man of reflection, of vast culture, a friend of the best-known writers and artists of the period'. More significantly, perhaps, in France's sickening anti-Semitic atmosphere, where an honourable Jewish army officer named Alfred Dreyfus was wrongly accused of the crime of treason on trumped-up evidence, Clemenceau was convinced of his innocence, although Dreyfus had already been tried and convicted and sentenced to prison on Devil's Island.

Clemenceau sought for eight years to have him released, by publishing articles in his two newspapers, *La Justice* and *L'Aurore*. For most of that time, the French military and the law courts continued to conceal the name and dishonour of the real culprit – a different officer altogether who had passed military secrets to the enemy for money to pay off his gambling debts. The innocent Dreyfus was scapegoated to prevent the national army being disgraced by one of its regular officers. As a consequence of Clemenceau's success, and the persistence of the novelist Émile Zola in having Dreyfus released and restored to his army career, Clemenceau was elected as a senator, and became Interior Minister in the Cabinet in 1906, before becoming Premier of France.

Worried and anxious about the indifferent attitude of the United States to the war, Clemenceau had appealed to the American public and to President Woodrow Wilson for aid, and was relieved at the entry of the US into the war as an ally in April 1917. Clemenceau single-mindedly pursued victory and, like Churchill, had no time for defeatists or traitors. He declared he would wage war 'to the last quarter hour, for the last quarter hour will be ours'.[9] He turned out to be right. General Ludendorff refused to give in until he ran out of weapons and shells, oil and other war material.

As soon as the armistice was signed by the defeated Germans on 11 November 1918, Clemenceau took care to ensure they were disarmed. Then he defended the French cause at the Peace Conference with conviction, working alternately with President Wilson and British Prime Minister Lloyd George. The Treaty of Versailles was signed in the Hall of Mirrors of the Versailles Palace on 28 June 1919.

Clemenceau fought for democracy to the end of his life, declaring, 'It is the only form of government which can establish equality for all, and which can bring closer the ultimate goals: freedom and justice.'[10]

He and Winston Churchill shared the same attitude. Where they differed was that Clemenceau was determined to punish the Germans for starting the war, whereas Churchill was magnanimous in his concern about future harmony in Europe.

Fear of Bolshevism

When British Prime Minister Lloyd George arrived in Paris, the British public expected him to impose harsh peace terms on Germany. Clemenceau was even more committed to making Germany pay for the war than him. But President

PRESSURES OF EVENTS

Woodrow Wilson had already determined that war costs would not be included in the reparations demand.

Most Americans considered Wilson to be high-minded and inspiringly idealistic, but he was unworldly, remote, unrealistic and stubborn to work with. He began by raising hopes at the conference with his original concept of 'self-determination', his fourteen points for the Treaty, and his belief that a 'League of Nations' could provide collective security against another war. But he was ignorant of Europe. He admitted afterwards that he had said things 'without the knowledge that nationalities existed, which are coming to us day after day'.[11]

Leaders of those new nations were appearing at the Peace Conference because of the collapse of the four great empires of which they had previously been a part. Germany, Russia, Austria and Turkey had controlled enormous territories in Europe and the Middle East before being brought to their knees by waging an unnecessary and self-destructive war against Serbia.

Churchill's position as Secretary of State for War and Air was quite different from Lloyd George's. Churchill emphasised the impossibility of Germany paying the full cost of the war, and told the British Cabinet that: 'It was important to get Germany on her legs again for fear of the spread of Bolshevism.'[12]

He was against the idea of the Kaiser being tried in a court for making war – which was the language of the popular news media – and insisted that the Allies should feed the starving Germans and get their economy in order to defeat the possibility of the Bolsheviks taking over Germany. Prime Minister David Lloyd George, on the other hand, was a populist who wanted the Kaiser tried and hanged. 'By every principle of justice,' he said, 'by the principles of justice which were recognised as applicable between individuals, the Germans were liable for the whole of the damages and the cost of recovering them.'[13]

'But, as a pragmatic politician and a statesman, he was well aware that, sooner or later, Britain would have to sell its goods to the Germans again, so he did not wish to destroy Germany.'[14]

Remarkably for someone who had proved himself to be one of Britain's greatest war leaders, Lloyd George was almost as vague about Europe and the Middle East as President Wilson. He leaned heavily on young Winston Churchill for advice when he was in the War Cabinet. Although they enjoyed a successful partnership as colleagues, Lloyd George already knew that Winston was ambitious for promotion and viewed him as a rival for popularity and fame.

Churchill was keen for an all-out war against the Communist takeover of Russia, but he never received support from the War Cabinet. Lloyd George went through the motions of supporting intervention but viewed it as a lost cause. He preferred to let Russia save itself by supplying the anti-Bolsheviks with arms, munitions, money and equipment. Churchill did not relish giving in when viewing the communist threat to Europe, but was forced to compromise with the Prime Minister, or risk being fired. And there was no doubt that Lloyd George was brought to the edge of impatience at Winston's obsession with Russia. It was not in Churchill's nature to compromise on the subject of social justice.

CHURCHILL'S CHALLENGES, 1918–1940

At the same time, the Liberal Lloyd George feared Winston could be a formidable opponent if he resigned and rejoined the Conservative Party.

Since Lord Milner was ready to retire as Colonial Secretary, Lloyd George hurriedly appointed Winston as Secretary of State for the Colonies. Churchill would now be engaged in redefining the Middle East after General Allenby had defeated the Empire of the Ottoman Turks, which left it without powerful leadership or control. The Middle East had become little more than a huge disputed tribal area, like Europe had been in the fourteenth century, with scores of predatory warlords plundering each other's territories with their private armies. Churchill was now tasked with creating suitable protective frontiers to pacify the region.

3

The World Crisis

Not surprisingly, with his instant grasp of foreign affairs and impatience for more responsibilities, Winston found little appeal in being limited to colonial affairs, and wished to enlarge his own department as some kind of Foreign Secretary. He proposed inflating his title to 'Secretary of State for Imperial Affairs', until Lord Curzon complained of his interference. Curzon had been chief negotiator for the Allies to end the war with the Turks. Lloyd George promised him he would put Winston in his place. Keeping him there was another matter.

Relations between Winston and the Prime Minister continued to be tense and disagreeable for Lloyd George, as they veered from arguments to cooperation and back again, with Churchill still angling to be Chancellor of the Exchequer, a position closest to the Prime Minister at 10 Downing Street – whereas Lloyd George wanted to keep his distance from Winston.

'The Prime Minister now believed his wayward minister was not above bidding for the supreme office.'[1]

The Prime Minister became even more wary of Churchill, who foresaw that Lloyd George's popularity as a wartime leader would soon wane. The Welsh Wizard's fortunes were gradually dwindling in the post-war confusion that hindered a return to the familiar lives that people hoped to take up again.

The remnants of territory in Mesopotamia were left in chaos from the battered and crumbled Turkish Empire. They were leaderless and disorderly sheikhdoms competing for power through tribal stirrings and conflicts. Only the British Empire remained a world superpower, but it was not as affluent or as powerful as most people imagined it was. Budget restraints were now a priority.

The Tsarist dynasty had been toppled by the Bolshevik revolutionary Lenin, who had exploited the wartime opportunity to take control of Russia by making peace with Germany. The Habsburg dynasty of the Austro-Hungarian Empire had aged and made a fatal judgment in going to war against the tiny Serbian nation it had falsely accused of threatening it. The Hohenzollern dynasty, which had ruled the German Empire, had ended when they lost the war and the Kaiser fled to Switzerland for safety.

Churchill would be obliged to pick up some of the pieces of the former empires, which were now leaderless, leaving Austria, Hungary and Czechoslovakia as tiny independent and defenceless states.

The old Emperor had not been wrong when he had said ruefully that Austria generally lost its wars. Even so, he had foolishly declared war on tiny Serbia in what had since turned out to be a suicidal act. He had died in 1916, and been mourned by his most loyal subjects, the Austro-Hungarian Jews whom he had shielded from Austria's and Hungary's anti-Semites, who were motivated by malice arising from their backwardness and superstitious beliefs.

As an Anglo-American historian and intellectual professor would remark, 'The true Austria was not the Austro-Germans in Graz or Salzburg: it was the Slavs, the Muslims, and the Jews ... Only they bore true allegiance to the crown.'[2]

Perhaps that was why Jews were ostracised and discriminated against by others who had always jockeyed for more power. The emotional disease of anti-Semitism still clung to the tribal Teutonic and Magyar cultures that kept it alive with tales from the rural past of witches and hobgoblins and primitive gods who appeared to inhabit the dark domain of their minds.

Austria's Dilemma

The Austrians found themselves left on their own as a tiny fragment remaining from what had been a vast empire. Its disintegration had come about after a combined force of German and Austrian troops had overwhelmed and defeated the Allied Italian 2nd Army in the foothills beneath the sharp peaks of the mountain range at the Eleventh Battle of the Isonzo, where the Italians had lost 40,000 dead and wounded and 280,000 taken prisoner, when fighting on their own on the Italian Front. German poison gas had played a key role in the Italian collapse.

Britain had been shocked to discover that their Italian allies had been reduced to half their military size. Churchill had swiftly advised Prime Minister Lloyd George to send eleven new divisions of British and French troops to their aid from the Western Front. They had arrived in Italy in time to turn the balance of power in the Allies' favour at the battle of Caporetto. Austria and Hungary were humiliated by their defeat and the Allied victory at the end of 1917, when 300,000 Austrians were killed around the Isonzo River. They had suffered in twelve almost continuous battles for over two years. The two combined kingdoms of Austria and Hungary collapsed and fell into a national trauma with sullen bitterness and smouldering rage, which would fuel the rise of Hitler and the Nazis.

When Sigmund Freud was asked by the Austrian government to study the mentally wounded, he diagnosed their traumatic dysfunctions as 'shell-shock'. Many survivors never recovered control of their senses. The stress of mental disorders contributed to the toxic post-war atmosphere in Austria, Hungary, and Germany.

That war was entirely different from all previous ones. Combat soldiers were confined from day to day in the insanitary conditions of trenches with constant illnesses under the threat of violence, terror and destruction from new mechanical weapons that hammered relentlessly at their incessant battle fatigue and dulled their senses. Young and inexperienced soldiers became trapped by exhaustion and diseases, and yet had to continue to survive dangerously with rotting corpses piling up as trench companions. It was a nightmare that burdened the combatants with grief and despair that the war would never end, while industrialised factories continued to manufacture and assemble even more lethal weapons for the battlefronts.

Most deaths in battle had previously resulted from the spread of infectious diseases, until the invention of the machine gun and the howitzer. Now the intensity of continual battles at the front and the extent of the slaughter from new and more deadly technologies caused something more than the typical combat fatigue and battlefront disorientation of the past. The effects would have to wait to be diagnosed more accurately at the end of the century as Post Traumatic Stress Disorder.

Many soldiers who were fortunate enough to return home were dysfunctional for the rest of their lives. Some managed to commit suicide. PTSD was suffered by more ex-serviceman than was revealed at the time. It was worse for the defeated armies. Nor was it recognised then what disastrous effects those mental conditions would have on post-war Austrian, Hungarian, and German politics, which were poisoned by the bitterness of defeat in the war.

It had not been over by Christmas 1914 as everyone had expected. The Hungarian Revolution exploded in 1918 and resulted in the final collapse of the Austro-Hungarian Empire, from which Hungarians disentangled themselves to suffer from their own war-crazed weariness.

Only Austria's capital, the city of Vienna, still pretended to imperial glory with its magnificent Baroque churches and facades that barely concealed the considerable post-war poverty and food shortages.

Other significant factors identified war psychosis as a source of future turbulence. There was, for example, the need for a large number of psychiatrists in Vienna's polyclinic for such a relatively small population of not much more than 1.5 million Viennese, apparently due to demoralisation and loss of identity. Many Hungarians and Czechs left for their native lands when the Empire no longer existed, and Vienna had lost over 197,000 dead during the war, including the results of a flu epidemic that began sooner than in Britain, and may even have precipitated Austria's defeat.

The Dead City

Freud's published case studies of some of his most colourful private patients created a sensation by suggesting, erroneously, that most were bourgeois married women, often sexually neglected by their husbands and overtaken by boredom, frustration, or hysteria. But the public clinic – managed for Freud by the twenty-three-year-old psychiatrist Wilhelm Reich – was occupied largely by vagrants and political agitators who were predominantly men. Middle- and upper-class male Viennese went to the extraordinarily over-abundant number of prostitutes instead of to the public clinic, in a search for identity, similar to post-war Berlin with its transvestite cabarets and post-war gender confusion.

The only lively elements in the otherwise lifeless city were its restless intelligentsia, most of whom appear to have been Jewish. So were most of its psychiatrists. Wilhelm Reich and the novelist Joseph Roth had been drawn to Vienna from Austrian Galicia to develop their careers. So had Manès Sperber, whose books, as well as Freud's, reveal the fermentation of ideas from their vivid experiences and fertile minds. Their problem was that there were too many successful Jews in Vienna and Budapest for the envious, unblinking and always watchful, anti-Semitic Austrians and Hungarians. Neither they nor the Germans could bear to see anyone successful when they were not.

Austria's Jews who were drawn to the capital city for work from Budapest and from small rural villages, soon realised that the Vienna seen on the surface was only a myth, and that all kinds of discontents seethed beneath it. 'Even the man who has only modest wealth is ... envied by his brother, who would not hesitate to do away with him in order to steal it.' That saying by tenth-century Persian explorer Ibn Rusta applied to most tribal societies who feared that the success of one might diminish the others.[3]

Being part of the Austrian Empire had given the Viennese a patronising sense of self-importance and self-aggrandisement. Now they were left stunned and confused at the way the empire had suddenly vanished and Austria had shrunk to only a tiny country on its own. Its only choice, like some of the other former provinces of the Empire that were now only fragments of their former size, was to attach itself to a bigger and more powerful ally. What they shared with Germany was not only a common language but a similar culture.

4

The Bolshevik Power-Grab

Churchill would also be drawn into the orbit of the Bolshevik Revolution when it had destabilised Russia after mutinies in the Tsar's army and navy. Russian troops shot their officers in order to escape from the war against Germany that Russia was unprepared for and its soldiers did not want.

While Lenin led the political arm of power, Leon Trotsky led the Red Army in a Russian civil war. Although Britain had sent a small number of troops to fight against the Bolshevik revolutionaries, they did so hesitantly, reluctantly and indecisively, claiming the war had ended at the end of 1918.

At the Paris Peace Conference the following year, French Premier Clemenceau had no doubts about who had begun the war, and forcefully managed to extract an agreement for reparations from Germany at the Treaty of Versailles; even though German politicians continued to claim that they were unfairly treated and were victims of a conspiracy.

It would take years to overcome the sadness and gloom that was the aftermath of the tragedy of the First World War, and view it in the light of the absurdity and ineptitude of the dysfunctional Teutonic would-be conquerors. Their irrational and bizarre behaviour had cost 9.4 million lives, and three or four times that number wounded.

Most historians tend to regard the Treaty of Versailles as the first step leading to the outbreak of the Second World War two decades later. General Pershing had been prescient at recognising it as a useful excuse by Germany to pause and rearm and train the next generation of young Germans for a continuation of the First World War. Churchill felt the same way and fully expected another world war as soon as Germany would be able to restore its necessary wartime level of resources. Britain's Secret Intelligence Service, with Lieutenant Colonel Stewart Menzies, who was second only to 'C' and training to replace him, was equally certain that they were simply waiting for the next world war.[1]

As for the war reparations that Germany was obliged to pay in the interim, they were not nearly as unfair as Germany claimed. And yet, according to Thomas Lamont – the banker representing the American Treasury – they 'caused more trouble, contention, hard feeling, and delay at the Paris Peace Conference than any other part of the Treaty'.[2] Someone had to foot the bill for the war. If Germany could not pay, then the British taxpayers would be presented with it.

As American diplomat Richard Holbrooke wrote of historian Margaret MacMillan, she 'corrects the widely held view that the reparations payments imposed by the victors were so onerous as to have caused the wreck of the German economy that paved the way for Hitler'.[3] It was another delusion by the Germans, who did not like to be beaten in war or peace and always blamed others for their failure.

The Treaty of Versailles 'has become synonymous with disaster, for the troubles it started (or failed to stop) in Central and Eastern Europe, in Southeast Asia, and in the Middle East; for its contribution to the rise of fascism in Europe and to the Great Depression; for its inability to reckon with a newly Bolshevik Russia; for the fact that a Second World War ensued.'[4]

Every continent was involved. But the resulting shambles of what had been intended to be a reasonable and practical conference to plan the future turned into chaos and incoherence, largely resulting from ignorance. Meanwhile, economist Keynes, who abandoned the conference in disgust and despair, knew that a plan was needed to save the world from revolution, and that starvation would lead to riots, anarchy, terrorism, and Communism.

Churchill's Secret Agent

Among the advisers and specialists reporting to the British delegation in the Paris Peace Conference was Flight Lieutenant Sidney Reilly of Canada's Royal Flying Corps. He wore a captain's insignia. He was lean, long-legged, and always immaculately dressed and groomed, with the self-confident air of a man of the world accustomed to overcoming opposition in order to achieve his goal. His personality combined both romanticism and sardonic charm. He was a great romancer of women. Most importantly, he could wheel and deal successfully with influential politicians, industry leaders, successful financiers, and leaders of the armed forces, and generally impress them and get his way with them.

Reilly was one of Winston's spies when he had been Home Secretary in 1911, before being appointed Minister for War. His secret agent had changed his name in accordance with his new profession, which had begun with infiltrating the rebellious Irish Fenians. His audacity as a spy, and his leadership qualities, were so extraordinary that he would be regarded as the greatest spy of all time. According to his biographer, Reilly had killed a German colonel and impersonated him at a confidential meeting of the Kaiser and his General Staff at his headquarters, while they discussed whether to seek an armistice with the Allies or continue the German war beyond 1918 by concentrating on U-boat attacks on Allied shipping.[5]

Far-fetched though it might appear, the high calibre of British Intelligence agents was confirmed by Winston Churchill in *The World Crisis,* when he referred to Colonel Knox with his discerning dispatches from inside Russian Headquarters, and a similar situation with British Intelligence agents in German military headquarters. Churchill wrote that Britain's Intelligence Service reports of what was passing in the minds of the German Naval Staff were so efficient that they reached him even before the Kaiser saw them.[6]

Reilly had been born in Imperial Russia and had several important reasons for spying on communist revolutionaries on behalf of Britain's Secret Service. He never forgave the Soviets for destroying the lives of the Russian middle classes. Like Churchill, he knew that the Russian Revolution was not a grass-roots rebellion by oppressed peoples, but a coup planned in advance by a small gang of ambitious adventurers seeking power. For Reilly, planning and implementing a counter-revolution was an opportunity to right the wrongs they had unjustly and brutally perpetrated with indifference or contempt for the Russian people.

Russia had been vulnerable for anyone with the intelligence and audacity to exploit the opportunity of a nation in chaos and crisis with inept leadership. It could fall into the hands of anyone, or several of the White Russian warlords who were presently fighting for it against Trotsky's revolutionary Red Army. All it needed was an idea; since history has shown that groups, mobs, or masses, are more inflamed emotionally, and blocked intellectually by a myth, a superstition, or a conspiracy theory, rather than recognising the reality of the situation.

Reilly and his friend Boris Savinkov, who had been Assistant War Minister of Russia in 1917, were so well placed and confident with their influential contacts in Russia that they even considered it possible to take control of the country themselves and set up their own government.

At the height of his career between 1918 and 1924 Sidney Reilly acted on a large and heroic scale as a maker and breaker of governments. He had just failed to capture Lenin and Trotsky, and other members of the Bolshevik Central Committee in 1918, to overturn Russia's new Bolshevik government in its infancy. It 'paved the way for the Russian Civil War proper, in which he played innumerable roles'.[7]

Reilly met Boris Savinkov for the first time at the Paris Peace Conference in 1919, when he was a member of the Russian political delegation who acted for the White Russians. Reilly and Churchill both had great respect for him as a devoted fighter of freedom for the Russian people. Churchill met Savinkov in Paris when the Russian Civil War was over. Savinkov told him, 'I know them well, Lenin and Trotsky. For years we worked hand in hand for the liberation of Russia. Now they have enslaved her worse than ever.'

By September 1920, Savinkov had an army of 20,000 to 30,000 officers and men under the leadership of the Polish Head of State, General Piłsudski. According to Churchill, Savinkov 'displayed the wisdom of a statesman, the qualities of a commander, the courage of a hero, and the endurance of a martyr'.[8]

British Prime Minister Lloyd George wanted to believe that the Soviet government would drop its communist ideology when it was forced to govern the country and deal with food shortages and millions of starving Russians who were dying. But Savinkov warned him; 'Remember, that the collapse of Rome was followed by centuries of the Dark Ages.'

Public and Private Lives

Despite the traumatic shock and grief at the unprecedented tragedies on the Western Front, Churchill, more than most people, was particularly conscious of the immensity of the war on the Eastern Front, which had already cost Russia nearly 9 million casualties by 1917. As he would write in *The World Crisis,* 'The struggle upon the Eastern Front is incomparably the greatest war in history. In its scale, in its slaughter, in the exertion of the combatants, in its military kaleidoscope, it far surpasses in magnitude and intensity all similar human episodes.'[9]

On top of the wartime slaughter came the Spanish flu epidemic in its closing years that killed 20 million more, troops and civilians alike, to end in 1920.

England was now a very different country from what it had been only a decade earlier when David Lloyd George and Winston Churchill had been 'the most advanced politicians'.[10] Social order had begun to deteriorate with labour uprisings in the mines, in industry, the railways, and other transport unions.

All the advantages of being the first nation to invent and construct the Industrial Revolution were lost by political agitators and conflicts between social classes from 1911 to the outbreak of the First World War. Churchill had been the minister responsible for maintaining law and order in the face of rebellion at home and anarchy and Bolshevism from overseas. There had been little time for social life, even if he had wanted it.

Despite the pressures on his time, his mother – still known generally as Lady Randolph Churchill, in spite of her subsequent marriage to the much younger Montagu Porch – had turned sixty-five in January 1919. They were still devoted to each other. And she had become more and more admiring of Winston, who was the most interesting man in her life. She listened with silent awe when he talked intensely to others of affairs of state.

Five years earlier, when she had turned sixty, she had visited her sister Leonie after a dinner party, and sat on her bed. 'I shall never get used to not being the most beautiful woman in the room,' she admitted. 'It was an intoxication to know every man had turned his head. It kept me in form.'

She was still somewhat jealous of the time taken up in Winston's life by her daughter-in-law, Clementine, who now had a little daughter called Marigold. Winston managed to spend a few days with them before leaving London for his constituents in Dundee, as Prime Minister Lloyd George had called a General Election.

In spite of the enormous contributions that Jennie and Clementine made to Winston's life and his career, we would probably never have heard of them if Winston had not been so dynamically driven in his ambition to succeed and his eagerness to charge continually forward to joist with enemies wherever the most vital action was being fought.

5

The Russian Civil War
1920

Civil War had broken out in Russia soon after Lenin's October Revolution in 1917, and ended in 1923, when Mother Russia was replaced by the dictatorship of the Soviet Union and a new system of oppression was put in place.[1] The size of Russia's formidable population was 125,640,021.[2] It was estimated that some 80 per cent were, or had been, peasants and serfs and therefore illiterate.

One of the momentous situations that had made way for the communist coup by Lenin and his comrades was a wave of previous revolutions which had swept across Europe from February 1848, known as 'the Spring of Nations'. Although generally considered to be a series of uprisings against oppression in a number of European countries, it had been triggered by a potato blight that struck the Scottish Highlands and Ireland and most parts of the continent of Europe, causing famine for four consecutive years. Waves of emigration in flights from starvation resulted in the most widespread wave of revolutions in European history.

A million died in Ireland, which was the worst hit with 2 million refugees who were fortunate to be still alive. Many had been forced to graze in the fields like cattle, leaving them with green chins. Most other deaths occurred in Belgium and Prussia. It had taken a year for government troops to put down the food rebellions ruthlessly. Tens of thousands who escaped the battles with the military on the continent of Europe became refugees fleeing to Britain, or onward to New York Harbour.

The Statue of Liberty on Liberty Island would become a symbol of freedom for the oppressed masses that arrived by ship at the Federal Immigration station on nearby Ellis Island. A famous poem by American Emma Lazarus would be inscribed at the base of its pedestal.

> 'Give me your tired, your poor, Your huddled masses yearning to breathe free,
> The wretched refuse of your teeming shore.
> Send these, the homeless, tempest-tost to me.
> I lift my lamp beside the golden door!'[3]

Other refugees had ended up in countries as different as Syria and South America. Most turned out not to be 'refuse' after all, since they were quick to re-establish themselves in new countries that were welcoming, instead of oppressive like the ones they had left.

The desperate goal of revolutionaries in France in 1848 had been a hope of removing the absolute political rule of foreign royalty and aristocrats with their oppressive and brutal armies, backed by the Church and secret police. All had been indifferent to their subjects. The revolutionary wave was initiated largely by democratic intellectuals, socialists, and the middle classes who wanted more participation in government. They were joined by the working classes and peasants. They demanded the abolition of slavery, serfdom and forced labour, freedom of the press, and the reorganisation of the class structure.

There had been numerous rebellions in Russia before Alexander Kerensky's democratic February Revolution, and Lenin's violent and dictatorial October Revolution in 1917 that finally toppled the corrupt and incompetent Tsarist regime. Best known among them was the mutiny by sailors on the battleship *Potemkin* in 1905. So the October Revolution was not as unexpected at it might seem, because that vast and backward agricultural country, only now beginning to industrialise, suffered from weak leadership and was poorly managed by self-interested and ruthless officials with a tyrannical army that kept the nation subdued, and the secret police of the *Okhrana* who oppressed and terrorised its citizens.[4]

Despite the continued oppression and incompetence of the Romanov dynasty, statistics showed huge improvements in the Russian economy and society in general. But, as it turned out, they were too late.[5]

The Tribe and the State

Only three years before Winston married, a Treaty of Peace had been signed in New Hampshire between the Tsar of Russia and the Emperor of Japan, which had ended the Russo-Japanese War. It was a manifestation of what happened when other nations copied the English Industrial Revolution. Japan did so very fast while Russia was slower to follow suit, and disorganised. It had been unprepared for the pre-emptive strike by the Japanese navy at Port Arthur. What they did not destroy of Russia's brand new fleet at anchor in Manchuria, the Russian navy scuttled to prevent it from falling into Japan's hands.

The Times leader writer described with admiration the effective training of the victorious Japanese in the war as 'the subordination of the individual to the tribe and the State'. The Japanese military class had recognised remarkably quickly the urgent need to industrialise and modernise its army and navy. According to *The Times*, it was a lesson that the West had to learn from Japan, which was the first modern totalitarian state to succeed in the arms race. The incident signalled the approaching end of democratic liberalism, individual human rights, and reason, by replacing parliamentary democracy with nationalist dictators.

It was a moment of new reality that Winston Churchill apparently failed to notice at the time, as he was pleased to no longer have the responsibility of policing the China seas. It could now be left to Britain's Japanese ally.[6] He continued to view Japan benignly as no threat to the West. His friend General Ian Hamilton had worked closely as a military adviser to the Japanese, and one of Winston's favourite British secret agents, Sidney Reilly, had cooperated with them by providing the harbour plans to destroy Russia's new and modern fleet.

The Japanese pursued modernisation through industrialisation and nationalism with self-discipline and a sense of national destiny. Germany followed the same goal with the overwhelming armament industry and shipping production of Krupp. Each dominated its own sphere of influence, with Japan in the Pacific and Germany in Europe.

Apart from the ineptness of the Tsar's court, the Russian Empire had good reason to be slow. Its population was even more complicated than the ethnic and religious array that caused conflicts of envy and jealousy in the old Austro-Hungarian Empire. Multiculturalism made it difficult to rule. Categorised by religions, there were over 87 million devoted to the Eastern Orthodox Church, close to 14 million Muslims, 11.5 million Roman Catholics, 5.2 million Jewish, 3.6 million Lutherans, 2.2 million listed as 'Old Believers', more than a million Armenian Gregorians, and nearly half a million Buddhists and Lamaists. The remainder of the Tsar's subjects numbered far less than a million for each group, consisting of Reformed, Mennonites, Armenian Catholics, Baptists, Karaites, Anglicans, and other Christian and non-Christian denominations. It resulted in continual clashes between sullen peasants who demanded human rights and the authorities who denied them; and between religious minorities who bore grudges against each other; as well as persecution by local secret police who were constantly overwhelmed by their task of suppressing discontent that rippled everywhere.

Added to that were the ethnic clashes between more than 55.6 million Russian speakers, 22.4 million Ukrainians listed as 'Little Russians', 13.4 million Turkic Tatars, close to 8 million who spoke Polish, nearly 6 million Belarusian, and over 5 million Yiddish. 8.5 million spoke Finnish languages, 1.8 million German, 1.4 million Latvian, more than 1.25 million Georgian, Mingrelian and Svan speaking Kartvelian languages. 1.2 million speaking Lithuanian, nearly 1.2 million Armenian, and a similar number speaking Moldavian and Romanian. Over a million spoke Dagestani languages. The remainder in much smaller numbers spoke Bulgarian, Zhmud, Greek, Ossetian, and Tajik.[7]

One of the most serious blunders of the Tsar in the period leading up to the mutinies in the army and navy and the short-lived Provisional Social Democratic government headed by Kerensky in July to November of that year, was insisting on taking command of the armed forces and revealing his ignorance and incompetence, and his culpability for the mutinies and the revolution that followed.

There had been only strong and violent leaders before him and the new Minister-Chairman.[8] His officials treated the masses and each minority group with suspicion and contempt, and considered that the only way to prevent any group from rising up against their leaders was to hold them down by brute force and threats and periodic campaigns of terror. Otherwise there might be another revolution like the one in France.

The bloody results of the French Revolution were still on the minds of all Europe's leaders, encouraging them to crush all perceived opposition swiftly, as they had done so successfully in the wave of uprisings that had spread across Europe in 1848.

Now, with the rise of Bolshevism that swept the liberal Kerensky government aside, the random slaughter of millions continued in Russia. As in Revolutionary France, it was a bitter and angrily fought violent bloodbath of personal quarrels and opportunities for crimes and revenge.

Whatever romantic or patriotic motives were given for either revolution by poets, painters, and public intellectuals of the time, mob riots were far too massive for the limited police force, or even armed troops, to quell for some time to come. The leaders were discontented and ambitious professional revolutionaries. As the respected and persecuted author Alexander Solzhenitsyn would write many years later, when Soviet Russia was about to collapse, the rule of Lenin and Stalin was 'an utterly alien yoke forced upon the Russian people'.[9]

6

The Warlords

Vladimir Ilyich Ulyanov, known as Lenin, appeared to have a fixation on the Bolshevik ideology as a weapon to wage a personal vendetta to avenge a crime committed by the old Tsarist regime against his own family. His older brother Sasha had been hanged by the Tsarist government in 1887 at the age of twenty-one. Sasha had been the revolutionary of the family, joining the terrorist wing of the People's Will Party. He and his comrades had made an attempt to assassinate Tsar Alexander III by throwing a bomb into his carriage, just as Alexander II had previously been killed by the same group.

Sasha was arrested in the Nevsky Prospekt as a suspect before it could happen, then tried and hanged on 8 May. Evidently Lenin's motives were personal. He appeared to be determined to complete what Sasha had begun, if only to avenge his brother's brutal death.

It is an example of how history and politics often conceal what was really a personal and highly emotional matter beneath claims of an ideology. Most Russians were illiterate and had no idea what Bolshevism meant, except that it gave them permission to kill their landlord and steal his property.

If Sasha had been passionate, Lenin was glacial towards human beings. They were merely statistics. People had no place in his plans. His egotism was remarkably like Karl Marx, although Marx's emotions were overheated. People were units of production for both of them, and pawns in a political game for power. Lenin would ruthlessly exterminate millions in his climb to power, in order to dedicate himself to achieving Marx's programme.

Lenin was a political theorist and a communist who had been born into a middle-class farming family in Perm, and studied for a law degree. He was spurred to revolution even before his brother Sasha was arrested and executed. He became a prominent figure in the Russian Social Democratic Labour Party after moving to St Petersburg. He was arrested for sedition and sent into exile for three years. He moved to Western Europe on his release and split the Bolsheviks against the international Menshevik ideology of world revolution.

Support for the war and the Tsar began to falter once the mutinies began and soldiers shot their officers. The Tsar was ousted largely because he had hesitated for too long over whether or not to withdraw from the Great War. He was swept aside by Lenin, who formed a one-party Communist State that pulled Russia out of the war in a popular move. He promised to redistribute land among the Russian peasants, nationalise banks, and industrialise on a much larger scale to compete with Germany, Britain, the United States and Japan.

In spite of their horrendous cruelties and mass murders by starvation and bullets, Fabian and other socialist admirers of the regime in England veiled the communist leaders with a romantic persona derived from their wishful thinking. It enabled them to view communist dictator Stalin warmly as 'Uncle Joe'. Stalin encouraged it by posing for photographs holding a friendly curved pipe as a theatrical prop, and smiling benignly. The halo of the wishful idealisation of the previous Tsar by the masses as their 'Little Father' was passed on to Lenin and Stalin in turn, because they were wrongly thought to be liberators from tyrannical rule. The peasants could not imagine that anyone could reject humanity for the sake of a false economic ideology concocted and imposed on them by an emotionally dysfunctional leader. It was unthinkable.

Under Lenin's leadership, any opponents of communism were immediately targeted and suppressed, or terminated. Tens of thousands were murdered in the prisons of the Kremlin and elsewhere, or sent to slave labour camps in Siberia, known later as the Gulags.

At the same time, the Soviet government had to fight a number of anti-Bolshevik armies in a civil war, who were not the only ones fighting the new Bolshevik regime in Russia. As soon as the world war was over, the Allies not only supported anti-Bolshevik forces on the Russian continent, but launched a multinational expeditionary force in 1918 in an attempt to re-establish the Eastern Front. It was a half-hearted attempt to stall Bolshevism, because of war weariness, and partly a sense of relief at the overthrow of the oppressive Tsarist regime. There was lack of enthusiasm for its return. British Empire troops amounted to a total of 619,646 volunteers.

Leon Trotsky was a doctrinaire Marxist revolutionary who intended to spread communism globally. He had joined Lenin just before the October Revolution, to become one of the most powerful leaders of the communists, and one of seven members of the Politburo who managed the revolution. They were Lenin, Trotsky, Zinoviev, Kamenev, Stalin, Sokolnikov and Bubnov. Trotsky founded and led the Red Army as people's Commissar of Military and Naval Affairs. He and Lenin were intellectuals.

Joseph Stalin, on the other hand, had been born the son of a drunken and violent cobbler in Georgia. His mother was a serf. His little home town was violent with marauding street gangs. He studied at the Orthodox Theological Seminary in Tiflis. He learned Marxism and admired Lenin. He was code-named 'Koba', after the hero of a Robin Hood type of character in a novel and outlawed as a revolutionary by the Tsar's secret police, the brutal *Okhrana*.[1]

Growing up in the grim and hopeless culture of the Russian Tsarist Empire, he became brutalised by a life that was little more than squalid slavery for the majority, whose only solace might be a bucket of vodka left for them by a generous master to drink themselves senseless in the evenings.

Stalin would gradually manipulate his way to full and total power by the 1920s.

Winston the Overachiever

Churchill had already spent nineteen years in politics and had commanded a Scottish battalion as a lieutenant colonel on the Western Front in the war by the time he was forty-two. The years of being the butt of bickering accusations by opposition Conservative Members of Parliament were almost forgotten with the changes that had transformed Britain's post-war society. Class distinctions had not yet been narrowed, and certainly not dissolved, but had been conveniently fudged after the Great War. He felt at the peak of contentment with the purposefulness facing him as Secretary of State for War, since his greatest motivating force was the continual challenges to his intellect and his skills.

He was still an obsessively compulsive overachiever in his work, with a zest for new interests. He had already held a variety of offices in the government: President of the Board of Trade at the age of thirty-three, Home Secretary and First Lord of the Admiralty, Minister of Munitions, and Secretary of State for War and Air in the past world war. He had always shown considerable zeal and energy in reorganising and modernising departments, sorting out their problems, instituting innovations, raising their standards of efficiency, and reducing costs. He was also respected for the new legislation he managed to push through Parliament that contributed to a more egalitarian society.

He had been loyal to three Prime Ministers so far; as Under-Secretary of State for the Colonies under Prime Minister Henry Campbell-Bannerman; then to Herbert Asquith and David Lloyd George, who sought his advice in a crisis and found him not only knowledgeable but strong-minded and resolute.[2]

Young Winston Churchill enjoyed being valued by the nation's leaders, with his advice in demand, and he was eager and delighted to provide help in times of confusion or chaos. He was – as Field Marshal Sir Henry Wilson had called him – 'a real gem in a crisis'. It was partly a matter of temperament, but also the fact that he had thoroughly prepared himself for his destiny according to his research into the life's work of his successful and influential ancestor, John Churchill, the 1st Duke of Marlborough.

He was considered by colleagues now to be patient and resourceful. But, in fact, he had lost none of his impatience with fools or his ambition to achieve success. At the same time, he was always conciliatory in times of workers' strikes, and generous in settlements even with foreign enemies or rebels, since he possessed the gift of detachment in understanding other people's points of view. He also possessed an ability to compartmentalise his feelings and attitudes, and a low opinion of human nature; so that his cynical view of the past chaos and incompetence failed to erode his optimism about the future.

It was only when he was out of office that he would sometimes become pessimistic out of frustration at being unable to influence events. Fortunately, his skills were in great demand because of a continuous array of problems and challenges, and his mindset was formed primarily to recognise and solve them, and exploit opportunities wherever he could find them.

CHURCHILL'S CHALLENGES, 1918–1940

Even so, some of his many critics still bickered with their accusations of his mishandling such episodes as the strikes by coal miners in Wales when he was Home Secretary, the Antwerp escapade when he was tempted to lead the floundering army, and the aborted Dardanelles Campaign when First Lord of the Admiralty. Had his critics known the true circumstances and facts, as he had known them at first-hand, he should have been beyond reproach. But the political opposition and the public were unforgiving.

One of the reasons for the invective aimed at him was that he had campaigned for free trade because he felt it would create more jobs for the working classes, whereas the Conservatives were against it in order to protect their own business interests. But the main reason for the Conservatives' attempts to ruin him had been that they had considered him disloyal to his class by switching sides to oppose them in the Liberal Party in the House of Commons. It continued to rankle, and made him a target for their criticisms and barbed insults.

The Conservative Party at that time represented the interests of the aristocracy and landed gentry, who might each own 1,000 to 30,000 acres of land representing their wealth. Churchill had found their interests narrow and self-serving when he had first been elected as a young Member of Parliament in a Conservative government. It was only when he had studied the first authoritative research on Britain's living standards that he had discovered about half of the population were living below the poverty level. He had decided that they were his real constituents. Finally dissatisfied with the attitude of Conservatives towards the majority of Britons, he had crossed the floor of the House of Commons to the Liberal benches in 1904, where Prime Minister Lloyd George led the opposition to the Conservative government.

Churchill had already admired the attitude of the Liberals even before he struck up a mutually supportive relationship with Liberal Prime Minister Lloyd George, who showed the same interest and care towards the underprivileged and marginalised poor and needy as Winston did.

Perhaps the best summary of the attitude of thoughtful people in young Winston's time was quoted by his private secretary Eddie Marsh: "I think that one's first duty is to make life as pleasant as one can for the people one is thrown with."[3]

7

Justice for All

Two years after the end of the Great War, as it was still called, Churchill was asked for a message to be published in a book listing all Jewish men who had fought for Great Britain. He replied that there was no need, since the facts spoke for them: 60,000 had fought in the war in Europe, Africa and Asia, despite their small proportion of the population in the British Empire. 2,324 were killed in the war, 6,350 were wounded. Five Jewish soldiers were awarded the Victoria Cross for exceptional bravery under fire, and 1,533 won other awards for their courage or initiative in battle.

Nevertheless, General Denikin's volunteer White Russian Army fighting against Bolshevik Russian troops in the civil war in the south had 'turned savagely against the Jews in more than 160 towns and villages'. Thousands of Jewish civilians were killed. An anti-Semitic attitude was already deep-seated in southern Russia and the Ukraine during the Tsarist regime. Both regions had been torn by massacres and pogroms against Jews in the seventeenth and nineteenth centuries. Unarmed and without rights, Jews were an easy target for violence. So, after the Bolshevik Revolution erupted in November 1917, many Jews were tired of being terrorised and hoped for better lives if they joined the Bolsheviks as equals.[1]

Churchill knew that some were commissars and leaders, but condemned the anti-Jewish terror. Daily life for most people in Tsarist Russia had been an endless nightmare without hope of ever waking up from it. In that regard, Jewish people had been no different from the peasants, but they had one huge advantage in that they were often the only ones in a village who could read and write and studied to know the outside world, and maintained civilised values.

The main mass of Russians was eagerly drugged by the regular rituals and incense of the Eastern Orthodox Byzantine Church and its often corrupt priests. The perception of life by the peasants was half-stupefied from obsessive superstitions and comforting and supposedly magical rituals. They worshipped painted icons and repeatedly crossed themselves to ward off evil spirits, while looking forward to a kinder and less brutal life in an imagined future world that was promised and depicted for them by the Russian Orthodox Church.

Rescuing the peasants from the Bolsheviks would require a volunteer army, which the British government had rejected as unpractical and too costly in Britain's poor post-war economic situation.

Now that Churchill was Secretary of State for War, his responsibility at the War Office was to continue government policy, which had been established before he had taken office. It involved sending war material to Russia's anti-Bolshevik armies which were attempting to drive the Bolsheviks from Petrograd and Moscow.[2] Churchill, with a broader and more imaginative mind than most politicians or civil servants, saw a way to weaken the Bolsheviks by discouraging Russian Jews from supporting them.

Social Justice

Most, even probably all, of the Jewish population in Russia were literate and educated from an early age. However, Russian author Fyodor Dostoevsky had ridiculed the notion that 'by simply completing a course of study, young people become immune to falling under the sway of crafty scoundrels who have thoroughly studied the magnanimous aspect of the human soul – most often the soul of youth – so as to be able to play on it like a musical instrument'.

Dostoevsky admitted that he himself, when young, had fallen, with others, for the beguiling promises of the revolutionary Sergei Nechaev, and that 'almost the whole company [of his friends] had graduated from the highest institutions of learning'.

His intention was to illustrate how easy it was for adolescents to be swayed by discontented subversives without being aware of the consequences of their actions.

Young Dostoevsky had joined the Petrashevsky Circle, which was a socialist gathering for intelligent discussions aimed at emancipating the serfs, who represented about 80 per cent of the population at the time. But – as with all such well-intentioned circles – they were soon joined by a small group of extremists who discredited the group and led to their arrest.

As the leading book critic of *The Russian Word* wrote of the character of the nihilist revolutionary Bazarov in Turgenev's great novel, *Fathers and Children,* 'In every period there have been people in the world dissatisfied with life in general, or with some special form of life in particular; in every period these people have made up an insignificant minority. The masses, in every period have lived contentedly, and with their inherent placidity have been satisfied with what was at hand. Only some sort of material catastrophe ... jolts this mass into uneasy movement, into the destruction of its customary, dreamily tranquil, vegetative existence ...'[3]

To the Tsarist government and its secret police, it was education that jolted the masses into protesting at the appalling living conditions, disorganisation and corruption in the Russian Empire. In those days of mass illiteracy, anyone who could read and write was considered to be a threat by the government, at least a potential critic; so that any type of rebelliousness or complaint would be followed by mass arrests of teachers, liberals, socialists, Jews, and anyone who could read, or demanded an end to social injustice.

At the same time, in earlier rebellions, when Bolsheviks arrived at villages on horseback, they would press the only literate people, who were usually Jewish, into service as a secretary of a new local Bolshevik cell. Those they chose had no choice: so that many Jews were forced into joining the Communist Party. It gave hope of change and improvement to those who felt oppressed. Some Jewish secretaries rose to become communist commissars. Others managed to escape to Britain or the United States.

As Dostoevsky phrased it, there is a 'tipping point' before which a well-balanced person with integrity has an opportunity to step back and walk away from the edge of evil. Young Fyodor had been caught in that dilemma himself, and he had *not* walked away. As a result, he was sentenced to death. He and his friends were manacled and chained before being lined up for execution before a firing squad.

'The death sentence was read out to all of us, we were given the Cross to kiss, swords were broken over our heads, and last pre-mortem changes were made to our clothing (white shirts). Then three (of us) were placed by the posts for the execution of the sentence. We were called out in threes; consequently I was in the second batch and had not more than a minute to live.'[4]

Only minutes from death in front of a firing squad, they had been reprieved at the last moment before the order was given to fire. Instead, they were sentenced to several years in a Siberian labour camp. That would be the likely fate of Jewish liberals who went to the aid of the underprivileged that needed a helping hand, with the added disadvantage that traditional government anti-Semitism marked them out as likely rebels to be arrested by the secret police for their magnanimous spirit, which was a desire for justice for all.

Journalist and author Arthur Koestler admitted in his autobiography to that feeling of 'devoting my life to the cause of the persecuted', which took possession of him in 1924. He described it as the 'oceanic feeling' – an expression that Freud had coined to denote a mystical or religious experience of self-sacrifice.[5] It was a sentiment that he shared with Winston Churchill. The difference was that, whereas it took Koestler several years to wake up from his delusion before he finally rejected communism, Churchill immediately saw through its dishonesty and recognised its dangers at the outset.

Sensitivity to the Pain of Others

After living in a well-ordered and democratic society, the oppressive living conditions and the injustices of Tsarist Russia would be impossible to imagine but for the literature of Russian writers like Isaak Babel, Dostoevsky, Tolstoy, Pushkin, Maxim Gorky, Chekhov and other authors and playwrights whose writing became classics. They were sensitive to the pain of others. Their conscience and candidness compelled them to describe the grim and cruel life in the Russian Empire, far, far away from the parties and balls of the upper classes in St Petersburg that Tolstoy described in *War and Peace* and Alexander Pushkin depicted in his story of an anti-hero in *Eugene Onegin*.[6]

In *The Life and Adventures of Matthew Pavlichenko*, Babel related how a fellow officer had stamped a former master to death in the Bolshevik civil war, and remarks thoughtfully of the incident, 'With shooting – I'll put it this way – with shooting you only get rid of a chap … With shooting you'll never get at the soul, to where it is in a fellow and how it shows itself. But I don't spare myself, and I've more than once trampled an enemy for over an hour …'[7]

Babel also wrote of the Bolsheviks, 'an individual who cannot love may choose complete power over another person instead; to make him or her do what they want, feel what they want, think what they want … to transform the other person into a thing, my thing, my possession. The ultimate degree of this attempt to know lies in the extreme of sadism, in the desire to make a human being suffer, to torture him to betray his "secret" in his suffering, or eventually to destroy him.'

Such morbid, self-indulgent and remorseless cruelty seems to have been almost commonplace in Russia at the time. Dostoevsky remarked on it as being a particularly Russian kind of vicious and spiteful cruelty. He maintained that, for example, while other people typically beat their starving horses to get them to move, only a Russian would think of whipping his horse across the eyeball.[8] And only a Russian landowner or government official would defy common sense by punishing a lazy or sullen peasant working on his estate by flogging him with a knout that would be likely to break his back; or bury a woman upright in the ground, with only her head exposed, as punishment for killing her husband in self-defence when he beat her brutally out of drunken boredom.

It is unlikely that a cultivated man of history and literature like Winston Churchill would not have read at least some of those Russian authors – even seen some of the early Russian silent films – so that he would have understood clearly that whoever spread anti-Semitic attitudes had no respect for anyone else's life either. He admired the gallantry of Jewish people seeking justice for all, because it was a prime element in his own nature. Anti-Semitism was a litmus test; an alarm signal that revealed how everyone else was in danger and would certainly be the next to be victimised if they allowed the Jews to be persecuted.

As for Russian Jews who believed there was no hope for Russia except with Bolshevism, Churchill felt that they should be offered an alternative of a Jewish National Home. One of the appeals of Zionism would be that it would open a door of hope after thousands of years of persecution. Churchill, with his own magnanimous spirit and his aspiration for justice, became an ardent Zionist himself.

8

The Soul of Nations

Churchill wrote about the revolutionaries who finally tore down the Tsarist regime and transformed Russia into an even more brutal and bloodthirsty nation than before, 'In the East of Poland lay the huge mass of Russia – not a wounded Russia only, but a poisoned Russia, an infected Russia, a plague-bearing Russia, a Russia of armed hordes not only smiting with bayonets and with cannon, but accompanied with and preceded by swarms of typhus-bearing vermin which slew the bodies of men, and political doctrines which destroyed the health and even the soul of nations.'[1]

To display his skills at coining short and snappy slogans, he wrote impishly to his intimate lady-friend, Violet Asquith, by remarking that his policy now was, 'Kill the Bolshie. Kiss the Hun.'

With the ever-depressing news coming out of Germany, he would change his mind about kissing the Huns. But it revealed his conviction and the general feeling in government that the spread of communism was by far the biggest threat at the time. It was only later that Europe and the world would be caught between two powerful police states imposing two different forms of persecution, and he would have to choose the most effective tactics by selecting which enemy to defeat first: the political enemy on the left or the military enemy on the right.

As Russian anti-Bolshevik forces continued killing Jews in the civil war, Churchill wrote instructions on 21 October to be sent to a senior British officer attached to the anti-Bolshevik forces in the south that everything must be done to prevent indiscriminate or wholesale executions. Above all, he explained that anything like a Jewish pogrom could do considerable harm to the Russian cause.[2]

He added that General Denikin could go to the length of refusing further ammunition or supplies to the Russian forces in order to secure the safety of innocent Jews. After hearing from Lloyd George of the continued persecutions, he wrote directly to Denikin to act immediately to vindicate the honour of the Volunteer Russian Army to gain support in Parliament for the Russian National Cause.[3]

British Prime Minister Lloyd George had chosen not to support the anti-Bolshevik Russians with ground troops, since the British public were tired of war, and Allied soldiers fighting only recently on the Western Front would resist being sent to another distant battlefield. British troops who had already been sent to Russia were withdrawn.

CHURCHILL'S CHALLENGES, 1918–1940

Lloyd George remarked to his colleagues that great armies would have been required if the Allies had decided to defeat the Bolsheviks, which they did not have. Anxious as the West was about the spread of Bolshevism, nor did they want to see the return of a Russian Empire with all the old social and economic inequalities and frictions.

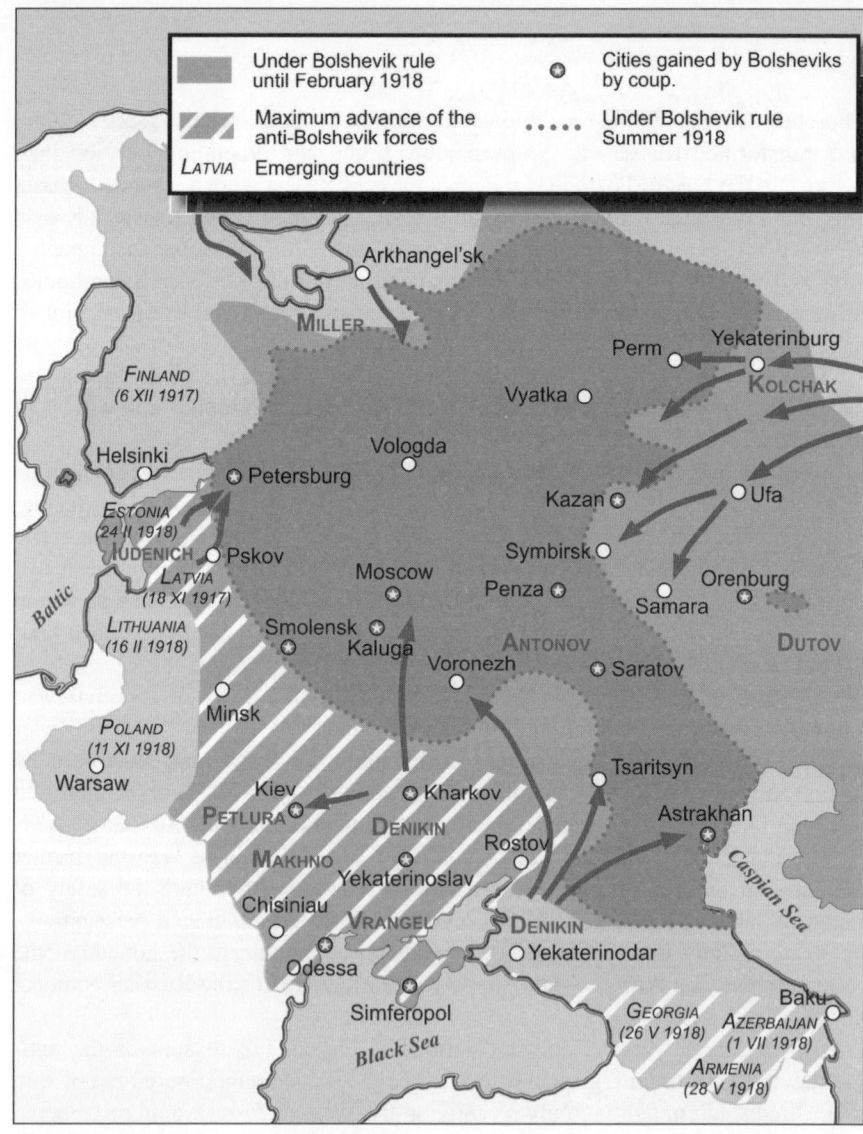

Russian Civil War in the West (1918-1920) with Red Army gains over patriotic generals and Admiral Kolchak.

Russia's Anti-Bolshevik Forces

There were more than half a million anti-Bolshevik Russian forces to begin with. Denikin's army advanced north-west towards Moscow from the Ukraine and South Russia, supported by Cossacks. General Yudenich in the north-west was intent on controlling the Baltic area and advanced within striking distance of Petrograd with heavy artillery. Admiral Kolchak's troops in Siberia advanced into the Russian interior, reaching Kazan on the Volga. Cossack troops advanced between the Ural Mountains and the Caspian Sea towards the Volga River. But their forces were not united, and the overwhelming question throughout the summer and autumn months was whether they could defeat Trotsky's Red Army, which was now well organised and well led.

The weakness of White Russian forces became clear by the summer, when one of Kolchak's Ukrainian regiments mutinied and murdered all its officers. In another mutiny in July, a Russian regiment handed over their section of the line to Red Army troops who confronted them.

Churchill placed considerable confidence in the Russian anti-Bolshevik leaders and used his special agent Reilly to keep him in personal touch with events in Russia, not only on the battlefields and with influential politicians and leading families, but also with the main Russian banks. Reilly's reports on the Volunteer Army, the Don Cossacks and the French military, proved to be 'accurate and far-sighted'.[4]

Even so, 'There is a lack of political guidance and co-ordination,' observed the British Foreign Office. 'But this might be discussed in Paris and Lt Reilly can throw interesting light on the situation (he goes there tomorrow).'[5]

Reilly arrived in Paris in Royal Flying Corps uniform to offer his advice at the peace conference on 30 March.

The Times reported on the civil war by attacking the Bolshevik leaders on 1 April, and followed up with a story about the possible recognition of a Lenin–Trotsky 'government'. On 4 April came a report that the French military were demoralised and the French general in command had ordered a withdrawal of Allied troops.

Reilly sailed to the United States after his visit to the peace conference, with a mission to persuade American banks and businesses to consider an Anglo–Russian business scheme by Karol Jaroszynski for an industrial combine, and to cooperate with it. He wired Picton Bagge at the British Foreign Office on 10 May to state that American bankers and industrialists were interested in the Russian market and prepared to raise capital in order to replace the anticipated stagnation of their export trade by equivalent new trade in Russia. They were only waiting for order to be restored.

Restoring order in Russia and planning its economic and political future were the mainsprings of Winston Churchill's post-war strategy. Armour and Ford and the American International Corporation had already made 'tentative agreements' with a Russian financier who possessed a fleet of ships on the River Volga; also with hundreds of agencies in the grain regions of Siberia and Ukraine, and several other banks.

Reilly sailed back to England on 15 May. On 3 July he noted that the activities of several anti-Bolshevik leaders in South Russia continued, but it was difficult to separate the bandits on each side from patriots. When Reilly called on Churchill for support, he was met with enthusiasm. Churchill wrote a minute to his staff at the War Office: 'A conference should be held tomorrow at the War Office on the Trade possibilities in the Denikin area.'[6]

Churchill believed that if Denikin could hold on to the territory he had won, there would be greater prosperity there than in the areas under Bolshevik rule; in which case Manchester, Sheffield, Leicester and other manufacturing cities in England could gain new markets for their goods. It was an opportunity to trade with millions of Russians. He firmly believed that the capitalist system was another way to fight the communists in war-torn Russia.

British diplomat Sir Ronald Graham wrote to Lord Curzon, 'If the scheme is economically sound, it should be worth supporting and may form a barrier to the economic penetration which the Germans are already organising.'[7]

But pertinent questions needed answering, such as 'how is this network of banks and societies to be set up in a country in a state of chaos and in the hands of murderous ruffians?'

Churchill circulated a paper by one of Jaroszynski's aides to the War Cabinet, pressing for British economic help for Admiral Kolchak and General Denikin, and warning that otherwise they will perish and Germany will step in. To prevent German control, it was in Britain's interest to help combine the Russian banks 'into one powerful organisation'. With enough finance, Kolchak's and Denikin's causes could then be considered safe.

Battling for Survival

General Denikin continued to advance his troops on Moscow throughout the summer and autumn. But Admiral Kolchak's autumn offensive in Siberia lasted only a month before he was forced to retreat at the end of September. Inadequate supplies from Britain and incompetent leadership stalled General Yudenich's assault against Petrograd. The Red Army rallied under Trotsky and pushed back Yudenich's forces.

'By October, a total Bolshevik force of 460,000 was facing 630,000 Whites.' Lenin and Trotsky controlled the interior lines. Troops and supplies were moved by rail to whichever sector of the front needed them urgently.[8]

Anti-Bolshevik forces murdered at least 100,000 Jewish people in 1918 and 1919: Cossacks and General Denikin's army in particular, causing material support from the Allies to shrink. Nevertheless, British tanks, aeroplanes and artillery pieces were still being shipped to General Yudenich's forces, with rifles and equipment for

20,000 men in mid-October. Even as Denikin's troops neared the outskirts of Tula, the British government agreed to send him surplus British munitions and other supplies valued at £17.5 million.

Then, unexpectedly, a Ukrainian peasant army attacked Denikin's forces while attempting to seize territory for itself. A few weeks later, several Cossack units that Denikin depended on transferred their allegiance to the Bolsheviks. Soon afterwards, Trotsky's Red Army reached Petrograd and counterattacked against Yudenich's troops, which continued their advance to the heights of Pulkovo, overlooking Petrograd. General Yudenich intended to prevent the Red Army from reaching Moscow.

'Lenin made every effort to ensure that Yudenich was likewise beaten back. On October 22 he instructed Trotsky; "It is *damnably* important for us to finish off Yudenich (just that – finish him off: dispatch him)." To ensure a successful offensive, Lenin asked Trotsky: "Cannot 20,000 or so Petrograd workers be mobilised, plus 10,000 or so of the bourgeoisie, machine guns to be posted to the rear of them, a few hundred shot, and a real mass assault on Yudenich assured?"'

Trotsky launched his counterattack against Yudenich and drove his forces from the Heights the next day. The anti-Bolshevik troops retreated on all fronts. Nations like France cut off all financial and military aid. A Polish army advanced against Denikin and obtained considerable territory in Western Russia and Eastern Galicia, which they hoped to hold on to as part of Poland.

By Christmas of 1919 Red Army forces stalled Denikin before he could reach Moscow, and he was forced to retreat. White Russian morale broke down. General Wrangel took over, but was finally forced to leave the Crimea with his forces.

French Premier Clemenceau met with Lloyd George on the same day that the Red Army drove Denikin from Kharkov. Trotsky and his army entered Kiev four days later. It took only another two weeks for the White anti-Bolshevik armies to retreat in complete disarray from Trotsky's overwhelming and unforgiving Red Army forces.

The Russian Civil War was now over, and British Prime Minister Lloyd George refused to back Churchill's schemes any longer.

9

Churchill's Obsession
1920

Palestine was part of Churchill's responsibility as Secretary of State for War, because it was under British military administration after being freed from Turkish rule three years previously by General Allenby. Chaim Weizmann, the head of the Zionist Executive in London, wrote to Churchill suggesting that the next Chief Administrator might be someone sympathetic to Zionism, and mentioned General Wyndham Deedes.

Field Marshall Allenby – as he had since become – had previously expressed sympathy at the Paris Peace Conference with the idea of appointing Deedes. Weizmann wanted to send several experts to study the country and make recommendations with plans, so that when political decisions were finalised in Paris, the Jewish people could begin to reconstitute Palestine as their National Home without loss of time. The whole point of the conferences was not only to obtain war reparations from Germany but to support self-determination for smaller nations left orphaned by the collapse of empires. Churchill passed on the letter to Allenby.

Allenby replied on 15 October 1919, 'However much we may sympathise with Zionist aims, it must be borne in mind that Palestine is as yet merely occupied enemy territory, under a purely military administration.' He pointed out that it was entirely the concern of the War Office.[1]

Churchill was concerned about the viability of the Middle Eastern provinces now that the Ottoman Empire, which had administered them, had been defeated and left a vacuum in its place. He feared that the proposed British Mandates for Palestine and Iraq would result in endless and costly conflicts with the Arabs. Bearing in mind that Prime Minister Lloyd George had emphasised that his aim was economy of military involvement and costs, Winston wrote a memorandum for the Cabinet that the former Ottoman Empire should not be divided between the victorious powers, but kept intact under the authority of the League of Nations.

Doing so would bring to an end the British Mandate in Palestine and abandon the pledge of a Jewish National Home according to the Balfour Declaration. He reasoned that the French were about 'to over-run Syria with hordes of Algerian troops'. Consequently they would soon be involved 'in a protracted and bloody struggle with the Arabs who are defending their native land'.

Britain would be bound to sympathise with the Arabs, causing 'serious injury' to Anglo–French relations. As far as Palestine was concerned, there were some Zionists who were convinced that the local population would be cleared out to suit them. He went on to explain that Britain was 'the greatest Mahommedan Power' as a consequence of the 20 million Muslims in British India. Considering Lloyd George's warning about economy, Churchill envisioned considerable expense and anxiety in partitioning the Turkish Empire, and said he thought it would be a mistake.[2]

Lloyd George thought otherwise. He wanted Palestine to continue under British rule, and he was committed to the Jewish National Home. It took Churchill four months of studying the situation more deeply before he agreed with the Prime Minister and became a committed advocate of Zionism and the Jewish National Home.

Conflict between Activists

When Churchill spoke in Sunderland on 2 January 1920, he attempted to sweep communism away with ridicule. But the introduction of Bolshevism in Russia was the result of oppression and persecution on a massive scale over generations, even centuries. It could not be so easily scorned. It would become an emotional issue for both sides.

Once again Churchill's emotional identification with a need for justice for the underdog would become a political obsession. What may have loomed in Churchill's mind was the murder of his friend Captain Cromie by the Bolsheviks. Young, noble and courageous Captain Francis Cromie of the Foreign Office had been a submarine commander when only twenty-four. He was shot to death on the steps of the British Embassy in Petrograd when a Bolshevik mob and the Soviet secret police (the CHEKA) attacked it. It reinforced Winston's determination to root out the Bolsheviks before they could do more harm.[3]

The leader of the Red Army, Leon Trotsky, was born Lev Davidovich Bronstein in a small Ukrainian village, one of eight children of a relatively successful farmer in a remote rural area. He became a revolutionary at seventeen and organised the South Russian Workers' Union a year later, for which he was imprisoned for two years. He exchanged ideas with other revolutionaries while behind bars. Trotsky too had developed an *idée fixe,* for which he would sacrifice his wife and daughter to the cause of Bolshevism. His daughter would commit suicide after following him to exile in Berlin. His wife would disappear much later on, during Stalin's Great Purges, when she would be murdered by Stalin's forces.

Lenin and Trotsky were prepared to endure and inflict unimaginable hardships on their families and everyone else for the sake of a problematic cause, because the injustices and cruelties of the Tsarist regime had hardened their hearts.

There were a few Russian writers who were prepared to risk their lives by revealing the truth about Russia under Romanov rule. Most were trapped into choosing

Bolshevism because there was no other alternative. Trotsky claimed that revolution was the only way to destroy the intolerable nightmare that was Tsarist Russia.

The Colonial Office

Churchill had not wanted the Colonial Office when it had been offered to him. He already knew the problems of trying to obtain reasonable agreement from volatile nationalistic leaders whose primary aim was to achieve more power. Their discontented and emotional followers had no intention of agreeing or compromising with anyone. Their overheated emotions prevented any consideration of the advantages of cooperation or compromise. But after Churchill had reviewed the situation and its challenges, he did what he had always done with new responsibilities; he had researched as much information as he could, and then dived in with all his senses and emotions, and his knowledge of history with its endless examples of fair governance.

Prime Minister David Lloyd George considered that young Winston spent more time than he should on problems he viewed as priorities, like International Communism, the Balfour Declaration, Home Rule for Ireland, and discontented Indian Nationalists who caused mischief for the administrators of the country. Lloyd George was a pragmatic and wily politician who attended to immediate priorities one at a time, and could not understand the young man's overdeveloped sense of responsibility or his broad sweep of knowledge of multiple events.

Winston's obsessive compulsion to help those who would otherwise be helpless was driven by a romantic notion of obtaining justice for vulnerable people who lacked the assertive power and influence to protect themselves. He was motivated by common decency rather than political ideology.

It was not the case with Winston's pragmatic political colleagues and the civil servants tackling their daily administrative routines patiently, objectively and unemotionally. They were amazed and put out by his total commitment to the affairs of Russia and the troublesome colonies and mandated territories. Lloyd George thought him mad to become so deeply involved with such emotive and often insoluble problems, and his way of attempting to turn them into opportunities for Britain. It involved the two friends and partners, who were still rivals for political greatness, in merely tiresome disputes about justice and liberty, free speech, authority, and human rights for all.

The disputes over Churchill's fixed position on the Russian Bolsheviks were often far more heated than tiresome. Maurice Hankey, the new Secretary to the Cabinet, noted that Churchill '(who had drunk a great deal) lectured us at enormous length & great brilliancy about Russia, spreading maps all over the floor. He is quite balmy in his enthusiasm for the anti-Bolsheviks.'[4]

Prime Minister Lloyd George was afraid that Churchill wanted to declare war on Bolshevik Russia, while *he* planned to begin formal negotiations with the new

Soviet Russian government in the traditional manner, in order to trade with them. The Prime Minister was twenty years senior to Churchill. He remarked a few days later, 'I don't know what to do with the boy.'

'The Prime Minister protested again that his appeals to Churchill to concentrate on cutting spending had fallen on deaf ears. He claimed that the previous Friday he had entreated Churchill "to let Russia be for at least 48 hours" and spend the weekend preparing for the Cabinet's Finance Committee.'[5]

Nevertheless, Churchill continued to investigate the nature and structure of the organisation in Moscow, determined to do his best to crush Bolshevism in Russia before it could spread to the British Isles. He knew the names and origins of Lenin and Trotsky. He decided that there were three options for any Russian Jews swept up in the Bolshevik Revolution – to emigrate to Palestine or the West; to attempt to hold on to Jewish social, religious and cultural values in Russia; or to join the Bolsheviks. It was only a minority who joined them, mostly the gullible for a romantic ideal, and others pushed unwillingly into communism.

To prevent the latter option, Churchill appealed to Russian Jews, and Jews from anywhere else, in a popular Sunday newspaper, the *Illustrated London Herald*, to choose between Zionism and Bolshevism. In one paragraph of the article he wrote, 'We owe to the Jews in the Christian revelation a system of ethics which, even if it were entirely separated from the supernatural, would be incomparably the most precious possession of mankind, worth in fact the fruits of all other wisdom and learning put together.'

Since he did not want to create stereotypes, he added, 'there are three main lines of political conception among the Jews, two of which are helpful and hopeful in a very high degree...' First were those who live in every country and identify with that country in which they regard themselves as citizens of the State which received them: so a Jew living in England would say "I am an Englishman practising the Jewish faith."'

He pointed out that even in Russia Jews had managed to play an honourable and useful part in the national life, despite the hostility levelled against them.

He made his own admiration of the Jewish people evident when he wrote, 'no thoughtful man can doubt the fact that they are beyond all question the most formidable and most remarkable race which has ever appeared in the world'.[6]

Even so, Jewish Bolsheviks saddened him. But he was convinced that the offer of a Jewish National Home after all those years would change their minds. Fortunately, Palestine had fallen into British hands as a result of Britain's conquest of the Ottoman Empire.

A Dangerous Man

Britain's victories during the war had resulted in a necessity to include new territories in the British Empire, particularly after Allenby's successful campaign against the Turks in the Middle East. At the same time, Churchill also had to pacify the Irish nationalists who never ceased rebelling against England. And there were nationalistic protests against British rule in India, as well as rebellion against British rule in Egypt, which was another part of the former Ottoman Empire. His task was not an easy one. But with his gift for compartmentalising, he was able to concentrate on each situation with his full attention. He already knew the political, economic and social problems of all those countries.

Nevertheless, Britain's colonial military forces were limited by Lloyd George's pressure to reduce spending. At the same time, troops who had been conscripted in the war were now pressing for speedy demobilisation, which would shrink the size of the British Army.

Above all, Churchill was obsessed by the Bolshevik threat, since the revolutionary Leon Trotsky, who led the Red Army, was still demanding and instigating communist revolutions all over the world and, in particular, in the British Empire. It caused abrasiveness from the start of the Russian Revolution, between Lenin, who was intent on industrialising Soviet Russia, and Trotsky, who planned to spread communism worldwide.

Now, industrial unrest in Britain sparked fears of Bolshevism taking hold in England like the spread of a plague. It was the main threat that obsessed Churchill during his post-war period in office with Prime Minister Lloyd George, who had already described Winston Churchill privately as a dangerous man who had Bolshevism on the brain.[7]

Churchill disagreed with Lloyd George's more pragmatic political approach to events with one eye always on the electorate, and plunged enthusiastically into every new challenge, as if Britain's life depended on him: 'in his eyes, they failed to recognise the severity of the issues at stake. He claimed that Lenin, Sinn Féin (the Irish Republican Party) and the Indian and Egyptian extremists were all linked in a joint effort to overthrow the Empire.'[8]

That conspiracy theory brought out all his heroic impulses to protect Great Britain from its enemies. As usual, he veered from coercion to conciliation as his driving ambition compelled him to excel.

In such a topsy-turvy world, it was no wonder that Churchill had not been at all keen to accept his government appointment to the Colonial Office.

'I am afraid this venture is going to break me,' he had said gloomily of the problems in Ireland.[9]

According to Sir Henry Wilson, who was Chief of the Imperial General Staff and an old friend from the war years, 'Winston told me he took the Colonies because he would not have lasted much longer in the WO owing to differences with LG.'[10]

10

The Middle East Upheaval
1921

Mesopotamia was still in a state of chaos as a consequence of the political and military upheaval in the Middle East. Britain had defeated the Turkish Empire, aided by Arab Irregular forces and Bedouin guerrillas led by the so-called Laurence of Arabia, but left a leadership vacuum. British troops had already been forced to put down a rebellion in Iraq, and there was real fear that unless the Middle East could be stabilised, Turkish forces might recognise an opportunity of weakness to return and retake it.

'In the spring of 1921,' wrote Winston Churchill, 'I was sent to the Colonial Office to take over our business in the Middle East and bring matters into some kind of order.' Preserving order in an Arab rebellion had cost more than 40,000 troops and £30 million a year.

'This could not go on. In Palestine, the strife between the Arabs and the Jews threatened at any moment to take the form of actual violence. The Arab chieftains, driven out of Syria with many of their followers, all of them our late allies, lurked furious in the deserts beyond the Jordan. Egypt was in ferment. Thus the whole of the Middle East presented a most melancholy and alarming picture.'[1]

Winston's bland remark about his appointment was phrased as if it were his due. In fact, wheels of influence had been turning and meshing with other wheels of necessity and destiny over which he'd had no control.

'Lawrence's press campaign against the government's policies in the Middle East not only had been successful, but had been followed with close attention by the prime minister, David Lloyd George, who watched with rising concern the cost of putting down Arab and Kurdish rebellions in Iraq – estimated at £20 million there alone – of separating Jews and Arabs in Palestine, and of trying to prevent Feisal's older brother, Emir Abdullah, from attacking the French in Syria.[2]

Lawrence had even visited 10 Downing Street in an attempt to have the interfering Lord Curzon removed from the Foreign Office. That, Lloyd George told him, was impossible. But Lawrence's idea of removing the Middle East from Curzon became lodged in the Prime Minister's mind. Implicit was Lawrence's proposal that one man should take charge of the Middle East. It was he who had recommended Winston Churchill.

CHURCHILL'S CHALLENGES, 1918–1940

Churchill had already been involved in crushing the rebellion in Iraq as Secretary of State for War and Secretary of State for Air.

> Lloyd George had always treated Churchill with the respect most sensible people reserve for a fused hand grenade. They were friends and rivals, both of them fiercely ambitious for power; of the two, Churchill was the more volatile, and at this point by far the more politically vulnerable, and Lloyd George, for all his fabled Welsh charm, did not conceal from his old friend the fact that only his personal intervention had persuaded the reluctant members of the Liberal and Conservative coalition to allow Churchill back into the government at all. Churchill was in the cabinet on suffrage, and at the pleasure of the prime minister, never a man to confuse good intentions with political self-interest. In any case, Lloyd George concluded that Churchill was the obvious man for the job – a choice which had the additional advantage that if Churchill failed, the prime minister could lay the entire responsibility on him.[3]

Churchill set up a new department of the Colonial Office to deal with the problems. Like the Prime Minister, he saw his responsibility was to maintain all of Britain's interests in the Middle East. They were to protect the Suez Canal, guard the oil in Iraq, and protect 'the safe air route to India across Arabia from Cairo to Baghdad'. He was also ordered to slash the heavy expenses of keeping hordes of troops in the area by using a few aircraft instead.

He made it abundantly clear that his preserve was no longer the responsibility of Lord Curzon, the Foreign Office or the War Office, by establishing a 'Middle East Department'.

He formed a preliminary nucleus of staff from a dozen 'very able' officers from the India Office, and some who had served in Iraq and Palestine in the war. He had not met T.E. Lawrence until the war was over.

'It was the spring of 1919 when the Peacemakers, or at any rate the Treaty-makers, were gathered in Paris and all England was in the ferment of the aftermath. So great had been the pressure in the War, so vast its scale, so dominating the great battles in France, that I had only been dimly conscious of the part played in Allenby's campaigns by the Arab revolt in the desert. But now someone said to me: "You ought to meet this wonderful young man. His exploits are an epic."'[4]

He invited Lawrence to lunch. Lawrence generally wore his Arab dress in London and Paris to publicise the interests of the Emir Feisal, since the Arab claims were being harshly and bitterly debated during the Peace Conference. He wore civilian clothes on this occasion. He looked at first sight, remarked Churchill afterwards, 'like one of the many clean-cut young officers who had gained high rank and distinction in the struggle. We were men only and the conversation was general.'

It was only later that Winston heard Lawrence had been invited to meet the King, who had planned to bestow a decoration on him, which Lawrence intended to refuse as a protest at the shabby way the Arabs had been treated and were regarded at the Paris Conference. The King had received Lawrence on 30 October to chat with him and bestow the honour of the Commandership of the Bath and the Distinguished Service Order (DSO) to which he had already been gazetted. Their conversation had taken place in private, and 'Lawrence begged that he might be allowed to refuse them'. Otherwise the Arabs might no longer trust him.

Churchill felt that, in his official position as Secretary of State for War at the time, he must at least tell Lawrence that his conduct had been wrong. Lawrence had accepted his rebuke in good humour during lunch, by remarking that it had been the only way to impress on the highest authorities that the honour of Great Britain was at stake when the Arabs had been betrayed to the demands of the French over Syria. He felt that the King should be made aware of what was being done in his name.

His remark made an impression on Churchill, who felt he should find out more about the grievances of the Arabs: 'I called for reports and pondered them. I talked to the Prime Minister about it. He explained that the French meant to have Syria and rule it from Damascus, and that nothing would turn them from it.' The Sykes–Picot agreement made in the war had confused the matter of principle: only the Paris Peace Conference could decide the outcome. 'This,' wrote Winston Churchill, 'was unanswerable.'[5]

Winston did not see Lawrence again for several weeks after their lunch. He wore his Arab robes in Paris. 'The gravity of his demeanour, the precision of his opinions, the range and quality of his conversation, all seemed enhanced to a remarkable degree by the splendid Arab head-dress and garb. From amid the flowing draperies his noble features, his perfectly chiselled lips and flashing eyes loaded with fire and comprehension shot forth. He looked what he was, one of Nature's greatest princes. We got on much better this time, and I began to form that impression of his strength and quality which since has never left me.'

Winston began to hear more about Lawrence from friends who had fought with him. There began to be continual talk about him in military and diplomatic circles, and academic ones. 'It appeared that he was a savant as well as a soldier, an archaeologist as well as a man of action, a brilliant scholar as well as an Arab partisan.'

No doubt some of the gossip was brought to Winston by his Private Secretary, art connoisseur Eddie Marsh, who was considered to be so sympathetic that just about everyone he met confided in him.

But Colonel Lawrence's Arab cause was not being viewed sympathetically at the Paris Peace Conference. He was almost inseparable from Feisal, as a friend and as his interpreter. He ignored the British in favour of the Arabs, and was rude to the French, whom he despised for their treatment of the Syrians. He clashed with the formidable Clemenceau in long and intense conversations.

'The old Tiger had a face as fierce as Lawrence's, an eye as unquailing and a will-power well matched. Clemenceau had a deep feeling for the east; he loved a paladin, admired Lawrence's exploits and recognised his genius. But the French sentiment about Syria was a hundred years old.'

CHURCHILL'S CHALLENGES, 1918–1940

The tiger in Clemenceau fumed at the idea that France had lost more dead in the trenches and No-Man's-Land than any of the other Allies. It was too much for him to bear, and he knew that his countrymen would never accept any other award for their pain than Syria. They would not let that prize fall from their grasp.

Everyone knew what followed. After long and bitter controversies both in Paris and in the East, the Peace Conference assigned the mandate for Syria to France. When the Arabs resisted this by force, the French troops threw the Emir Feisal out of Damascus after a fight in which some of the bravest

New frontiers in the Middle East.

of the Arab chiefs were killed. They settled down in the occupation of this splendid province, repressed the subsequent revolts with the utmost sternness, and rule there to this day by the aid of a very large army.[6]

Churchill would write those words in 1935. Lawrence did not know what to do about what he thought of as a betrayal. He felt frustrated and desperate. As a highly principled man, he was disgusted with the treacheries of life. He wrote that all personal ambition had died in him even before he had entered Damascus with his ragged guerilla forces in triumph in the final stages of the war.

Churchill's view of the treatment meted out to the Arabs at the Peace Conference was more pragmatic, because so many other people had suffered in the aftermath of the Great War, by the end of which four great empires had collapsed and millions of refugees were milling in and out of cities in search of food and shelter and loved ones. Many of them were orphaned children who were starving.

Their different attitudes to the aftermath of war were based on a simple fact that the whole point of igniting an Arab Revolt against Germany's ally was to end the war and slaughter on the Western Front as quickly as possible by breaking the deadlock – whereas for the Arabs it was a risky matter of seizing liberty from the savagery of Turkish oppression.

Mapping the Middle East

Winston decided to persuade Lawrence to join his staff in the new Middle East Department at the Colonial Office. He had no idea that it had been Lawrence who had recommended *him* to Lloyd George in the first place. He needed practical experts who knew the terrain and the people intimately. Colonel Lawrence was still greatly admired as the statuesque 'Lawrence of Arabia', and most of the staff knew him well. Some had even served under him at the battlefront. But they were aghast at the idea of saddling a wild beast of the desert. Some undervalued him while others were jealous of him. Some others genuinely thought that, with his edgy temperament, he could never be pinned down to a desk.

Winston persisted by offering him an important post. And, much to the surprise of the staff, Lawrence accepted his offer. The pay of £1,200 a year was modest, but Winston believed that Lawrence had run out of money. And the self-contained man who did not believe in material possessions or money led a frugal life. Even so, Winston had upped it to £1,600 a year.*

---

* Michael Korda wrote that Winston's Private Secretary Eddie Marsh first suggested the idea to Lawrence in December 1920, when he had hesitated, but thought better of it after talking it over with Feisal.[7]

CHURCHILL'S CHALLENGES, 1918–1940

As the situation worsened in the Middle East, Winston arranged an imminent conference in Cairo with most of his experts. He wrote, 'Accompanied by Lawrence, Hubert Young, and Trenchard from the Air Ministry, I set out for Cairo.'

They stayed there and in Palestine for over a month, submitting proposals to the Cabinet: 1. They would placate the Arabs and the House of the Sherifs of Mecca by placing the Emir Feisal on the throne as King of Iraq, and place the Emir Abdulla in charge of Trans-Jordan's government. 2. They would remove most of the troops from Iraq and place its defence in the hands of the Royal Air Force instead. 3. They suggested that the immediate difficulties between Arabs and Jews in Palestine should be adjusted as a foundation for the future.

Their first two propositions were met with powerful opposition and the French government was angry at Feisal being favoured after they thought they had got rid of him as a rebel. Britain's War Office had not yet adapted to air superiority and were shocked at the proposal to get rid of boots on the ground. Hugh Trenchard, founder of the Royal Air Force, was a different matter altogether: he could always be trusted to proceed with orders. When their proposals were finally accepted, Winston thought it would take a year to implement them.

Lawrence had advised installing a native king in Iraq. Who would be suitable? The answer boiled down to either the Emir Feisal or Ibn Saud, both of whom claimed the throne of Syria. Which could be trusted to be amenable to guidance, and which could be controlled by Britain's Foreign Office had still to be decided.

Lawrence was now a civil servant, and became Winston's chief adviser at the conference in Cairo in March 1921, to decide on how to draw up a new map of the Middle East. Another new adviser who attended the conference was the archaeologist and travel writer Gertrude Bell. Both she and Lawrence believed in Arab self-rule under Britain's guidance.

Winston did not mention her name when writing about the event, possibly because she was not a permanent member of his staff, but worked as a secret agent on special assignments, and he was punctilious about keeping absolutely silent where secret service matters were concerned. He had met her several years earlier when they had spent a day together touring archaeological sites.

He could now claim to have listened to several expert opinions. In addition, he took the advice of Sir John Shuckburgh, who joined his staff with Sir Gilbert Clayton, and Richard Meinertzhagen, who was an ardent Zionist. All were experienced in Middle East diplomacy and desert warfare.

Gertrude Bell was the first woman ever to be commissioned as an officer in the British Army and held the official rank of a major. She was known as an explorer of great courage who knew the territory and customs of the Arab tribes exceptionally well. Her familiarity with them and the respect they showed her appears to have been her greatest asset to Britain's Secret Intelligence Service. Deference was also shown to her by British administrators because of her knowledge of politics and her personal contacts with influential personalities at the top levels of government. It had been achieved partly because her father, Sir Hugh Bell, was a leading industrialist in steel and the sixth wealthiest man in Britain, and she was his heiress.

Unknown to many at the time, she was a trained spymaster who taught other secret agents in Britain's SIS, like the enigmatic St John Philby. Besides English, she spoke fluent French, Italian, German, Arabic, Persian and Turkish. 'Her around-the-world trips gave her enough Hindustani to dispense with an interpreter, and a smattering of Japanese and Urdu.'[8]

She was a self-assured and formidable woman who was not afraid of anyone. According to one of her biographers, 'From the time she took up her post as "Major Miss Bell"' in the Intelligence Bureau in Cairo in 1915, when she no longer had time to keep a diary, she told her father that her letters to the family would in future be her diary and asked them to keep them.'

She and her father and stepmother were an unusually affectionate family who took great interest in each other's work and were supportive of each other's abilities. She wrote very long letters home almost daily, and their replies were almost as long as hers. Her father had known he had an exceptionally intelligent and learned daughter almost from the first. Her academic studies and grades at Oxford University were most unusual for a young woman at that time. Her intellect could be challenging to most men who were not as bright as her. It led to several tragic relationships. She had already developed a close intellectual relationship with Lawrence before the Cairo Conference.

Major Miss Bell attended Winston's conference in Cairo in March 1921. When the Emir Feisal arrived in Baghdad in June, Gertrude met him and established a personal friendship. It was the same month when Prince Ibn Saud invaded and took the town of Hayyil, which Gertrude had explored in her travels. The Shammar tribesmen from Hayyil fled into Iraq.

'She made seven expeditions into the vast regions of the Middle East and Turkey, first as a wealthy tourist, but soon as an archaeologist, explorer and information gatherer for the British government. She described them as the happiest times of her life.'[9] She yearned for adventure and loved mountain climbing. Long before the Cairo Conference, in her youth in 1899–1900, she had made explorations to Petra, Deraa, Palmyra, Beirut and Damascus.

11

The Kingmakers
1921–22

Winston met up with Clementine in Marseilles. They had been married for thirteen years, which had been hectic for him and stressful for her. He had considered himself well enough established in his dual careers as politician and author to buy a country house to 'add great happiness and peace to our lives,' as he would write to her after the event. So arduous had been her life ever since she had agreed to marry him on that rainy day at Blenheim Palace that the stresses and strains of living with such a dedicated, ambitious and obsessive individual forced her to separate herself from him from time to time to recover her health and composure.

They took a steamship from Marseilles to Egypt, where they arrived on 9 March 1921. Three days later he joined the Cairo Conference with Britain's first High Commissioner to Palestine, Sir Herbert Samuel, and T.E. Lawrence.

Their first days were spent acclimatising themselves to Cairo, and the discomfort of the excessive heat, the irritation of persistent flies, sweat that ran down their faces and accumulated in every crevice of the body, and the hysterical rioting crowds of demanding Arabs that confronted Churchill at every opportunity. On the other hand, the Arabs venerated Lawrence with awe and slipped to their knees to kiss his feet whenever he appeared in his Arab garb of white silk that shimmered in the sunlight.

Always present was the official plainclothes bodyguard appointed to Churchill by Scotland Yard. Walter Thompson had not yet become accustomed to Winston's ways, which were still the self-assured ones of an aristocrat, despite Clementine constantly reminding him to behave more considerately to others who were not used to his seemingly flippant imperious manner. Thompson had been born in the East End of London as one of thirteen children and had so far led an entirely different life from Winston. But from now on they would share significant and often critical moments together; and initially weighed each other up with caution.

Thompson was impressed by the robust health of the sun-tanned Jewish farmers working in the *kibbutz*, despite the fact that some had been born in the same neighbourhood of Whitechapel as he had, where most East End denizens were pale and undernourished, short and physically undeveloped.

'Heat and a swarm of flies hit us as we tied up... a huge crowd of tarbooshed Egyptians and Arabs collected on the dock, and the sight of Winston and his party coming down the gangway made them yell with fury.' Lawrence had said that 'the Arab masses were dangerous and inflammable'.[1]

On the train, 'a huge mass of ugly-looking Egyptians fought for a hold on the outside window ledges ... All the while Winston sat totally unperturbed in the corner, calmly smoking a cigar. I was alone behind, holding his dispatch box, when a stone whizzed through the broken window and hurtled between us. Winston turned to me and said, "Thompson, you'd better give the case to Archie [Sir Archibald Sinclair, his parliamentary secretary]. You might be wanting both your hands soon."'[2]

Lawrence had warned Thompson at the beginning of the trip that Churchill's life would be at risk 'from the instant we were on Arab soil'. When they reached the hotel, Lawrence took Thompson aside and told him, 'Churchill is in great danger. Never, on any account, let him out of your sight. Trust nobody, black or white. Guard him as you would your own life – even in the sanctuary of his own bedchamber.'*

Lawrence and Winston got along remarkably well. Both were original and independent thinkers, and yet had a great deal in common; particularly their sense of adventure and self-reliance. Lawrence praised Churchill's imagination and courage – perhaps because Churchill's policy was almost identical with his plan and that of the other officials on the spot, like British Administrator Sir Percy Cox. He was High Commissioner of Mesopotamia, which would soon be formally named Iraq. Bell was one of Cox's staff. The result was that she or Winston would frequently be criticised later on for putting together populations who had nothing in common.[3] In reality, Churchill did not jump in with his own preconceived ideas, but generally agreed with the Middle East specialists, so that major decisions on Iraq and the Middle East were collective ones by experts who knew and loved the region and the way of life of its inhabitants.

Their first decision was that Transjordan should be separated from Palestine. The Emirate of Transjordan was created on 11 April after Winston's discussion with Emir Abdullah in Jerusalem, who was recommended by Lawrence. He was the second son of Sharif Hussein, leader of the Hashemite dynasty. The previous government was dysfunctional and the region was believed to be ungovernable as a backwater of the former Ottoman Empire.[4]

'Cox, Gertrude, and Lawrence had no problem convincing Churchill that Emir Feisal was the best candidate for king of Iraq. Not only was he a war hero and brave ally of the British during the revolt, but Gertrude Bell was convinced that he presented the strongest hope for success and stability in Iraq.'[5]

As Gertrude would write to explain to her father, 'The rank and file of the tribesmen, the shepherds, marsh dwellers, rice, barley and date cultivators of the Euphrates and Tigris, whose experience of statecraft was confined to speculations as to the performances of their next-door neighbours, could hardly be asked who should next be the ruler of the country, and by what constitution.'

---

* Thompson would save Churchill's life no fewer than twenty times over the years when targeted by assassins and mutinous crowds.

It was her job to make sure that 'nobody suffered as a member of an oppressed minority in a country split by racial, religious, and economic differences'. And yet, if they aimed at representative territories and institutions, there would be a majority of Shias. 'We as outsiders can't differentiate between Sunni and Shi'ah ... The final authority must be in the hands of the Sunnis, in spite of their numerical inferiority; otherwise you will have a mujtahid-run state, which is the very devil.' She claimed that you could never have three completely autonomous regions, because of their different geographical situation and resources, like Mosul with its oil. And the tribes and the townsmen feared and hated each other. The big landowners would keep the tribes out.[6]

Lawrence's close friendship with the Arab leaders, and his sympathy with their aspirations, convinced him that British overall control east of the Jordan with an Arab ruler, and Churchill's own enthusiasm to see the Zionists help the Arabs forward to modernity and prosperity in Palestine and elsewhere in the Middle East, was the ideal solution for both parties. He considered the Jewish Zionists to be the natural conveyors of Western democratic culture, which he felt necessary in the Middle East. What he hoped for was that 'the lines of Arab and Zionist policy' would converge in the not too distant future.[7]

Colonel Meinertzhagen was another Briton who was a dedicated Zionist, and was critical of the effect of Lawrence voicing the Arab claim to the territory, particularly with Abdullah ruling Transjordan, because it effectively reduced the Jewish homeland under Whitehall's pro-Arab plan and the Balfour Declaration to one third of its original size of Biblical Palestine.[8]

Churchill put forward a proposal for Kurdish autonomy in northern Iraq, to prevent any possibility of oppression of a Kurdish minority. But he was ready to change his view and support Cox, who had reconsidered his own attitude and was given due respect as the man on the spot who knew the region and the situation better than anyone.

Even so, Churchill would frequently be blamed as the whipping boy when anything turned out wrong, because of his customary habit of travelling to the spot himself and inevitably being photographed or written about in the newspapers. Self-publicity was frowned on severely by the Foreign Office and English society in general as vulgar and suspect. Too much self-importance was considered untrustworthy and even dangerous.

Churchill had special responsibility for three British Mandates as Secretary of State for the Colonies: Transjordan, Palestine and the future Iraq. Britain had been awarded the mandate to organise Palestine in April 1920. It changed Britain's previous military administrations into a civil one.[9] But whatever he considered appropriate was limited by Lloyd George's policy, which was to find ways to reduce administrative costs. These were, after all, desert regions inhabited by only a sparse and constantly moving tribal population, where little happened as a consequence of the warnings in the Q'ran against innovations. Prayers took up most of the days.[10]

Winston's second priority was faithfully to implement the terms of the Balfour Declaration in order to facilitate the establishment of a Jewish National Home.

To implement the dual needs of political progress and economic administration, the Middle East Department of the Colonial Office was headed by John Shuckburgh. He understood the Muslim mindset and its aspirations after serving in the India Office for twenty-one years. T.E. Lawrence was Churchill's main adviser on Arab affairs, since he had been attached to Sharif Hussein of Mecca in the Arab Revolt to drive the Ottoman Turks from the Arabian Peninsula in 1917 and 1918; since when Hussein bin Ali had been appointed King of the Arab countries by his father.

Lawrence also negotiated with Arab leaders outside of Palestine. He informed Churchill that Hussein's eldest son, Emir Feisal, had now 'agreed to abandon all claims of his father to Palestine', in return for Arab sovereignty in Baghdad, Amman and Damascus.[11]

Churchill was happy not to be involved in Damascus, because it was part of Syria where the French had installed themselves and could not be dislodged. But he thought it good news that the Arabs accepted 'the Jewish position in Palestine'.[12]

'Churchill favoured a scheme whereby Feisal would accept the throne of Iraq, and his brother Abdullah the throne of Transjordan, in return for Western Palestine, from the Mediterranean Sea to the River Jordan, becoming the location of the Jewish National Home under British control.'[13]

The Arab Revolt

Prince Feisal was an aristocrat, as the third son of the Hashemite Hussein Ibn Ali, sharif of Mecca and self-proclaimed king of the Hejaz; the western region of the Arabian Peninsula. Hussein came from the bloodline of the Prophet Muhammad, through his daughter Fatima. His mother was also descended from the Prophet – an auspicious beginning for a prince of the desert, where blood is everything. Feisal was removed from his mother's care when he was seven days old and taken to the black tents of the Bedouin to be brought up hardily in the desert, until the age of six in 1891. His mother died while he led a nomadic life.

The political atmosphere at that time in Constantinople was tense with conspiracies and secret societies. The Sultan Abdul Hamid – like most autocrats who were feared, and feared everyone else – had become paranoid; so that enemies, whether real or imaginary, had to be murdered for his peace of mind. To make sure they were dead, the Sultan demanded their head in a box on each occasion.

When Feisal turned six, he was taken with his brothers to meet his father. Hussein lived in a house on the Golden Horn with thirty-two women in his harem. Each had her suite and her slaves. Feisal had to take considerable care to be on his best behaviour, because children were punished as a matter of routine, with their feet tied and beaten. Despite that, and the extreme shortage of food because of the cost, he was well educated by tutors.[14]

By the age of eighteen, Feisal was in the Turkish army in 1903. At first, he patrolled the desert with the Turkish camel corps. A few years later, he commanded the Arab camel cavalry. He was ordered by the Turks to put down a rebellion by Arab tribesmen in Asir, where the Turks burned villages and mutilated Arab rebels.

Somehow in the shuffle of power after the Sultan was deposed six years later, Hussein had achieved the title of Emir of the holy city of Mecca, with the rich perquisite of fees from pilgrims that he obtained from supervising the annual hajj. Feisal now represented Jidda in the Turkish parliament.

When the Great War erupted in 1914, the Turks had ordered Hussein to proclaim a jihad by all Muslims against Christians. He refused on the grounds that the most powerful ally of the Turks were Germans and Christians. Now, as always, Hussein found himself in a dangerous position. He sent Feisal to Damascus to incite a military uprising against the Turks.

Feisal's friends in the nationalist political clubs might well have betrayed him any day as a traitor to the ruling Turks, even though he sent messages to Hussein for support in covert ways, by using invisible ink on wrapping paper. His life was in even greater jeopardy when he was obliged to stay with the Turkish Governor, General Djemal, whenever he was in Damascus. For General Mehmed Djemal Pasha suspected that Feisal was up to something treasonous, and put him continually to the test of making him watch public hangings of scores of his Syrian friends. They suffered their deaths without giving Feisal away, while Feisal had to avoid betraying himself and his aim, which was Arab independence from the Turks.

Hussein ordered Feisal back to lead the Arab troops raised by his brother Abdullah. Even though Feisal did not believe the time was right for an uprising, he managed to tear himself away from Djemal Pasha.

On 2 June 1916, Hussein fired the first shot that would commence the Arab Revolt. It was like a starting pistol for a race against 22,000 Turkish soldiers in the garrison at Medina. Feisal's few thousand rebels were poorly equipped. After ascertaining the strength of the Turkish artillery up close, Hussein hurriedly withdrew his forces. Even so, he had earned the admiration of his men by leading from the front when battling with the Turks, and they continued to follow him.

The Sykes–Picot Agreement

Unknown to Hussein or Feisal at the time, others possessed a secret influence over their destiny. The most significant was Mark Sykes, who was an amateur adviser to the British government. The British loved their amateurs, who tended to patronise professional diplomats and politicians. Amateurism, to them, was a proud boast that they were dedicated to doing something for the love of it rather than for money or ambition, which were frowned on as vulgar.

Sykes did not have to concern himself with money. He had grown up on a 30,000-acre ancestral estate as the only child of a Yorkshire aristocrat, and been educated at Cambridge. He had travelled extensively throughout the Ottoman

Empire, written four books, and served as a soldier in the Boer War. Sykes had also been parliamentary secretary to the chief administrator of Ireland and honorary attaché to the British embassy in Constantinople. Those were just the highlights prior to age twenty-five. 'He had served as the Conservative member of Parliament for Hull central since 1912.'[15]

Lord Kitchener had appointed Sykes as an adviser to an influential committee that was intended to guide the British Cabinet on Middle Eastern affairs. His intelligence, self-assurance and initiative soon made him the dominant member. He embarked on a fact-finding trip of the region and turned up in Cairo, where Lawrence had taken an immediate liking to his breezy manner. T.E. had not yet recognised the other side of Sykes's duplicitous nature, while Sykes was soon holding court in Cairo.

At the same time, a German secret agent named Curt Prüfer was working for General Djemal Pasha, to discover where the Syrian people's sympathies really lay. Was it with the Ottoman Empire, the British, the Germans, or the French?

> By that autumn, the need for an unbiased assessment of Syrian public opinion was becoming acute both for the governor and his German advisors. With the Allied misadventure in Gallipoli showing signs of winding down, there was once again the threat of an enemy landing somewhere on the Syrian coast. If the Allies put ashore in Lebanon, how would the Lebanese Christians and the Druze religious minority respond? And what of the Jews, centred just below in Palestine? With the persecution of the Armenians in Anatolia continuing unabated, surely many in Syria's Jewish community were worried they might be next. Above all, what of the Arabs? Djemal Pasha had already begun to move against the Arab conspirators unmasked in the French consulate documents, and Emir Hussein in Mecca was a continuing source of concern, but what of the great masses of Arabs elsewhere?[16]

Prüfer had made his way through Syria for five weeks in a variety of different disguises. He had talked to Jewish and Arab shopkeepers, Christian landowners, 'westernised aristocrats and Bedouin sheikhs and fellaheen. He had reported what he had learned to the German embassy in Constantinople and Djemal Pasha: Christians were discontented but in such a small minority that they were too cowardly to resist.' The Jewish population, particularly Zionists, took a different attitude – they aimed to create an independent Jewish State in Palestine. 'It was more likely to be supported by an Allied victory than a German one. But they would not dare to commit subversive acts until an armed military force had already landed. The biggest problem might have been the biggest group who were the Arab Muslim community. But Djemal's operations against them had weakened them and their resolve. The bulk of the population appeared to support the Turkish Government whom they were accustomed to living and trading with. That, at any rate, was Prüfer's conclusion.'

If the Arabs were capable of launching an uprising, Prüfer suggested in his usual incisive way that it would be unlikely to gain mass support, because of the 'frivolous nature of the population'. However, the German spy added, if the British landed in Syria, they might feel emboldened to act.

Prüfer's report encouraged Djemal to leave the meeting in a more optimistic frame of mind.

'Encouraging the Arabs to revolt had of course been a British operation from the outset, and one that had made the French leadership with their imperial design on Syria and Lebanon, very nervous when they'd caught wind of it. Their concerns had been eased by the signing of the secret Sykes–Picot agreement, codifying their Middle Eastern claims, but had come rushing back when the Arab revolt had become a reality.'[17]

The secretly framed Sykes–Picot agreement had legitimised the division of Arab territories in the former Ottoman Empire into independent spheres of influence to be administered by Britain and France. Russia would acquire three Armenian provinces and some Kurdish territory. France would have Lebanon and the Syrian littoral. It would result in the dismemberment of Turkish-held Syria into Iraq, Lebanon and Palestine. Mark Sykes had organised the carve up in secret with François Georges-Picot of France. Russia was the third signatory to the entente. It was the implementation of that agreement that was being thrashed out at the Peace Conference in Paris after all the sound and fury of the 'Arab Revolt' had now died down and passed away.

12

Feisal's Reward

According to Lawrence, Turkish revenge against unarmed Arab inhabitants in Awali for the rising had been swift and ruthless. They had massacred every living thing within the walled town. Rapes, fire and butchery were typical. Bodies were thrown into the flames of burning houses, whether they were alive or dead.[1] Shock spread across Arabia as the Turks slit the throats of their captives. The only leader that Arab villagers could turn to was Feisal. Tall, graceful, handsome, picturesque and charismatic, Feisal Ibn Hussein ibn Ali was, according to General Allenby, 'the very type of royalty'.

While Feisal began to win a victory here and there, the atmosphere did not change in the Paris Peace Conference, which continued carving up the Middle East between the British and French, as before, even while the Arabs led by Feisal fought for their independence. He was elected King of Syria by Arab nationalists, but expelled by the French Army when they took over Syria as a colony in July 1920.

Gertrude Bell, with her secret informants, knew exactly what was going on in Paris and London, in Arabia and France, as if all were puppets in her hands. She had studied Feisal from near and far, and made her own assessment of him. She decided she liked him.

In July, Gertrude Bell announced the result of a referendum in Iraq, where the naqib declared Feisal king-elect on behalf of the Iraqi Council of State.

Feisal Ibn Hussein ibn Ali had arrived in Iraq in June 1921. The Jewish community gave him a great reception in the Grand Rabbi's official house. He was popularly crowned Feisal the First of Iraq in August. Having unanimously been declared king, Cox knew that there had to be a referendum to confirm King Feisal as the 'people's choice'.

The Unending Conflict

Churchill and Prime Minister Lloyd George, the British administration, and Lawrence of Arabia, all firmly believed that the introduction of modern agricultural and industrial methods by Jewish settlers would bring the primitive and changeless seventh century Arab culture into the present and make the barren deserts bloom. So did King Feisal of Iraq, King Ibn Saud of Saudi Arabia, and King Abdullah of Transjordan. Feisal and Abdulla were brothers and descendents of the Prophet through the Hashemite bloodline of Ali Hussein of the Banu Hashim tribe. All three were cultured modern men. King Ibn Saud obtained his power, not by bloodline, but from the swords of his Wahhabi iqhwan warriors, and then from oil. Only the superstitious and illiterate Arab mobs and *fellaghin* were against modernization from the first visit that Winston Churchill made to Jerusalem as the new British Colonial Secretary in 1920. He was welcomed by hysterical riots and violence that continued for four days, which were stirred up by the anti-British nationalistic political revolutionary, Amin al-Husseini.

Feisal's initial condition of being crowned king of Syria could not be met, because the French had taken possession of the territory in accordance with the Mandate by the League of Nations, and would not have him. He was subsequently happy to be crowned King of Iraq instead. But clashes would continue between educated Arab rulers and the unruly Wahhabi Puritan sect for centuries. At the same time as Amin al-Husseini had instigated the April riots in Jerusalem in 1920, he had formed small groups of suicide squads known as *fedayeen,* who became martyrs for death in unending terrorist riots to push nations to their limits that would continue until present times.[2]

Major Miss Bell had a great deal to do with Feisal's enthronement. She had taken an immediate liking to him when they had first met, and used her considerable influence to get him on the throne. They shared the same impish sense of humour and would smile at each other when their eyes met at official functions. She loved being a king-maker and a power behind the throne. She and Feisal treated each other with affection. He called her his sister. Since she knew he had never visited the great archway at Cresiphon, she invited him there for breakfast, where they sat in the cool of the day on fine carpets, 'drank coffee, and ate eggs, tongue, sardines, and melons'.[3]

One of Gertrude Bell's assignments had been to persuade the Shiites and the Jews of Baghdad to accept a Sunni king.[4]

'Oh father,' she wrote home from her office in Baghdad on 6 August. 'Isn't it wonderful. I sometimes think I must be in a dream.'

Lawrence was still maintaining his composure as a newly hired civil servant. He astonished all his colleagues by his patience and tactfulness, and was happy working with others. According to Winston, Lawrence seemed content to sink his own powerful personality and become a humdrum official if it could redeem the promises he had made to the Arab chiefs. The situation certainly seemed to begin to improve by the end of the year. All their measures were implemented one at a time: 'The Army left Iraq, the Air Force was installed in a loop of the Euphrates, Baghdad proclaimed Feisal as king. Abdullah settled down loyally and comfortably in Trans-Jordania.'

Jewish Legitimacy in Palestine

Since T. E. Lawrence viewed the Jews as the "natural importers of Western leaven so necessary for countries in the Near East," he had taken the Zionist leader Chaim

Weizmann to see the Emir Feisal in the desert in 1918. Feisal had no problems with their ambitions. He "accepted the possibility of future Jewish claims to territory in Palestine." It had been their homeland as the two kingdoms of Judea and Israel before they had been annexed as a province of Rome in 63 BCE. "Feisal agreed that Palestine could absorb "four to five million Jews without encroaching on the rights of the Arab peasantry." He approved a Jewish majority in Palestine" if he should become king. His Syrian rule would be short-lived, since the French government expelled him as an inconvenience when they had a Mandate to rule Syria themselves.

When Feisal became king of Iraq, he was true to his word in treating all his subjects of whatever tribe, Kurds, Druze, or other religions equally. He did not differentiate between citizens; as would be confirmed by one of his happy Jewish subjects, Avi Shlaim, who would describe the small but active Jewish community of what he called Arab-Jews.[5]

But, regardless of the attitude of educated Arabs who led society, there was always a clash between leaders and led. The main mass of Arab peasants were illiterate and knew nothing of the outside world because of their daily focus on prayer and the Q'ran, and its injunction that nothing must change. In April 1920 at the Nebi Musa Festival in Jerusalem, Arab mobs of nearly 70,000 began a hysterical pogrom against Jews. When religious leaders incited the Arabs to use force, they began attacking Jews in the Old City, shouting slogans like "Palestine is our land, the Jews are our dogs!"[6]

Terrorism against Jews was glorified to the younger generation of teenage rebels who used it gleefully as an outlet for violence. Murdering peaceful and unarmed neighbours who were Jews was a relief from constant prayer and a rehearsal for the traditional attacks on weaker tribes and caravans passing through their land.. It was part of the same bloodlust that had existed in the desert for centuries. The question that arose in the mind of the High Commissioner of Jerusalem was how much of the 1920 pogrom was fermented by the Mufti of Jerusalem.

The distinguished Liberal politician and former Home Secretary Samuel had made the cardinal error of appointing Haj Amin al-Husseini as Grand Mufti of Jerusalem as a gesture of goodwill towards the Arabs, when unaware that Amin was pro-German and a sworn enemy of the British and all Jews.

Meanwhile, since Lawrence was still Feisal's intelligence officer and represented him at the Paris Peace Conference, he drafted a formal agreement known as the Feisal-Weizmann Agreement, which he read to Feisal in his private suite at the Carlton Hotel in Paris on January 1919, and countersigned Feisal's signature as a witness. It was the official document he presented formally to the peace conference as evidence of an accord between the Zionists and the Emir Feisal, which supported an Arab Kingdom and Jewish settlement in Palestine, It met their official aim to approve the self-determination of smaller nations that had been cut adrift from established economies by the fall of four empires.

Weizmann's services to Great Britain in the First World War have become largely forgotten. One day in March 1915, when the war had reached a stalemate on the Western Front, he found a summons waiting for him from the Admiralty. The First Sea Lord, Winston Churchill, was the same age as him; forty-one. The Admiralty was faced with a severe shortage of acetone, which was vital for a propellant known as cordite, used for heavy artillery, including naval guns. He was soon brought to discuss the problem with the "brisk, fascinating, charming and energetic" Winston Churchill.[7]

"Well, Dr. Weizmann, we need thirty thousand tons of acetone. Can you make it?"

It was the beginning of Weizmann's close relationship with the leaders of Britain's wartime government. After a considerable amount of ingenuity for which he asked no reward, and which had earned their admiration, he was regarded by them as a genius. He was summoned into the presence of Lloyd George, who was by then the Minister of Munitions. Weizmann had avoided the risk of the imperial army and navy being unable to use its heavy artillery for want of a propellant.

"You have rendered great service to the State," Lloyd George told him, "and I wish to ask the Prime Minister to recommend you to His Majesty for some honour."

Weizmann famously replied, "I would like you to do something for my people."

It was the origin of the National Home for Jews in Palestine, which would ultimately become the State of Israel.[8]

The Colonial Office

Winston asked Lawrence what he would like to do when everything was put in place. He envisaged a great career opening up for the military hero who was still known as 'Lawrence of Arabia'. Lawrence gave his usual cryptic smile, and said his work there would be finished in a few months. 'All you will see of me is a small cloud of dust on the horizon.'

Winston, now in good favour with the government, could have appointed him to great commands, but Lawrence was not interested. He appeared to want to disappear into the landscape.

What would he look for now? He could not put it into better words at the time, but he wrote a letter soon afterwards to military strategist Liddell Hart on New Year's Eve.[9] Their extended friendship was largely a matter of intellectual chit-chat by correspondence. He ended this letter by saying, 'For myself I am going to taste the flavour of true leisure in "a great Sunday that goes on and on".'[10]

Most likely Lawrence meant visiting the sites of lost civilisations in the English countryside on a bicycle, or hiking alone in the hills and dales and meditating on the peculiarities of human beings – since many battle-hardened generals upon retirement absorbed themselves in studying the beauty of butterflies or became ardent bird-watchers with binoculars, nurtured a rose garden, or quietly followed the footprints and spoor of badgers, or other wild animals, to their lair. Those generals and other wartime officers with their solitary quests for beauty were done with the frenzied antics of men seeking order in the civil service or fighting regiments. Now, at long last, they were free to choose more spontaneous and random forms of life, and no longer obliged to be a cog in a machine, but rather a free spirit.

Winston must have considered the opinion of many people who believed that Lawrence was nothing but a fake. He knew he was not. Those who thought Lawrence was a vain peacock, a show-off who exaggerated his importance, were wrong too. He was neither. Lawrence was genuine. But now he had had enough of the limelight, and mixing with ambitious people, and taking and giving orders in the army, he wanted to be rid of it, and needed time to figure out how to escape from the man-made world, and what to do to achieve some sort of contentment.

Despite Lawrence's pose as someone who did not like to give orders or take them, he developed the same deep 'mixture of affection, loyalty, and respect' for Winston Churchill as he'd previously enjoyed with General Allenby.

The cynical Colonel Richard Meinertzhagen, who worked with Lawrence in the Department, was still an imaginative ideas man in the fine art of military deception as he had been when a captain. He noted a few observations about Lawrence in his diary. He admitted he had begun by being sceptical and patronising, not realising that T.E. needed his grand poses as protection because he was a shy man. The colonel changed his mind while working with him, noting that Churchill's attitude towards Lawrence 'almost amounted to hero-worship,' and that 'Lawrence was a most remarkable man, with a most remarkable record, but as unscrupulous as he is dangerous. His meek schoolboy expression hides the cunning of a fox and the intriguing spirit of the East … We all know that Lawrence is a humbug, though as able as a monkey.'

He and Lawrence worked well together because each enjoyed the mastery of deception. They understood the value of a legend wrapped in a myth that would unfurl when the time was ripe. If he was a humbug, as Meinertzhagen suspected with admiration, how was it that so many people were either ready to listen to Lawrence's advice or prepared to follow him?

Churchill's normally bluntly spoken bodyguard from Scotland Yard, Inspector Thompson, was somehow convincing about T.E. when he wrote in retrospect, 'Lawrence was the man. No Pope of Rome ever had more command before his own worshippers … Colonel Lawrence raised his hand slowly, the first and second fingers raised above the other two for silence and for blessing. He could have owned the earth … Every man froze with respect, in a kind of New Testament adoration of shepherds for a master … We passed through these murderous-looking men and they parted way for us without a struggle. Many touched Lawrence as he moved forward among them. Far off, drums were beating, and a horse neighed …

Lawrence was so greatly loved and respected that he could have established his own empire from Alexandretta to the Indus.'[11]

No doubt their adulation was based on a desperate hope and plenty of prayers that Lawrence would go to war again in Syria and lead them in a revolt that would sweep out the French.

The Seven Pillars of Wisdom

Lawrence undertook one more mission for Winston, which was a success, as usual. He left the colonial service after a year, as he had said he would. The next thing that Winston heard about him was that he had begun to write a book, which would become a classic of literature. He would name it *The Seven Pillars of Wisdom*. After reliving his adventures by inscribing them on each page, he must have felt an awful anticlimax in his life that he was unable to escape from. Nothing could live up to what he had experienced and written about, with maybe an artful touch or two to his scenarios that might not have been entirely accurate, but were needed to achieve perfection on each page. There were close to 700 of them, which still retain his nostalgia for the nomadic life of the Arab tribes.

Winston, who may have been responding to the approach of middle age, always got on well with Lawrence and admired the young man for the adventurous spirit he had always possessed himself, and for his curiosity about people and places and incidents, which had made Winston such a good war correspondent. Churchill identified himself with Lawrence in the profile of him that he would write in 1935, where there is evidence of the difficulty he had of describing Lawrence's unusual nature and his independence. Churchill covered page after page with admiring words and phrases as he searched for the right one, and could not leave the subject of Lawrence alone. Winston was rarely in awe of anyone. He was, after all, a trained professional soldier and a successful politician himself.

That time – so soon after the war with its gruesome deaths of millions of young men on the battlefronts – was an age of hero-worship; a nostalgic recognition of their value when put to the test, and an attempt to bring them back to life again. T.E. was only thirty-two, while Winston had reached the age of forty-six and seemed spellbound when he wrote of Lawrence's exploits and his charming but genuine personality. And Lawrence admired and respected Winston.[12]

It is likely that Lawrence reminded him of Savrola, the hero of the novel he had written two decades earlier, although it had been based on his own wishful thinking about himself. Winston always wrote himself into every book, whether in *Savrola* or as his father in his biography of Lord Randolph, or his ancestor John Churchill, the 1st Duke of Marlborough. It was characteristic that he enlarged on his characters to make them what he felt they *ought* to be, which was more like *him*. 'He saw himself in the great Duke, too; like Marlborough he loved the sound of bullets, the clash of sabres, the applause of nations and of sovereigns, and of history, and his vindication of Marlborough from neglect and contumely was in a sense a vindication of himself.'[13]

Savrola was a patrician on the side of the people. So were Winston and Lawrence. Young Winston described what motivated Savrola as follows: 'The life he lived was the only one he could ever live, he must go on to the end. The end comes often early in such men whose spirits are so wrought that they know rest only in action, contentment only in danger, and in confusion find their only peace.'

No wonder he was in awe as he watched his own fictional creature, Savrola, come to life before his eyes in the person of Lawrence of Arabia! What a disappointment it must have been for Winston Churchill, after their experiences together, to see Lawrence finally vanish in a small cloud of dust on the horizon, as he'd said he would, and as if he had never been there at all.

13

Gertrude of Arabia

Gertrude Bell's privileged life had been taken up with a great deal of travelling, some mountain-climbing, hunting, society, gardening, and learning archaeology, before she had been spotted by Britain's Secret Intelligence Service. They viewed her as an asset because of her languages – particularly Arabic and Persian – and her first-hand knowledge of the Arab tribes.

'Yet, as the prospect of marriage and children receded, she felt an increasing need for self-fulfillment. As an independent woman of great ability she was driven by the need to test herself, veering towards challenges tinged with danger and excitement. When she conquered Arabic and discovered desert travel, the challenges proliferated into an all-embracing personal experiment of which she would never reach the end. There was the risky business of staying alive and reaching her goal and the intoxication of asserting her own identity far from the world that regarded her as a spinster, an heiress, and a Bell.'[1]

We know every detail of her travels as a consequence of her regular long descriptive letters to her parents.[2] Wherever she travelled, she studied people and archaeological sites, and made notes of any Turkish barracks she spotted. She would be accompanied by male guides and camel drivers. After spending ten to twelve hours in the saddle of her camel, she would write carefully descriptive letters home and complete her abbreviated diaries. On arrival at a town or city she would stay in a consulate or an embassy. She would send her secret information to the Foreign Office by diplomatic bag.

She was recognised throughout Britain as their best-known traveller as early as 1905. To understand her emotional make-up and her intelligent sense of curiosity and mischievous humour, it is only necessary to read a paragraph or two from some of her own books, which brim with the joys of life.

> With the silence of an extinct world still heavy upon us, we made our way to the upper end of the valley, but at the gates of the plain Life came surging to meet us. A wild hollyhock stood sentinel among the stones; it had spread some of its yellow petals for banner and on its uplifted spears the buds were fat and creamy with coming bloom. Rain had fallen in the night, and had called the wilderness itself to life, clothing its thorns with a purple garment of tiny flowers; the delicious sun struck upon our shoulders; a joyful little wind blew the damp, sweet

smell of the reviving earth in gusts towards us; our horses sniffed the air and, catching the infection of the moment, tugged at the bit and set off at racing speed across the rain-softened ground. And we, too, passed out of the silence and remembered that we lived. Life seized us and inspired us with a mad sense of revelry. The humming wind and the teeming earth shouted 'Life! life!' as we rode. Life! life! the bountiful, the magnificent! Age was far from us – death far; we had left him enthroned in his barren mountains, with ghostly cities and outworn faiths to bear him company. For us the wide plain and the limitless world, for us the beauty and the freshness of the morning, for us youth and the joy of living![3]

Gertrude had made her first visit to Persia when she was only twenty-four. She was thirty-six when she wrote that tribute to life. She worked for British Intelligence in the Arab Bureau in Cairo from 1916, when she was forty-eight. One of her assets for Britain's Secret Intelligence Service was drawing up maps of territories that she knew intimately from travelling there, and may even have photographed. She was a Member of the Royal Photographic Society and took two cameras with her into the desert.[4]

A Multi-Ethnic Society

Their biggest problem that faced her now, and particularly Winston Churchill and Lawrence, was how to divide up Mesopotamia into stable territories with new frontiers to contain and protect the mass of different Arab tribes, and the nomadic pastoralist Bedouin, without conflicting religions or religious doctrines or ethnic groups that could not tolerate one another. There were Muslims of several different sects like the Sunni, which included Kurds. There were Alawis, who were Arabic-speaking Turkmen; Arabic-speaking Ismailis; Arabic-speaking Syrians, Lebanese, Iraqis and Iranians. There were also Christians and Jews, Druze and Circassians, and Sunni Muslim Greeks. There were Shia Arabs too. Their only link was the Arabic language.

Mesopotamia has been a melting pot of races since civilisation began. Its frequent conflicts were inevitable. So she knew that Iraq would continually be prone to violent disruptions. Her task was to fulfill Britain's promise of self-determination according to the League's mandate. And she had another important reason to establish a functional Iraq. If Britain had evacuated Mesopotamia as Winston Churchill had originally advised, the Turks would have surged back from the north to reinstate themselves as corrupt rulers and take revenge on the population. There was also a very real threat from the Red Army planning to drive the communist revolution south into the Middle East. Ibn Saud and his fearsome Wahhabi warriors were already attacking the southern borders.

'Without Western endorsement and British support, Iraq would have faced three powerful enemies without an army to defend it. The peoples of the Middle East who had failed to make their case for nationhood or political identity at the time of the Paris Peace Conference – for instance the Kurdish people – remained at the mercy of massacres and incursions by their neighbours.'[5]

> The western border with Syria was fixed by a previous agreement with the French, the southern border was an invisible line in the sand between Iraq and the vast empty desert Ibn Saud claimed, and the eastern border was that of the old Ottoman Empire with Persia; but to the north was the territory inhabited by Kurds, Arab-speaking non-Arabs, supposedly of Indo-European descent, who passionately desired an independent Kurdistan. Unfortunately for them, the grand prize of Iraq from the British point of view was Mosul, right in the middle of the Kurdish homeland, with its rich oil deposits. Accordingly, commercial interests and realpolitik combined to create a country with a Shiite majority, a Sunni king, a disappointed Kurdish minority and a small but wealthy and cosmopolitan class of Jewish merchants in Baghdad.[6]

How to keep them at peace with one another and stop the traditional raiding parties for cattle, slaves and girls or young women, on one hand, and protect them from the machine guns and artillery and butchery of invaders from outside?

Gertrude Bell contributed to the defeat of the Ottoman Empire through her position in Britain's Arab Bureau, and founded Iraq, in company with T.E. Lawrence and Winston Churchill.[7] She had known the territory well from her travels beforehand. More than a decade earlier, in February 1909, she had sat on a hilltop for an hour in Ashur, northern Mesopotamia, some 60 miles south of Mosul, looking down on the territory that would someday become Iraq.[8]

'I ... considered the history of Asia that was spread out before me. Here Mithridates murdered the Greek generals, here Xenophen began to have his command, and just beyond Zab the Greeks turned and defeated the archers of Mithridates, marching then on to Larissa, the mound of Nimrod. Where Xenophon saw the great Assyrian city of Calah standing in ruins.'[9]

A basic aim was to preserve Lebanon for Christians, Palestine for Jews, Syria for Sunni, and Saudi Arabia for at least twenty other ethnic tribes. And there was the matter of how to deal with the nomadic tribes who travelled regularly across borders all year round, led by the seasons to search for better pastureland for their goats or cattle.

They were an example of the evolutionary process in which weaker or more peaceful tribes became victims of the raiding parties of more powerful tribes who stole their cattle, their women and their slaves. It was how subsistence farmers had made a surplus, as their traditional agricultural pattern was to 'sow one place this year and go and live somewhere else lest their animals should eat the growing corn. Next year this lies fallow and the fallow of the year before is sown.'[10]

Right: Winston received his commission as a cavalry officer from Queen Victoria in 1895. *Imperial War Museum Collection.*

Below left: Lieutenant Winston Churchill, age 24, fighting with Kitchener at Khartoum.

Below right: Winston Churchill in 1900 when he became a Member of Parliament at age 25.

Above left: Known as "the terrible twins," Lloyd George when President of the Board of Trade, with Winston Churchill as Colonial Under-Secretary of State in Sir Henry Campbell-Bannerman's government in 1907.

Above right: Winston and Clementine Hozier engaged before marrying.

Winston Churchill shakes hands with the Kaiser when invited to observe Prussian military manoeuvres near Breslau in 1906.

Above: Clementine Churchill age 24 with Winston on manoeuvres when a reserve territorial officer in 1910. *Photo used with thanks to Hillsdale College, Michigan.*

Below: Home Secretary Winston Churchill takes charge when police are killed by anarchists in London's East End. The "Siege of Sidney Street" was a watershed case of violence arriving in England in 1911 from revolutionaries. *Illustrated London News,* January 11.

Above: Russian revolutionaries arrested by Tsarist secret police soon after this photo was taken of Vladimir Lenin at centre of the League of Struggle for the Emancipation of the Working Class. February 1897. Lenin left for Switzerland in 1900.

Below left: Winston Churchill when First Lord of the Admiralty in 1912.

Below right: Photo montage: Karl Marx in 1867 and Friederich Engels in 1856.

Right: Annie Kenney and Christabel Pankhurst used violent revolutionary tactics as members of the Women's Social and Political Union in Britain in 1908.

Below: March 1917 attack on the Tsar's palace in the first days of the Bolshevik Revolution.

Russian Civil War. Lenin speaks in public with Red Army troops. 5 May 1920 in Moscow. Trotsky and Kamenev stand on the steps of the platform at right.

Admiral Alexander Kolchak: Russian patriot and hero of the civil war.

Above left: Minister of Munitions Winston Churchill visits workers near Glasgow after leaving the Western Battlefront in World War 1. *The Imperial War Museum, UK.*

Above right: Major General Sir Percy Cox. Highly regarded British Administrator in the Middle East and officer in Britain's Secret Intelligence Service, played a prominent role in creating Iraq with Gertrude Bell, T. E. Lawrence and Winston Churchill. (1916 photo).

Above left: Lieutenant-Colonel Winston Churchill of the 6th Battalion, The Royal Scots Fusiliers, in the lines behind Ploegsteert in Belgium in 1916.

Above right: British archaeologist, travel author and Intelligence Officer Gertrude Bell in Babylon in 1909. She mapped Arabia and invented Iraq with T. E. Lawrence and Colonial Secretary Winston Churchill.

Above: Giza March 12, 1921. Left to right: Clementine (beneath smaller pyramid), Winston, Gertrude Bell, T.E. Lawrence, and bodyguard Thompson, with others participants in the 1921 Cairo Conference.

Below left: Éamon De Valera was an admirer of Hitler. De Valera led the Anti-Treaty Sinn Féin until 1926.

Below right: Irish revolutionary soldier and politician Michael Collins was ambushed and killed by IRA gunmen after signing a treaty with Britain in December 1921.

It was said that the very reason why the Prophet Muhammad created Islam was to prevent Arab-speaking tribes from killing each other. He planned to unite them instead, by designing a religion that forbade Muslims from worshipping idols and slaughtering each other. It was a frontier country in which every stranger was an enemy until you were able to distinguish who were your friends. Suspicion ruled, and there were plenty of blood enemies. No doubt the Prophet had recognised that they could be a force to be reckoned with by others if united by Islam.

Zionism

Prime Minister Lloyd George's foreign secretary, Lord Balfour, had issued a declaration in November 1917 that sympathised with the Zionist cause for a permanent homeland for the Jewish people. They had been uprooted by invasions from the Roman Empire some two thousand years previously, and had wandered the earth as victims, like Armenians or Kurds or Nabatians, and other nations whose territory had been annexed by invaders. To complicate their claims for the restoration of their traditional homeland, it had been occupied subsequently by Muslims and Ottoman Turks.

Gertrude Bell explained the problem in bald statistical terms in a secret document that she passed to the Secretary of State for India: 'Not least among the denationalising forces is the fact that a part of Syria, though like the rest mainly inhabited by Arabs, is regarded by non-Arab people as its prescriptive inheritance. At a liberal estimate the Jews of Palestine may form a quarter of the population of the province, the Christians a fifth, while the remainder are Mohammedan Arabs.'[11]

She argued on behalf of the Arab majority, yet Zionists claimed that not only was it their traditional homeland that had been stolen from them, but nothing had been there when more recent Jewish immigrants had set up farming communities. It could be proved simply from photographs. Subsequent Arab migrants had moved in after Jewish development, because of the better living standards created by Jewish farmers and an opportunity to trade with them.

Winston's first commercial commitment to Zionist enterprise in Palestine provided jobs for eight hundred Jewish and Arab workers and managers. It was a concession for harnessing the waters of the Jordan and Yarkon rivers to provide electrical power for the region. It also enabled the Zionists to plan for new urban and rural developments.

Churchill planned a four-week trip to visit Cairo and Jerusalem in April 1921, in order to establish 'the nature of British rule' in Palestine and Iraq. He was informed before leaving 'that there was no conflict between Britain's wartime pledges to the Arabs and to the Jews'.[12] They would be fulfilled when 'the land east of the Jordan became an Arab State, and the land west of the Jordan up to the Mediterranean Sea became the area of the Jewish National Home'.[13]

The formation of a Jewish National Home was not simply a matter of territory, it was their historic homeland before it had been invaded, annexed, and destroyed by the Roman Empire. After which the former Roman province had been invaded by the Ottoman Turks. Their empire, or Caliphate, no longer existed, after its defeat by Allied military forces in 1918. But apprehension remained that if Iraq was not seen to be settled and protected, the Turks might decide it was time to return and take it back.

Speaking on behalf of the Zionists, Chaim Weizmann hoped that Churchill would modify the boundaries of a future Palestine in accordance with the historic site of the Jewish people, by explaining that 'the rich plains to the north have been taken away from Palestine and given to France'. They were Lebanon and Syria. And that, 'Transjordan has from the earliest time been an integral and vital part of Palestine.' He went on to remind Churchill that it was east of the Jordan that 'the Israelite tribes of Reuben, Gad and Manasseh first pitched their tents and pastured their flocks'.

It was yet another emotive issue over which Churchill was obliged to preside with the wisdom of King Solomon. To help him, Weizmann referred to Arab national aspirations that, he claimed, 'centre on Damascus and Baghdad, and do not lie in Transjordania'.

As compensation for Britain's agreement with France, which had fixed the northern border to cut Palestine off from the waters of the Litani River, which the Zionists had planned to harness for electric power for industry, Weizmann urged Churchill to set Palestine's southern boundary down to the Gulf of Akaba. Although historically and intellectually sound, Churchill did not allow himself to be swayed by Weizmann's proposals. The political implications were far too complex and possibly dangerous in the long run.

Dynamics of Power

Churchill had been well aware from his early twenties, if not before, that wars always occurred as a normal part of life, and were caused by discontented rebels who were hot-headed with grievances. The dynamics of power arose in the personal drives of zealous individuals with the imagination to conceive whatever criminal activities they thought they could get away with. Predatory leaders always tested others for signs of weakness. The eminent French social psychologist Gustave Le Bon remarked on the minds of revolutionary leaders, like Robespierre in the French Revolution, as well as to the mass hysteria of the mobs he incited.

From the moment in 1919 when the League of Nations mandated one part of the Middle East to Britain and another to France, each eyed the other's new territory covetously, and tribal rivalry arose between them. The Official Secrets Act prevented the exposure of the underlying realities of that time until official documents were declassified and described by James Barr, who wrote, 'In the summer of 2007 I came across a sentence in a newly declassified British government report that made my eyes bulge.'[14]

It was written by a British security officer in MI5 who had just returned from the Middle East at the beginning of 1945. Terrorism, he announced, 'would seem to be receiving support from the French'.[15]

He added that he knew from top-secret sources that French officials in the Levant had been secretly selling arms to the *Hagana*, which would become the nucleus of the official army in the future State of Israel. The alliance between French government officials and Jewish terrorists in Palestine was part of France's secret war against Britain that would continue until 1948 as a consequence of their grievances.

A part of the equation of rebel leader and the led was a mystical attribute that might be called 'national destiny', in which nationalism became a cult or religion. It generally involved a great deal of flag-waving and cries for 'freedom', which concealed a desire to victimise other people. From a sociological point of view, it could be described as the timeless jostling of tribes that always seek to get the upper hand. As German Chancellor Bismarck described it, 'It is the destiny of the weak to be devoured by the strong.'

Such tribal jostling was taking place during young Winston's time as Colonial Secretary, not only in the Middle East but also in Soviet Russia, and very soon in the Weimar Republic of Germany.[16] His hands would be full while attempting to sort out the problems between Arab and Arab, Arab and Zionist, and Arab and French. The Arabs wanted the French out of Syria and Lebanon, while the French were determined to remain. The Arabs particularly wanted to dispose of Zionists in any way they could, while Churchill was tasked by the British government with implementing the Balfour Declaration of November 1917, which was based on the Sykes–Picot Agreement of May 1916. The first guaranteed a Jewish homeland in Palestine, while the second was a secret agreement made between Britain and France during the Great War, to fill the power vacuum after the defeat of the tottering Turkish Empire. The Arabs disagreed with both policies, while the British supported Arab self-determination. The amalgamation of different and intractable problems resembled a vast Gordian knot that could never be untied. But they did their best.

The rival ambitions of the French triggered revenge atrocities against Britain in the Middle East that ended only in 1948, when it was the Zionists who controlled Tiberias and Jaffa. Britain was discredited, and forced to leave in May.[17]

Tribal jostling between France, Britain, Arabs and Zionists, formed and reformed one shape of events after another in those three decades, while young Winston – according to his own accounts of his portfolio – appeared to be on top of all the problems. In reality, he was always scrutinised by the unblinking eyes of every tribe and political group, and buffeted by the dynamics of power from every source. Despite his short time in office of only twenty-one months as Colonial Secretary, he would leave a deep impression on the Middle East, before taking up the new appointment he had really wanted as Chancellor of the Exchequer.

He would have to wait for it while out of office in a government reshuffle until appointed by Prime Minister Stanley Baldwin in 1924.

Meanwhile, young Churchill observed the evolutionary process play itself out with the sharpest minds watching for weakness, hesitation, or defeatism in others, while the more foolishly unprepared left their future survival to chance. And, as any gambler learns, the odds rarely if ever favour the inattentive and unprepared.

The Druze Minority

Only four months after Winston took office as Colonial Secretary on 13 February 1921, General Gouraud was ambushed by assassins on 23 June while being driven in his vehicle from Damascus to the Golan Heights. It was two days after Emir Feisal had landed in Basra on his way to Baghdad, with the support of the British. The French general viewed him as 'a monster who would eventually devour us'.[18]

The assassins had been dressed as Syrian gendarmes. Although every bullet missed the general, his interpreter lay dead. Gouraud was determined to find the killer who had wanted to have him assassinated. His investigations settled first on Ahmed Marawed, who had fled to Transjordan and was 'living under the indulgent eye' of a British political officer. Merawed appeared to be under the protection of Abdullah's followers. Churchill sent Lawrence to find out the truth.

Gouraud had seized Damascus for the French in 1920. He had hived off Lebanon as a Christian enclave and divided Syria into four provinces to recognise the Druze and Alawite minorities. Although the French were required by the League to prepare the Arabs for self-rule, his aim was to divide and conquer. The French still had an eighteenth- or nineteenth-century attitude to suppressing 'natives' and treating them as primitives, while 'Syria was milked of its more profitable resources'. As a result, Lawrence reasoned that the British should not be seen as propping up the French.[19]

Since the British refused to help the French trace the general's assassins, the French made their own arrests. They were led to the home of the formidable Sultan Atrash – a Druze hero of British explorer Wilfred Thesiger. The Atrash family was the largest and most powerful in the Jabal Druze. Whereas the Turks had respected their reputation for ferocity, the Druze were viewed as heretics by other Muslims. The French attempted to bring the fiery Druze under control, in the belief that they consisted of only 50,000 inhabitants. They did not know that 10,000 were armed.

It was not until July 1925, after Winston had already left, that shots were fired and the Druze Uprising began. Some British officials were claimed to have exclaimed, 'Damn good show! Fancy a few tough Arabs taking on France – they must be real sportsmen.' The French were convinced that the British were actively helping the Druze rebels, and even prolonging the uprising in the hope of forcing the French out of Syria.[20]

GERTRUDE OF ARABIA

Commonwealth of Independent States - European States

Land grab of Ukraine in 1923 Russian Civil War by Lenin's Red Army. Map produced by CIA.

Kill the Bolshies

Back in January 1919, Lloyd George had been in Paris to work at the Peace Conference on the final terms of the Treaty of Versailles. Although they had decided to invite the Russian Bolsheviks to discuss trade, Churchill was still anxiously attempting to drum up support for Denikin's retreating armies. Lloyd George's secretary, Frances Stevenson, wrote about Churchill in her diary that, 'At times he became almost like a madman.' Churchill admitted to Sir Henry Wilson, the Chief of General Imperial Staff that he thought of resigning.

Churchill had written an article for the *Illustrated Sunday Herald* describing Lenin's 'diabolical purpose', and declared that, 'All tyrants are the enemies of the human race.' Now, hearing of General Denikin's probable doom at the hands of the Red Army, he authorised General Holman to part from Denikin and leave Russia, while urging Denikin to give up fighting and attempt to negotiate with the Bolsheviks for a small area where he and his troops might live in peace. But General Denikin and his followers continued fighting the Bolsheviks, despite thousands of losses. They finally fled to the Crimea with 35,000 troops on the same day that Admiral Kolchak was captured and imprisoned by the Reds.

'I am frankly in despair,' wrote Lloyd George to Winston. In spite of the young man's promise to let the subject of the anti-Bolsheviks rest for a while, 'Your reply is to send me a four-page letter on Russia, and a closely printed memorandum of several pages – all on Russia.' He then cast doubt on Winston's assertions: 'You confidently predict in your memorandum that Denikin is on the eve of some great and striking success. I looked up some of your memoranda made earlier in the year about Kolchak, and I find that you use exactly the same language in reference to Kolchak's successes.'

Since Admiral Kolchak was locked up in a Bolshevik cell in Irkutsk, the Prime Minister added, 'I wonder if it is any use my making one last effort to induce you to throw off this obsession which, if you will forgive me for saying so, is upsetting your balance.'[21]

Winston Churchill Timeline

1874: Winston Spencer Churchill born at Blenheim Palace.
1895: Commissioned as second lieutenant in the cavalry by Queen Victoria.
1895: His father Lord Randolph Churchill dies.
1898: Publishes first book of his experiences in Pakistan & Afghanistan Frontier War.
1898: Cavalry charge at Battle of Omdurman in the Sudan River War.
1899: Taken prisoner by the Boers in South Africa and escapes.
1900: Elected Conservative Member of Parliament for Oldham.
1901: Visits North America when Queen Victoria dies.
1904: Gives his maiden speech in the House of Commons.
1904: Winston switches to Liberal Party.

1905: Colonial Under-Secretary of State with Liberal Campbell-Bannerman as PM.
1908: President, Board of Trade.
1908: Marries Clementine Hozier.
1910: Home Secretary.
1911: First Lord of the Admiralty in Asquith's government.
1915: Gallipoli Campaign fails.
1916: Military service on Western Front as lieutenant colonel in Royal Scots Fusiliers.
1917: Minister of Munitions in Lloyd George's coalition government.
1919: Secretary of State for War and Air.
1921: Secretary of State for Colonies.
1922: Loses seat in Parliament when coalition government voted out.
1924: Chancellor of the Exchequer.
1925: Rejoins the Conservative Party.
1932: Visits Munich and warns of a rearmed Germany.
1939: First Lord of the Admiralty in Chamberlain's government.
1940: Prime Minister of Britain and Minister of Defence at age 66.

From the furthermost corner in the west of Turkey where Ancient Troy once stood, to the Khyber Pass in the east, and south as far down as Yeman and the Gulf of Aden, a vast terrain spreads out, which all types of tribes had previously swept through from the time of Alexander the Great. They had conquered or been overcome and left bitterness in their wake. Now it was Winston Churchill's turn to meet the challenges along the ancient trade routes, and paths of glory and tragedy, followed by an extraordinary array of warriors who had come and gone. Only occasional heaps of stones from the remains of collapsed walls showed from their inscriptions that earlier civilizations had once existed there. In spite of his impatience to undertake his mission and move on to become Chancellor of the Exchequer, there was no doubt that he enjoyed the intellectual battles with his adversaries. But victory over the desert wastes was by no means a foregone conclusion.

14

Churchill's Middle East Ambition
1921–23

Churchill had left Cairo for Jerusalem by train on 23 March 1921. There was a short stop at Gaza early the next morning when he was welcomed by a large crowd of shouting Arabs. Churchill's spirits were raised by the zealousness of all the cheering at his arrival, and felt he had an enthusiastic audience shouting 'Cheers for the Minister!' 'Cheers for Great Britain!'

Other mobs showed even greater enthusiasm with their hopeful cries of 'Down with the Jews!' and 'Cut their throats!' But Winston had no idea what they were saying as the train continued on its way to Jerusalem with him feeling as optimistic in his assignment as he usually did.

Arabs rioted in Haifa the day after he arrived, demanding a stop to further Jewish immigration. Police opened fire to disperse frenzied mobs. A Christian Arab boy of thirteen and a Muslim Arab woman were shot in the chaos and confusion. Churchill put in an appearance at the British Military Cemetery overlooking Jerusalem, at a service of dedication for two thousand British soldiers buried there in the war. They had given their lives, he said, to liberate the land and bring about peace and friendship among the inhabitants. It was the responsibility of those present to see the task completed.

At dinner that evening, he told the Emir Abdullah that he looked forward to seeing him installed as ruler of Transjordan, and pledged him not to undertake any activity against France or the Zionists. He informed him that, while Jewish immigrants would be allowed to enter Palestine, 'the rights of the existing non-Jewish population would be strictly observed'.

Abdullah accepted his assurance, but the unruly local Arabs did not. Instead, they warned Churchill that if Britain took no notice of their cries for an end to Jewish immigration, 'then perhaps Russia will take up their call some day; or perhaps even Germany.' The Arabs claimed, imaginatively, that the aim of the Zionists was to establish a Jewish kingdom in Palestine 'and gradually control the world'.

Churchill did his best to put Abdullah's mind at rest by telling him that Jewish immigration would be a very slow process and emphasised again that the rights of the existing population would be preserved. He had already received full support for his plans from Lloyd George.

Winston was still on good terms with LG, as he was known by his more intimate friends. They had travelled to the south of France together at the end of the previous year, and Lloyd George had read Winston's early draft of a new book on the train from Paris to the Mediterranean. As Winston told Clementine, 'He praised the style and made several pregnant suggestions which I am embodying.'

He had already received an advance of £9,000 from a British publisher and expected another £13,000 from an American one.

Lloyd George took the opportunity to disembarrass himself of the Irish problem by passing it on for Churchill to deal with. Winston remarked to Clementine how well they got on whenever Lloyd George needed him. But he had been obliged to interrupt his work on the Irish troubles to make this trip to Cairo to meet the Emir and other leaders.

When Abdullah visited the Mosque of Omar, he was assailed by a hostile crowd with shouts of 'Palestine for the Arabs' and 'Down with the Zionists'. Hysterical mobs had to be dispersed by British police. Evidently the crowds did not trust their leaders and the leaders despised the rioting mobs.

Churchill spoke at the site of the proposed Hebrew University, declaring that, 'Personally, my heart is full of sympathy for Zionism.' He made a deep impression on Jewish Zionists, who had rarely heard a kind word spoken on their behalf for over two thousand years.

At Government House the next day, Churchill received a delegation from the Executive Committee of the Haifa Congress of Palestinian Arabs. Their threatening message was that, 'The Arab is noble and large-hearted; he is also vengeful, and never forgets an ill-deed. If England does not take up the cause of the Arabs, other powers will.'

They meant Fascist Italy and Germany.*

The threat not only came from Muslims in Palestine, but also from Muslims in India and Iraq. They had decided that Palestine belonged to the Arabs, and presented Churchill with a five-point memorandum: Firstly, the whole principle of a National Home for the Jews should be abolished. Secondly, a national government should be created and be responsible to a parliament elected by the Palestinian people. Thirdly, Jewish immigration should be halted.

Fourthly, all laws framed after the British occupation should be annulled. Fifthly, Palestine should not be separated from her sister states – including Syria, which was now under French rule, and Egypt, which was still under British rule. Nothing else would satisfy them.

---

* It was an era of nationalism not only across the Middle East, but also in Soviet Russia, India, Ireland, Italy and Germany. The Mufti of Jerusalem Amin al-Husseini would eventually arrange a secret deal to supply oil to the Nazis in return for expertise in developing murder camps to destroy all Christians, Jews and other non-Muslims in the Middle East; ultimately known as Hitler's 'Plan Orient'.

CHURCHILL'S CHALLENGES, 1918–1940

Churchill told them candidly that he had no power to repudiate the Balfour Declaration, and, even if he had, he would not: it had been ratified by the Allied Powers in wartime, 'when victory and defeat hung in the balance'. Money from outside had been contributed for the general prosperity and welfare of Palestine. And there was no reason why Palestine should not support a larger population. He urged them to think positively: 'Instead of sharing miseries through quarrels you will share blessings through cooperation.' He finished by announcing that 'a bright and tranquil future lies before your country'.[1]

While talking to the Jewish delegation, Churchill was concerned about Jewish immigrants from Russia who might possibly include Bolsheviks, and reminded them that they should choose more acceptable ones. Groups of Jews were being trained on farms in Europe and in Soviet Russia to become farmers. It was only when they had mastered the arts of tilling the soil, animal husbandry and other rural skills that they would be sent to Palestine to establish new farming communities.[2]

By the end of his eight-day trip to Palestine, Churchill had been impressed 'by the enthusiasm of the Jews and the intensity of Arab hostility against them'.[3] What he would certainly have observed with a sense of irony was that little had changed in the region since Winwood Reade had travelled there in the 1870s. Winston had read the explorer and anthropologist's account when he had been a young man of twenty or more in 1896 or thereabouts:

> A people can never rise from low estate as long as they are engrossed in the painful struggle for daily bread. On the other hand, leisure alone is not sufficient to effect the self-promotion of men. His life is one long torpor, with spasms of activity. Century follows century, but he does not change ... the shepherd tribes roam from pasture to pasture; their flocks and herds yield them food and dress and 'houses of hair', as they call their tents. They have little work to do, their time is almost entirely their own. They pass long hours in slow conversation, in gazing at the heavens, in the sensuous, passive oriental reverie. The intellectual capacities of such men are by no means to be despised, as those who have lived among them are aware. They are skilful interpreters of nature's language and of the human heart; they compose beautiful poems; their religion is simple and sublime; yet time passes on, and they do not advance. The Arab sheikh of the present day lives precisely as Abraham did three thousand years ago ... [4]

Perhaps the most ardent enemy of change was Amin al-Husseini. He had been born in Jerusalem in 1897, when Palestine had been part of the Ottoman Turkish Empire. In 1910 he was an officer in the Turkish artillery and an enemy of the West, even before General Allenby defeated the Turks in 1918. After the Paris Peace Conference, when Britain accepted a mandate to administer Palestine in 1921, he played a leading part in resisting the return of the Jews to their former homeland, despite the post-war aim of self-determination. After the 1920 Nebi Musa riots, Amin fled to Transjordan and hid among the Bedouin tribes. By 1921 – after clashes for supremacy with other

Arab nationalists who continued to squabble with each other for dominance – Amin was appointed to the influential position of the Mufti of Jerusalem and President of the newly created religious organisation, the Supreme Muslim Council. He was a Sunni Muslim. The honour was bestowed on him by the Jewish High Commissioner, Sir Herbert Samuel, in the hope of encouraging goodwill between Arabs and Jews. Samuel had yet to recognize the pathological hatred in Amin's heart that would make him, in effect, the Adolf Hitler of the Middle East. He and his Arab opponents for power had one thing in common; they continued to demand a stop to Jewish immigration, and to prevent Jewish families and Zionist organisations from buying back land in what had been Jewish territory in Biblical times.[5] *

This Little Life

Churchill spoke in the House of Commons on his return to London, to explain that although he was enthusiastic about the optimism of the Zionists in Palestine, he was also discouraged by the negative form of Islamic extremism that had emerged in Saudi Arabia. A large number of followers of the new Saudi King, Ibn Saud, belonged to the fundamentalist Wahhabi sect. They lived austere lives and imposed their beliefs on others by force. It was their duty and their faith to kill anyone who did not share their opinions, and 'to make slaves of their wives and children. Women have been put to death in Wahhabi villages,' just for going outside their home into the streets. They are 'intolerant, well-armed, and bloodthirsty'. He warned the House, 'they are very dangerous'.[6]

The Commons voted overwhelmingly in favour of the government's policy on Palestine.

Two months later, at the end of June, Churchill was shocked and grieved by two family tragedies. On 29 May 1921, his mother Jennie broke her ankle in a fall downstairs. Gangrene set in, resulting in the need for amputation above the knee. Immediately his bodyguard Walter Thompson heard that Lady Randolph might die from loss of blood, he offered to provide his own. But, as Churchill wrote to a friend, Jennie died at the age of sixty-seven of 'old age, decrepitude, loneliness …' She was buried beside Lord Randolph in Bladon churchyard.

Six days after attending her funeral, he described to the Imperial Conference in London that what he envisioned was reconciliation between France and

---

* Amin would be forced to flee to Lebanon in 1937 by the Nashashabi family, who vied with him for total power. When the Second World War began in 1939, Amin would flee to fascist Italy, and Nazi Germany, where Hitler would hatch his Middle East policy called 'Plan Orient', and instruct Amin how to set up murder camps in the Middle East to destroy all non-Muslims. After the defeat of Nazi Germany in 1945, he would flee to Egypt to escape prosecution for war crimes, and from where he directed rebellions against the British.

Germany. He also addressed other problems in Europe, of removing grievances and inequalities of nations by negotiations and agreements. He announced to the Prime Ministers of British Dominions that his aim was to appease 'the fearful hatreds and antagonisms which exist in Europe and to enable the world to settle down'. Britain's role, he explained, should be that of 'the Ally of France and the friend of Germany'. Unless he could act to remove 'the frightful rancour and fear and hatred' between those two countries, they would most certainly result in a 'renewal of the struggle' in a generation or so.

Then, at the beginning of August, his two and a half-year-old daughter, Marigold, became ill with meningitis and died. Winston and Clementine were devastated: 'that this little life should have been extinguished,' he wrote to a friend, 'just when it was so beautiful & so happy – just when it was beginning.'

Churchill shared his grief with his bodyguard, and both took a last look at Marigold's tiny form that looked like a sculptured figure in white marble. If their friendship had been sealed by Walter's offer of a blood transfusion to Jennie, their grief over Marigold created a bond.

Meningitis was only one of several infectious diseases that still stalked the British Isles, like tuberculosis, and burst into epidemics from time to time. Churchill withdrew to Dunrobin Castle in Scotland, the home of his friend the Duke of Sutherland, where he agonised over her death in solitude. The Duke's brother had only recently died from wounds he had received on the Western Front.

Churchill painted and reflected on life, in isolation, while Clementine remained in London to be near Marigold's grave.

He wrote to her; 'Many tender thoughts my darling all of you & your sweet kittens. Alas I keep feeling the hurt of the Duckadilly. I expect you will have made a pilgrimage yesterday. Now Alastair is buried near his father's grave overlooking the bay. Another twenty years will bring me to the end of my allotted span even if I have so long. The reflections of middle age are mellow. I will take what comes.'

Continued violence in Iraq and Palestine resulted in heavy costs to maintain larger British military, police, and administration forces than he had budgeted for. In the north of Iraq, RAF planes had to be used to bomb ungovernable tribesmen when they continually attacked British garrisons. There was another Arab riot against the Jewish National Home in Palestine that left five dead. Nevertheless, he continually impressed on his advisers that his and their priority was to reduce costs, since his budgets were severely limited by the Treasury.

Ireland was another wound that still festered. Clementine had written to him at the beginning of the year, 'Do my darling use your influence *now* for some sort of moderation or at any rate justice in Ireland. Put yourself in the place of the Irish ... It always makes me unhappy & disappointed when I see you *inclined* to take for granted that the rough, iron-fisted "Hunnish" way will prevail.'

In reality, he had supported the possibility of a truce with Sinn Féin, hoping that a calmer tone would emerge from those who continued to murder for their political ideal of an independent and united Ireland, regardless of the bloody consequences.

He was still prepared to offer them Dominion Home Rule, and pressed Lloyd George to agree to negotiate without any preconditions.

Despite his own pain at the deaths of Marigold and his mother, he told Lloyd George how shocked he had been to catch sight in his constituency of 'some men in bare feet and some children in a savage and starving condition.'[7] He added that he doubted the wisdom of the government policy of deflation. Lloyd George responded by reproaching him with 'an attempt to lay the blame on your colleagues for present unemployment conditions'.

There was some truth in that, since Churchill had been passed over for the job of Chancellor of the Exchequer, which would have been a step closer to the position of Prime Minister at 10 Downing Street.

II

THE RUSSIAN CRISIS

15

The Enemy on the Left
1922–23

Winston Churchill was very much taken by Admiral Kolchak, and would describe his unfortunate circumstances as a Russian patriot in *The World Crisis* in 1929. The admiral had already demonstrated his leadership skills and courage when the revolution erupted and caused mutiny in his fleet. Kerensky's provisional government advised him to seek refuge in Japan until he was needed. He became Minister of Marine in the Omsk government. Winston Churchill wrote sympathetically of him:

> Kolchak was honest, loyal and incorruptible. His outlook and temperament were autocratic; but he tried hard to be liberal and progressive in accordance with what he was assured was the spirit of the times. He had no political experience, and was devoid of those profound intuitions which have enabled men of equal virtue and character to steer their way through the shoals and storms of revolution. He was an intelligent, honourable, patriotic admiral. He took no part in the movement or conspiracy which overthrew the civil power; but when the necessities of the time and the general demand of those with whom he was in contact thrust upon him the responsibilities of dictatorship, he accepted the duty.[1]

Kolchak became Commander-in-Chief of Siberia, the Cossack homeland, and Orenburg. His aim was to revive the fighting power of the White Russian Army and defeat the Bolsheviks, to restore law and order, and allow the Russian people to choose their own government.

It was a time, wrote Churchill, to justify his confidence in law and order, when, 'The mass remained sunk in Russian apathy and fatalism. He was the best man available.'

Kolchak directed General Gaida's Siberian Army of about 100,000 soldiers in a rapid advance of the entire front of 150 miles, and resumed the offensive on 1 March 1919. His aim was to join up in support of the Allied Armies at Archangel. At the same time, General Denikin's force of Russian volunteers in the Black Sea Region joined Krasnov's 100,000 Cossacks, to become a significant military factor.

On 26 May, the Supreme Council of Allied and Associated Powers: the 'Big Five', consisting of Clemenceau of France, Lloyd George, President Wilson of the US, Premier Orlando of Italy, and the Japanese delegate Salonji, sent a note to Kolchak clarifying their policy towards Russia. It was to avoid interference with communist Russia's affairs, and to let the Russians sort out their own problems in their own way in order to restore peace. They had decided by that time it was no longer possible to do so by dealing with the Soviet government in Moscow.

Kolchak replied that he had no intention of retaining power after Russia's interests were achieved. He would call an election at the end of the Civil War. The Big Five thereupon offered him their support.

The Siberian Western Army had been badly defeated in May and June. British Intelligence agent Colonel Knox observed and reported on Kolchak's collapse. And the Supreme Council of Five decided by August that it would not be prudent to provide Kolchak with any more help. According to Knox, 'The men are listless and slack, and there is no sign of their officers taking them in hand. The men do not want rest, but hard work and discipline ...'

Admiral Kolchak had evidently lost his grip by 24 December, when a revolution took place at Irkutsk, and Kolchak placed himself under the protection of the Czech Army. But they could not be relied upon in circumstances where officers and men changed sides according to the fortunes of war, sometimes simply to whoever offered them food; or they might starve to death. Sometimes armies of hundreds of thousands of men without food disappeared in the vastness of the Russian landscape, 'lost – dispersed, melted, evaporated ...'

Churchill had done his best to support and guide and provide aid to Kolchak through Knox, who also availed himself of the services of Colonel John Ward and his Middlesex Regiment. But now they sailed from Vladivostok to England on 8 September 1919. The Hampshire Regiment also left Russia, abandoning Kolchak to his doom.

On 14 January two Czech officers were ordered to hand Kolchak over to the local authorities, and the admiral was locked up in a jail at Irkutsk. Churchill's record of Kolchak's fate, from his spies, differed somewhat from the official one, by stating: 'On February 7, before it was light, the Admiral and his prime minister were murdered in their cells in the customary Bolshevik manner by the discharging of automatic pistols pressed against the back of their heads.'[2]

Death of a Hero

On 7 February 1920, on the bank of a tributary of the Angara called the Ushakovka, a Red Army firing squad prepared to execute a patriot. Admiral Kolchak had been the most effective of all the anti-Bolshevik leaders whom Winston had known. Kolchak had been captured and imprisoned in Irkutsk. He and a former prime minister of an independent Far Eastern region had been found guilty of treason by the Bolsheviks. Only Kolchak's mistress was allowed to go free.

'In the still, freezing night desultory shooting could be heard to the westward as guards under the prison commandant led Kolchak into the funnel of yellow light [from the headlight of a lorry which had brought the firing squad]. Pepeliaev [the former Prime Minister] had to be dragged. Both men were handcuffed.

'Kolchak was offered a bandage for his eyes, but refused. There are various accounts of his last words, none reliable. Only one has, for me, the ring of truth. In this version Chudnovsky asked whether he had a last request to make. "Would you be so good," said Kolchak, "as to get a message sent to my wife in Paris, to say that I bless my son?"'

"I'll see what can be done," replied Chudnovsky offhandedly, "if I don't forget about it."'[3]

The patriotic admiral was fortunate to be let off so lightly by a brutal regime that dealt as cruelly and ruthlessly with its followers as its opponents. His pointless murder ended the anti-Bolshevik activity by Russians. He had been the last hope for a return to civilisation, however imperfect it might have been. The volley of shots that rang out from the barrels of the firing squad would abandon the entire population of Soviet Russia to three quarters of a century of slavery under Stalin's erratic rule.

Lloyd George's policy now was to accept and live with the Soviet Union, and trade with them, since the battle against communism in Russia was lost. American troops withdrew from Siberia in April.

In view of the subsequent tyranny by Lenin, and then by Stalin, historian Margaret MacMillan believed that Churchill was right all along about the Bolsheviks, and that Lloyd George was wrong to view Churchill's championing of General Denikin and Admiral Kolchak simply as a personal obsession.[4]

Making Peace with the Bolsheviks

Russia's dwindling anti-Bolshevik military forces and Churchill had done all they could. Now that everyone wanted to make peace with the Bolsheviks, Churchill was left to find ways to avoid Britain and other nations being infected by International Communism. He wrote to Lloyd George that, although he did not believe that harmony was possible between Bolshevism and western civilisation, he recognised that a cessation of arms and the promotion of material prosperity were inevitable; so 'we must trust for better or worse to peaceful influences to bring about the disappearance of this awful tyranny and peril'.[5]

Although always the hero at the centre of his own adventures and dramas, Churchill was viewed as unreliable by some people who knew him, like Sir Henry Wilson, who wrote in his diary, 'So ends in practical disaster another of Winston's military attempts. Antwerp, Dardanelles, Denikin. His judgment is always at fault, & he is hopeless when in power.'

But the Russian Civil War was not quite over yet. The Polish army advanced on Kiev and drove out the Bolsheviks. General Wrangel took over from Denikin and opposed a powerful Bolshevik force. Nevertheless, the British government agreed to recognise Bolshevik Russia officially, in exchange for persuading the Bolsheviks to stop interfering in Afghanistan, Persia and the Caucasus, Central Europe and Britain.

Three hundred thousand combatants were killed in the civil war. Another 450,000 died of disease. It was only part of the human destruction. Cossack troops shot some 25,000 civilians in one province alone. The anti-Semitic White Army murdered 100,000 Jewish people in the Ukraine, while another unknown number were slaughtered in the pogroms in the south. The Red Army either shot or deported 500,000 to 700,000 Cossacks in revenge.[6]

As it would turn out, the Communist leaders and commissars were even more ruthless and incompetent at ruling Russia than the lazy-minded and half-hearted aristocrats and corrupt officials of the Tsarist regime had been. Lenin was furious at what he saw as resistance to his liberating policy by peasant forces loyal to the previous regime, and ordered grain to be confiscated in villages in the Urals, which caused the first of a number of deliberate famines that Russia would experience within the decade. One to two million people starved to death. Typhoid followed among the malnourished and weakened population, killing at least three million more.[7]

On top of that, Lenin's secret police, the CHEKA, executed another quarter of a million without trials.[8]

After three years of civil war and terror since the October Revolution imposed its rule on the countless villages in agricultural areas where four fifths of Russia's peasants were living, the Red Army and White Armies and Cossacks had plundered, burnt, killed and raped, and abandoned those Russians to die of starvation and disease. Even so, that cycle of terror was not new to Russia: 'Before 1917 the tsar's armies had engaged in the same periodic campaigns of terror in an attempt to control a population still living largely beyond the law: in a country of 160 million souls, the official police force numbered only about one hundred thousand, with everyday order maintained by the often brutal rule of village elders.'[9]

Terror in Ireland

At that point in Russian affairs, Lloyd George decided that he needed Churchill as a priority to suppress the crimes and disorder in Ireland, where Churchill found Sinn Féin's acts of terror towards the Irish population and the local constabulary repugnant.[10] Two members of the Royal Irish Constabulary had been murdered at the beginning of 1919, initiating the deadly Anglo–Irish War of Independence.

As Sinn Féin murders continued, Lloyd George asked Churchill's friend, General Tudor, to form a special Irish police force. Director of Military Operations Henry Wilson described it as 'a counter-murder association'. It consisted of eight thousand former soldiers from the Great War. Because of the odds and ends of uniforms left over from the war, they were named 'Black and Tans'. Their aim was to take terrorism to the terrorists by returning every murder of one of their comrades with the death of a terrorist.[11] Shooting, burnings and reprisals were part of the terrorist culture. As Wilson wrote in his diary, Churchill 'evidently had some lingering hope of our rough handling of the Sinn Féins'.

Churchill defended British officers in the Irish Constabulary and the Black and Tans as loyal and gallant in coping with such a repugnant situation in which no one could be trusted and violent criminality ensued. Field Marshal Sir Henry Wilson would be assassinated on his own doorstep in London by two IRA gunmen as a reprisal in June 1922. He had been commander of the British Army in Ireland in 1914. He had just unveiled a memorial to Britain's war dead. Police found a hit-list of other IRA targets scheduled for assassination, with Winston Churchill's name at the top. He was immediately assigned more security. It was not the first or last time that he would be targeted by assassins. His bodyguard, Inspector Walter Thompson, slept in the premises for several weeks. He saved Churchill's life many times. As for Winston, 'He longed to confront danger,' Thompson said.[12]

When the Churchill children, Diana and Randolph, returned from roller skating in Holland Park, they found their home surrounded by police, who were making a thorough search of the property for possible IRA intruders. Winston was now obliged to sleep in the attic with a metal shield to reinforce his bedroom door, and a service revolver in reach for months afterwards.

General Tudor was also earmarked for assassination by the IRA. He was followed to Newfoundland by an IRA gunman, where he armed himself in readiness with his service revolver and a brass knuckleduster, and waited to confront his assassin.[13] He was saved by the local Catholic priest, who turned the IRA gunman away from murder by warning him that he'd be unlikely to escape from the Canadian police afterwards.[14]

With reprisals by one side triggering reprisals from the other, Churchill privately 'acknowledged the failure of the policy of force'.[15]

The Irish rebel leaders finally tired of war and agreed to a truce. As with India, when offered Dominion status within the British Empire, they stubbornly demanded full independence instead. Churchill was convinced that in each case the inherent hatred between religious factions would cause them to exploit independence as an opportunity to murder each other. Dealing with the blind emotions that stirred up Irish and Indian nationalists meant that, whatever you attempted to do for the sake of peace, you could end up by supporting the wrong side.

Bloody Sunday

Nevertheless, Winston negotiated for eight weeks with the dashing and handsome young Michael Collins, who was the leading figure on the Irish Republican side. Collins had played a key role in the so-called 'Bloody Sunday'. when twelve

THE ENEMY ON THE LEFT

British officers were murdered on 21 November 1920. As they weighed each other up at their first meeting, Collins decided he didn't trust Churchill; he thought him bombastic and full of ex-officer lingo. But, as usual, when Churchill applied his charm, they got along well and Collins ended by admiring him.

Lloyd George was a different matter altogether as far as Collins was concerned. Collins wrote of him, 'Born poor is therefore shrewd. Was lawyer therefore crafty ... Would sell his nearest and dearest for political prestige.'[16]

Lloyd George viewed Collins more pragmatically since, in two and a half years, 1,300 people had been killed in the struggle against the IRA, including 550 troops and police.[17]

The first hurdle in negotiations was the right of the six northern counties to be excluded from Home Rule. Then there was Churchill's demand that Irish MPs in a new parliament representing the south would swear allegiance to the Crown. Both were overheated emotive issues, as all discussions between representatives of either side were. But Prime Minister Lloyd George was an expert at sweeping emotions aside and replacing them with pragmatic solutions. He gave the Irish delegates an ultimatum on 5 December 1921, either to sign the treaty as presented to them, with partition and the oath of allegiance, or return to war. Collins finally agreed after several indecisive hours – with Winston pacing in the background in evening dress, with a cigar clenched in his jaw.

Collins was evidently relieved at the offer of a truce, and admitted the IRA could not have lasted for more than another three weeks. He had done his best to save Ireland. The treaty he signed gave it scope to increase its freedom in the future. But 'he knew he was signing his own death warrant'.[18]

And so it would turn out, since Ireland's President Éamon de Valera was a pragmatic and a devious politician who had deliberately not attended the signing himself, so that he could repudiate the agreement afterwards. Despite the Irish government approving the treaty by sixty-four votes to fifty-seven, anti-treaty IRA gunmen ambushed Michael Collins's convoy a year later and shot him dead for signing it.

16

Realities and Illusions
1923–24

Winston Churchill stood firmly against Protectionism, which he considered self-defeating, and gave an entertaining speech in the House of Commons in November 1923. He described the leader of the Conservative Party, Stanley Baldwin, as a combination of two characters from *Alice Through the Looking Glass* – the March Hare, who was mad, and the Mad Hatter. It was his colourful way of defending free trade against the imposition of tariffs that created hurdles to exporting Britain's goods overseas.

Although the Conservatives were returned to office in the General Election soon afterwards, they had lost eighty-eight seats. In the following month, former Liberal Prime Minister Asquith decided to appeal more to Labour constituents than Conservatives. Churchill disagreed. Although he was a Liberal at heart, he recognised that a centrist party was no longer popular, and called on Liberals to support Conservative candidates in a by-election where there was no Liberal candidate. The *Glasgow Herald* noted that, 'Mr. Churchill seems a predestined champion of the individualism which he has served all his political life under both of its liveries.'

He had fought socialist candidates ever since 1908. He was cheered in the House when he claimed that, 'It is an absurd delusion that the industries of this country can be conducted through committees of elected politicians.' He reminded them how socialism had ruined Russia, and claimed it would 'kill Great Britain stone dead'. He abhorred men with doctrinaire views and a desire to impose notions on their fellow citizens as to what they should do and not do: they would bring untold miseries upon millions.

Nevertheless, Conservative Prime Minister Stanley Baldwin decided to call a General Election on November 1923, in which he would introduce protectionism. It was a rallying cry for Churchill, who still firmly believed in the economic and employment advantages of free trade. Several Liberal associations asked him to be their candidate. Speaking in Manchester, he said that Liberalism was the only 'sure, sober, safe middle course of lucid intelligence and high principle'.[1] Three days later, he accepted the invitation of the West Leicester Liberal Association to be their candidate.

The *Leicester Mail* was hostile to him, but the *Nottingham Journal* supported him and sent truckloads of newspapers with their recommendation to his new

REALITIES AND ILLUSIONS

constituency. His new young friend, the twenty-one-year-old Brendan Bracken, helped to distribute them. But the campaign did not go well. The *Leicester Mail* announced gleefully that Winston Churchill and Clementine 'were greeted by groans and hoots'. Nobody cheered. Whenever he opened his mouth to speak, they cried out, 'What about the Dardanelles?'

He managed to say to one of the hecklers, 'What do you know of the Dardanelles? The Dardanelles might have saved millions of lives. Don't imagine I am running away from the Dardanelles.'

Someone smashed his car window after one of his speeches in London, while he attempted to drive away from a hostile, hooting crowd. Someone else spat on the vehicle as it left.

Clementine did her best to support her husband by speaking at West Leicester. But Churchill's fame caused extremes of emotion – people either loved him or hated him. In any case, Baldwin had seriously misjudged his call for an election, and the Conservatives lost almost a hundred seats. Nevertheless, Churchill failed to return to Parliament as a Liberal.

The numbers showed that the Conservatives could be defeated if Labour and the Liberals joined in a coalition against them. But Churchill wanted the Liberals to join the Conservatives to keep Labour out. He was annoyed when Asquith refused. Asquith's daughter Violet told him privately that her father's reason was that joining forces with the Liberals could undermine commercial and business activity.

Liberals and Labour joined forces to defeat the Conservatives, as Churchill had feared, and forced Baldwin to resign. Labour Party leader Ramsay MacDonald became Prime Minister, and Churchill immediately congratulated him by letter. It was a normal act of courtesy between opponents even though he had a poor opinion of MacDonald. It was said of MacDonald that no one knew what he was going to say or what he had just said.

Although Churchill was invited to stand for Bristol West, he declined on the grounds that the Conservatives were too strong to oppose.

Two weeks later he had still not firmly made up his mind what course of action to take. He took a few months to write on holiday at Mimizan in the south of France. But, restless as ever, he was soon back in London for a long talk with Baldwin.

In May, the Conservative Association of Ashton-under-Lyne invited him to be their candidate, and several other invitations arrived from various Conservative associations. But Churchill hesitated to rejoin the Conservative Party. Clementine was a firm and convinced Liberal, and unhappy that he might return to the Conservatives. She wrote him, 'Do not however let the Tories get you too cheap. They have treated you so badly in the past they ought to be made to pay.'

At his election address on 9 March, the Labour Party had attacked him for his attempt 'to overthrow Bolshevik Russia'. And he was confronted with the usual cries about his wartime failure in the Dardanelles. But Thomas Jones, the Deputy Secretary to the Cabinet, remarked that, 'The Dardanelles pursues Churchill most unfairly, for it was one of the big conceptions of the war and if put through with vigour might have shortened the war by a couple of years.'

That had been Churchill's aim. But it had been handled badly by the half-hearted Admiralty and a War Office led by a distracted Kitchener who had seemed engrossed in other affairs once it had been approved.

Out of Office

With the collapse of the coalition government in 1922, and a surge of public opinion to the left, Churchill found himself out of office. He also lost his seat as a Member of Parliament when he failed to obtain support in the by-election in West Leicester in December 1923. No longer an MP, he was prevented from continuing to fight against socialism. There was a genuine fear that socialists were fomenting a Bolshevik revolution in Britain. The Communist Party of Great Britain had been founded several years previously.

The new Labour government would soon be undermined by publication in the newspapers of the infamous 'Zinoviev Letter', which purported to show the socialist government's links to the Soviet Union, which many Conservatives feared. The letter was revealed to be a forgery.*

Now, at last, Churchill had the leisure time to research and write his famous account of the complexities and confusion of the First World War, which had resulted in the collapse of four huge empires in Europe. He called it *The World Crisis: 1911–1918*. In it, he showed how the twentieth century was shaped, and described how he thought the world should make its way through a jungle of conflicting interests. It was published in five volumes. The first volume appeared in 1923 to considerable praise. His fifth volume would appear eight years later.

'As Churchill pressed ahead with the writing, he wrote to Clementine from Cannes of how the book was "a great chance to put my whole case in agreeable form to an attentive audience". It would also, he pointed out, earn enough money "to make us feel very comfortable".

'While on his writing holiday, he discovered the casinos in Cannes and Monte Carlo, which he visited frequently, losing more often than he won but winning enough to pay the rent on the villa.'[2]

'The more Churchill wrote, the wider became his interest and his reading. He devoured each new book on the war as it was published. Whole sections of his work derived, with acknowledgment, from the work of others, including British naval and war historians, and senior German and French and Russian participants.'[3]

He was still receiving threatening letters from Ireland, and asked his bodyguard if he had his revolver with him. When Thompson hesitated, caught off guard, Churchill demanded to see it before he was satisfied. Thompson had forgotten to bring it with him but, 'I never again forgot the revolver.'[4]

---

* Many years later, when top-secret information was declassified, the forgery was disclosed as having been organised by the patriotic Sidney Reilly of MI5 and some of his 'scallywags'.

REALITIES AND ILLUSIONS

Several months after the assassination of Sir Henry Wilson in London's west end, Churchill still received threatening letters, some telling him the exact date and time he would be killed. When in office, he was driven in an armoured car with bulletproof windows, and carried a revolver. His marksmanship with a Colt 45 was deadly.[5] While still in the Colonial Office, he was frequently followed by a car with three occupants who watched out for him to and from his destinations.[6]

Churchill attacked socialism, fascism and communism in his speeches intended for re-election, and his hustings were good sport for anyone spoiling for a fight. They attracted attacks from strong-arm thugs with knuckle-dusters and clubs. Churchill was guarded from them at the hustings by 'a group of protectors armed with mallets' organised by Commander Oliver Locker-Thompson and watched over by Walter Thompson, who had no reservations about getting involved by using his fists on any of the hoodlums. He enjoyed a good fight and was always on the alert from when he had been Policeman Number 459 at Paddington Green police station. He laid out a number of attackers with his fists and sometimes had to use a truncheon.[7]

Riots and Insurrections

Anyone who studied history with serious interest generally discovered that mankind suffered from a tendency to flee when confronted by insurmountable problems, and take shelter in the comfort zone of an alternative universe of illusions. Pioneer psychologists like Carl Jung realised that 'the pendulum of the mind oscillates between sense and nonsense, not between right and wrong'. To the gullible and misguided, nonsense often appeared to open up other possibilities. And a multitude of rosy illusions was always to be found at hand.

The scope of Churchill's keen studies as a young man and his scholarly research while writing his own books of history revealed how man's switch from reality into illusion in his quest for answers is only a very small step. As an example, Winston had immediately seen through the illusory claims of communism to its real motive, which was a means for unscrupulous adventurers to obtain power. George Washington had described it most succinctly in his 1796 *Farewell Address*, in which he warned that a political party 'agitates the community with ill founded jealousies and false alarms, kindles the animosity of one part against another, and foments occasional riot and insurrection'.

Political agitators Marx and Engels wrote the Communist Manifesto as a result of the successful English Industrial Revolution, which was something new and overwhelming. While it brought employment to the jobless and vastly improved Britain's economy, so that its standard of living was the highest in the world, it also spawned new problems with agitators, like anarchists who objected to being governed, socialists who wanted to steamroller everyone to make them all equal, and Marxists and Trotskyites who believed in imposing force to establish order by military and secret police.

Despite industrialisation's huge contribution to the success of Great Britain's economy and its creation of new jobs, Karl Marx in London and Friederich Engels in Manchester never stopped complaining about working conditions, even while factory owners were improving them, and after they had been improved. They warned that the evils of capitalism must be replaced with the virtues of communism, without any evidence for their claim. They published their Manifesto in 1848, twenty-six years before Winston Churchill was born. It would have looked like dense and foreign philosophising to him, with long drawn-out circuitous theories backed by propaganda, instead of evidence – whereas Churchill knew that English democracy had constantly been proven to work; so why take a terrible risk of disaster by changing it?

The communist world was not the real world. It was nothing more than a fantasy invented by a couple of discontented rebels with their own personal grievances. The communist regime had left a deep impression on young Winston when serving his term as Colonial Secretary, and being thrust into its quagmire because of his new ministerial position, in which he would be caught up in the turmoil of other peoples' tortured emotions.

Lenin's application of Marx's theories began to shape itself as a very real threat to the rest of the world after the Bolshevik Revolution in Soviet Russia and the end of the civil war in 1923. A foggy emotional appeal of mystical and illusory proportions was imposed on the uneducated Russian masses, like a bandage to relieve the traumas of oppression suffered under the Romanov Empire for three centuries. Most had no idea what Bolshevism meant, or any other of its meaningless politically weighted words or emotionally charged propaganda, like 'All power to the Soviets', which became the rallying cry of mediocrities who were given power over the illiterate masses.

The illusion of something called Bolshevism or communism would become in the twentieth century what fanatical religions had been in medieval times. Common sense was abandoned in the hysteria of what might be described as a form of hallucination, into which Churchill would be thrust as a minister of the Crown.

Marxist claims of a political paradise were particularly appealing to the millions of families in Europe who were starving from crop failures, while some fled to London Docks and New York Harbour to escape the misery and oppression that was autocratic Europe. Migrants who had suffered from waves of revolutions and oppression brought their grievances with them. They and the half-starved Irish, who had endured a similar fate from the potato blight, were the most likely nucleus for the spread of a communist ideology from Soviet Russia. Their American prophet was John Reed, because he claimed to have been an eyewitness to the October Revolution.

Dark Satanic Mills

Britain's working classes were not as naïve and impressionable as Marx and Engels had hoped. They enjoyed the highest living standards in the world. They knew that, despite the communist urge to revolution and the overthrow of capitalism, capitalised industries provided more jobs in the cities than could be found in rural areas. Little had been written of people who lived and died in anonymous poverty, misery, and tragic ill-health in the English countryside. Thomas Hardy's and Sir Walter Scott's best-selling novels relied on romance against the background of rural England, as those of the Brontë sisters and Jane Austen did, to attract readers, whereas illness, desperation and starvation had been far more typical. The truth about the horrible working conditions in some factories was that, awful though they were, they were superior to work in the countryside; otherwise hundreds of thousands of unemployed would not have fled from rural area into the cities, to escape from farm owners who could afford to pay only subsistence wages.*

Country folk, who had felt attached to the soil, viewed industrialisation as tantamount to 'the disintegration of civilisation'. The poet William Blake complained that the beauty of the countryside was being spoiled by introducing 'these dark Satanic Mills' with belching chimneys, and noisy heavy industries that left black soot everywhere.

Austrian economist Joseph Schumpeter, who worked in America, took a more realistic view when he wrote that new technologies are always disruptive, as part of an evolutionary process of creative destruction. New technologies all but destroy society, but they may benefit by initiating progress in the long run.

Churchill's attitude was one he achieved by distancing himself emotionally so that he could view situations on a more lofty historic scale, from which he knew that, in any case – regardless of some people's emotional demands – there was no alternative to the consequences of judgments that had already been taken; whether they were intended or unintended consequences. Nor were there precedents to call on for ideas that might improve industrial conditions. Although he had not managed to restrain his emotions at the injustices of the Russian Revolution, young Winston had learned, first from *The Martyrdom of Man,* then from the communist regime, that most people behaved irrationally, and that life was a tragedy.

---

* The attraction of higher wages for fewer hours in the towns, mechanization in the 1850s and 1860s, and depression in the last quarter of the century, all led to extensive rural depopulation – a great exodus mostly to Scottish and English towns, some to the coalfields (especially in Wales), some to the colonies, some to the army.

17

Political Rivals

Lloyd George was well aware of Winston's ambition, and frequently snubbed him to keep him in his place. He was probably the only man who could: he was the older of the two by twenty years, intelligent and experienced, and Winston respected him. Although LG recognised Winston's brilliance and his drive and ambition, he was acutely aware that Churchill wanted to be on top. He had even suspected on several occasions that Winston was planning to topple and replace him. It was not simply Lloyd George's imagination, or the paranoia of a national leader; Winston had spent his entire life pursuing political leadership, and finally seemed ready for the top spot. But he was confronted by the mistrust of colleagues.

The fact that both his parents were dead now did not discourage him from wanting to prove his worth. He had been rebuked several times by his father and felt neglected by his mother when he had been a schoolboy boarder at Harrow. Being Prime Minister seemed to be the mechanism for his need to excel and be appreciated, to prove his parents had been wrong to underrate him.

His brilliance needed an outlet, an opportunity to flourish. And nothing was going to stop Winston, because his ego was too great to permit it. All that held him back now was that his colleagues, and even his friends, were afraid of his ruthless ambition. But Lloyd George was an outstanding leader, praised by all. Winston had admired Lloyd George as a brilliant war leader, even to imagining he was the Prime Minister's partner, as well as his friend. Now he had reached a point where his admiration for Lloyd George was so strong that he apparently wanted to *be* LG – or, at any rate, be the Prime Minister who would replace him.

Their differences had come out into the open with their clash of opinions about the Bolsheviks, when Churchill wrote him a letter accusing him of 'altogether failing to address your mind to the real dangers that are before us'.[1] In response, Lloyd George said he thought that Churchill envisioned himself riding on a white charger into Moscow 'in a triumphal procession after the defeat of the Bolsheviks, and being acclaimed as the saviour of Russia'.[2]

H.W. Wilson, the leader writer of the *Daily Mail*, had remarked to the newspaper owner that, 'It is a question whether Winston would not make a better Prime Minister than Lloyd George … slippery though he is, he is less slippery than Lloyd George whom no one trusts.'[3]

There was another driving force that charged Winston's energy, too, and propelled him to be on top. He had become aware of it at age twenty-one, when he had been a soldier in training, and was bored by the limitations of the daily routines in the military barracks and stables of his cavalry regiment, and recognised a huge gap in his education. He had asked Jennie to send him an assortment of history books and books on philosophy, because he'd wanted to know more about ethics.

She had sent him Macaulay's works in twelve volumes. He was already on to Plato's *Republic* and Winwood Reade's *Martyrdom of Man*, Hallam's *Constitutional History* and Adam Smith's *Wealth of Nations*. He read history and philosophy for four or five hours every day – Schopenhauer on Pessimism, Malthus on Population, and Darwin's *On the Origin of Species,* 'interspersed with other books of lesser standing', as he described his new reading material when he wrote his memoir.

Schopenhauer's famous essay begins; 'Unless *suffering* is the direct and immediate object of life, our existence must entirely fail of its aim. It is absurd to look upon the enormous amount of pain that abounds everywhere in the world, and originates in needs and necessities inseparable from life itself, as serving no purpose at all and the result of mere chance. Each separate misfortune, as it comes, seems, no doubt, to be something exceptional; but misfortune in general is the rule.'[4]

He resisted Schopenhauer's pessimism, while the result of his eager studies had awakened him to the fundamental character of the world beyond the sound of horses' hooves in the stables and the jingles of bridles, and military exercises in his army barracks. Since his studies often involved the revelations of Jewish ethics, he had admired the Jewish people ever since.

What the young Winston had discovered through the narratives of classical history books and the outlook of the great philosophers was a recognition of the conflict between cruelty, bigotry and injustice – the forces of darkness that don't want their fearful powers taken from them – and the forces of enlightenment and justice that opposed them. Winston always championed against injustices. Injustice was his trigger. He saw the need for justice everywhere; in Russia against the Bolsheviks, in Ireland against the gunmen of the Republican Army, in India against the cruelty to different religious groups and the Untouchables, in Germany at the present time, in Palestine and Saudi Arabia, in Iraq, and throughout Britain and the British Empire. It was an anxious and worrying challenge to find himself fighting for justice everywhere.

Opposition only made him more determined in his quest for justice, because he knew the poor calibre of his opponents. Despite the fact that he admired Lloyd George, he was also obliged to battle with him for supremacy against his political pragmatism, which involved turning his back on the injustices in Soviet Russia. Churchill was a romantic and a sentimentalist. That was why they made such a good team. But they were also rivals for the limelight. And the world allows only one hero to emerge at a time, particularly in politics, where leaders do not like to be upstaged by rivals.

As the author of *The Good Soldier* wrote, 'All good soldiers are sentimentalists. Their profession is full of big words, like courage, loyalty, honour, and constancy.'[5]

Although Lloyd George was well aware that Churchill was a dangerous man – he had already said so – he was fascinated by him; almost like gazing transfixed at a king cobra about to strike.

Winston had already become the hero of his own romantic imagination as a child, when he had been born in Blenheim Palace. But reading Darwin, Macaulay, Reade, and other explorers of the intellect and the emotions, had broadened his mind and established his character, his world view, and his place in it, as a romantic knight in dazzling armour, who would fight to bring justice everywhere.

Military adviser Sir Henry Wilson had already perceived and noted it succinctly in his diary several years earlier: 'Winston all against Bolshevism, & therefore, in this against LG.'[6]

Misfortune the General Rule

Lloyd George had managed to patch up his differences with Winston over the communist threat during the years following the outbreak of the revolution, perhaps because he was receiving plenty of opposition to his leadership by 1922. He needed a friend as a sparring partner who would enhance his prestige. As he was gradually bypassed, he was even considering resigning.

His secretary, Frances Stevenson, made a note in her diary on 3 February, 'Winston and F.E. will be furious when they learn of D.'s [David's] plan to go out and leave the field to the Conservatives. That will not suit their book at all.' She added, 'Winston is still nursing his ambition.'[7]

Sir Philip Sassoon remarked to Lord Esher that Lloyd George should resign at once: 'But Winston (whose views are always personal) advises him to hang on because Winston does not wish to give up his job & I am sure he means to join the Tories at the earliest possible moment.'[8]

Churchill's incautious impatience showed itself on 20 February, when he spoke to Lloyd George at a Cabinet meeting in a manner that appeared to show want of respect.[9] Winston hurriedly wrote to him the same day to apologize: 'The word "ungrateful" ought not to have been used, & I hope you will efface it from your memory.'[10]

Lloyd George reacted by excluding him from a Cabinet Finance Committee meeting.

Their argument now centred on Lloyd George's determination to officially recognise the Soviet Union, whereas Churchill was set against it, and was thought to be determined to resign if he could not have his way. But at the conference with the Russians in Genoa in April, the Soviets told LG they had already engaged with the Germans instead of the British; so Lloyd George's conciliatory meeting was aborted.

On 19 October, it was noted that an independent Conservative had beaten the coalition candidate at the Newport by-election, showing the danger of being associated with LG's current and unpopular coalition government. A majority of Conservatives met immediately at the Carlton Club in London to decide if they should remain in the Coalition or not. They voted against it and against Lloyd George, by 187 to 87.

LG had been living on his hallowed record as a respected wartime Prime Minister. The public had liked his six-point programme then: 'Try the Kaiser; Punish all those guilty of atrocities; Squeeze the maximum indemnity from Germany; Britain for the British, socially and industrially; Rehabilitate the broken in war; And provide a happier country for all.'

It was a different story now. For one thing, the public did not like to hear of repression in Ireland. And the Conservatives would not forgive LG for recognising the Soviet Union. It was unfortunate for him too that unemployment had rocketed from 400,000 to 2 million from April to December in that year. Then there were revelations of his practise of selling political titles of honour. It planted distrust of all his actions.[11]

The result was that a body of die-hard Conservatives no longer considered a coalition of parties in government was useful or necessary; which meant dropping Lloyd George as the Prime Minister. As was customary in such loss of confidence, Lloyd George left for Buckingham Palace to tender his resignation. It ended his relationship with Churchill.

Churchill was unaware of the final vote of no confidence, since he was unexpectedly removed from the scene for a sudden operation on his appendix. He only learned of the fall of Lloyd George when he recovered. As he wrote in October 1922, 'I had lost not only my appendix but my Office as Secretary of State for the Dominions and Colonies.'

18

The Most Terrible Event
1922–23

Bonar Law was re-elected as leader of the Conservative Party and became Britain's new Prime Minister in 1922, placing the Conservatives in power for the first time since 1905. Churchill was excluded from Parliament for the first time in twenty-two years. But, for the moment at least, he was glad of the rest.

Now there was no longer a coalition government, Churchill found himself out in the cold. The Liberal Party was no longer in the ascendancy, whereas he was a Liberal free trader. It was essential to keep his constituents in Dundee happy with him and his political record.

Still confined to his sickbed, he dictated a list of election statements for Clementine to use when she travelled up north to speak for him in Scotland, despite the fact that their newborn daughter Mary was only seven weeks old. He still had his stitches in and his doctors refused to let him travel until six days before polling.[1]

'I find what the people like is the settlement of the Irish question,' Clementine suggested. 'The idea against you seems to be that you are a "War Monger", but I am exhibiting you as a Cherub Peace Maker with little fluffy wings around your chubby face.'

The reason why Churchill was being blamed for war once again was Britain's campaign for Greek independence against Turkey. In reality, Winston had pressed Lloyd George to make peace with the Turks, while the *Daily Mail* reflected public disfavour with the war by printing a headline that said 'Get out of Chanak'.

Britain's intervention in a dispute between the Greeks and the Turks was about a piece of land that Turkey had surrendered in 1918. Foreign Secretary Curzon had persuaded the Cabinet that the Turks should not be allowed to take Gallipoli and Constantinople. Consequently, Churchill and Lloyd George had provided a press release about the urgency of protecting the Dardanelles and the Bosphorus against 'violent and hostile Turkish aggression'.

But Bonar Law, who led the Conservatives out of the coalition, where they had felt frustrated, announced that it was wrong for Britain, as the leading Muslim power (with 60 million Muslims in India), to show any hostility or unfairness to the Turk.' He added the most crucial point for Britain: 'We cannot act alone as the policeman for the world.'

Right: British intelligence officer Lieutenant Colonel T. E. Lawrence at Rabegh, north of Jidda in 1917. He became known as "Lawrence of Arabia" after leading irregular Arab forces to victory against the Ottoman Turks in Palestine, as part of General Allenby's army.

Below: Prince Feisal's party at the Peace Conference in Versailles in 1919.
Left to right: Rustam Haidar, Nuri al-Said, Prince Feisal (front), Captain Rosario Pisani (rear), Colonel T. E. Lawrence, Feisal's slave (name unknown), Captain Hassan Khadri.

Above left: Prime Minister Andrew Bonar Law, tasked by the Conservative Party to ruin Winston Churchill. *The United States Library of Congress's Prints and Photographs division.*

Above right: General Sir Ian Hamilton commanded the failed Expeditionary Force in the Gallipoli Campaign in the First World War. (1910-1915 photo). Highly regarded, highly awarded.

Britain's Labour Prime Minister Ramsay MacDonald, 1924 and 1929-1931. *Punch* magazine cartoon implies Communist sympathies.

Above left and above right: Iconic Kitchener recruitment poster in Britain and American imitation.

Above left: Stanley Baldwin, Conservative Prime Minister in the 1920s.

Above right: Portrait of General John Churchill, 1st Duke of Marlborough (1650-1722).

Above: American Jennie from New York. Lady Randolph Churchill with her two small sons.

Below left: Lord Randolph Churchill in 1883. Former Chancellor of the Exchequer and Leader of the House of Commons.

Below right: Cartoon of Colonel Sir Henry Hozier who had adopted Clementine. *Vanity Fair* magazine, 10 February 1883, "Men of the Day," when a director of Lloyds of London.

It was a reasonable argument that continually arose whenever the British government was brought in as a referee for another match between neighbours or other bellicose nations, and when inevitably short of funds. But, as British High Commissioner Sir Horace Rumbold declared on the day that an agreement was signed by all parties, 'Factors which probably determined the Turks to sign were our display of force, and their knowledge that we would use it in the last resort.'

It confirmed Churchill's continued insistence that diplomacy only had value when it could be seen to be backed by machine guns or battleships.

He reached his forty-eighth birthday two weeks after being defeated at the polls. Six months later he remarked on how 'the Government moulders placidly away.' His complacency at the turn of events came from having plenty of writing to do for the first volume of his war memoirs.

His five-volume work, entitled *The World Crisis,* would be his account of the First World War. It would be released over the next ten years. The reviewer for the *New Statesman* described his first volume as remarkably egotistical, but it was honest and would long survive him. Lord Asquith's wife, Margo, liked it and gave him some political advice: 'Lie low; do nothing in politics, go on writing all the time & painting; do not join your former colleagues who are making prodigious asses of themselves in every possible manner.'

He spent the summer supervising the final work for his improvements to Chartwell, the country home he had bought only fairly recently and to which he kept adding. Clementine felt uneasy about it because of the maintenance costs of such a large house that soaked up money and showed few results. He wrote to her not to worry about money or feel insecure, since a cousin had just died and left him a property in Ireland that produced an annual income of £4,000.

He was back in London for the release of his second volume. He had managed to include in it documents in his favour that the Dardanelles Commission had never released. Leo Amery, a contemporary from Harrow who was now First Lord of the Admiralty, praised its skill and sympathised with Churchill's former position in the Admiralty, where he had been hemmed in on all sides by irresolution.

Enemies of the People

It was time for Joseph Stalin to recognise the grim necessity of bringing Soviet Russia into the twentieth century. Russia under the Romanov Tsars had been, arguably, the most backward rural country in Europe, except for Ireland, when more virile nations, like Germany, Japan and the United States, had already followed Britain's example by industrialising. The result of being unready in the eternal battle for survival had stared the Romanovs in the face only seven years previously, when Imperial Russia had been defeated in the Russo–Japanese War of 1904–05.

Despite the communist revolution, or because of it, Soviet Russia was still vulnerable to attacks from any belligerent industrialised nation, and a mood of intense suspicion against possible internal or external enemies pervaded Moscow, even though such enemies did not exist. Wilfully disobedient internal forces, like sullen peasants, stubborn Kulaks, or complacent middle-class Russians, were disposed of by the million if they showed signs of not cooperating with Stalin to the utmost. All would be sacrificed to Stalin's aim of independence through industrialisation, because of the limited time he felt he had to arm against a possible military attack from an aggressive enemy.

Although he could not know it then, Stalin would have only nineteen years to industrialise and rearm his country with enough high-quality weapons, tanks and aircraft to repel and defeat a military invasion. Even so, he would be taken by surprise at the speed and enormity of the actual event when it occurred.

Stalin's overriding tactic for fulfilling his ambition to remain in total power over the Soviet Union was to eliminate anyone he suspected might threaten his aims and his position in future. He now indulged in a series of public show trials of so-called 'enemies of the people', which became part of a ritual of trumped-up 'confessions' aimed at justifying himself to the public for his persecutions of innocent people.

Everything was carefully stage managed in each of his show trials. The opening one on 18 May, which ended on 26 July, was performed in an impressive Moscow building named the Hall of Columns. 'Death to the Wreckers!' was spelled out on banners hung on a number of public buildings.

Confessions were read out at the trial. Two of the accused tried to tell the court that they had been extracted by force and fraud, but were derided and sneered at. They had been tortured, then promised their freedom if they signed confessions that implicated themselves and others. 'The twelve-year-old son of one of the accused demanded the death penalty for his father.'[2]

The objective of the trumped-up trials was to identify the so-called 'class enemy'. It introduced identity politics into the range of Stalin's propaganda weapons in order to hold on to power. A fictional individual or group would be linked with other fictitious overseas enemies who would be accused of planning to undermine Soviet Russia. It was no more than a conspiracy theory. Most of the charges against the accused were implausible, but the trials would warn bourgeois men and women not to harbour reactionary thoughts or ideas, but to keep quiet and conform. Otherwise they would be identified and executed.

In the case of the Shakhty trial, five out of fifty of his victims were engineers. They could be sentenced to long terms in prison, or to forced labour camps, which were known as Gulags. The numbers of such slave labour camps in the north and in Siberia were growing.

A Most Terrible Event

The major post-war theme of discontent in Germany had been the matter of war reparations. It was a problem that provided Hitler with a popular subject for his

THE MOST TERRIBLE EVENT

anti-government speeches and rallies. The topic promoted such heated fury that it swelled the sizes of his audiences. When the German government showed its reluctance to pay, the Allies demanded compensation payment immediately. But Germany was suffering from a severe economic crisis and could not pay.

Loss of industrial territory and of men from war casualties, coupled with the demoralisation of defeat, combined to create loss of confidence and a shrinking economy. The Weimar government was obliged to explain to the Allies that it did not have sufficient financial or material resources to pay the reparations they demanded.[3]

The Supreme Allied Council met in an emergency session in Cannes to discuss the stalemate.

The German government claimed that they were cooperating as an equal nation, not as a defeated one – that it had been the Kaiser and the military that had been beaten in 1918, not the Weimar Republic.[4] Walther Rathenau, the head of the German delegation, summarised their financial problems in such a reasonable way, and created such a positive impression, that the Council granted a postponement of the first two monthly payments for a year. It also agreed to a reduction in the scale of payments.

While further discussion ensued in Paris on a moratorium on all German reparation payments for 1922, to the German government's huge satisfaction, there occurred in Berlin what a British commentator called 'the most terrible event in the history of the German republic'. Soon after leaving his home in an open car on the morning of 24 June, Walther Rathenau was murdered by three nationalist extremists who viewed him as a traitor to Germany because he was a Jew.

The tragedy was a reaction to what extremists had been shouting in the streets for weeks since he had managed to postpone and reduce reparation payments: 'Knock off Walter Rathenau, the Goddamned, filthy Jewish Sow.'[5]

The murder was motivated by a very large and intimidating number of people of the extreme political right, who had no intention of paying even a cent of the war reparations. It was intended to warn off anyone who disagreed with them about not paying the German war debt. But the result of Rathenau's murder was not what the nationalists had expected. Evidently there was still some sanity left in Germany, because hundreds of thousands of workers poured out of factories and shops to merge into a column, four deep, and marched solemnly through the streets of Berlin, holding up socialist mourning banners They passed silently between dense crowds of supporters from early afternoon to sunset.

The nationalists had hoped to trigger a rising that would have to be forcibly suppressed. Then they could claim they were victims and prepare the way for a dictatorship to impose order. But, instead, the assassination created support for the Weimar Republic, which was continuing to work well at that point. But 1922 and 1923 in Germany would be described as nightmare years. They were the beginning of a period of delusion. Those years would be known for mass joblessness and hunger, with urban street fights between the increasing number of fascist agitators and the political left.

Chancellor Dr Wirth denounced the extremists in the Reichstag, and all organisations that spread anti-Semitism, chauvinism, nationalism, and monarchism.

'The real enemies of our country,' the Chancellor said, 'are those who instill this poison into our people. We know where we have to seek them. The enemy stands on the right!'

19

Troublemakers
1923

As a man who was driven by the desire for justice, and determined never to stop working for it, Winston continued to encounter flawed and apparently hopeless human nature all around him, and a crumbling world economic system. He had expected the same Calvinist attitude that he had followed instinctively by leading a purposeful life. He felt that people 'had no right to remain idle, even if contented in their activity'.[1]

Considering his attitude, he showed remarkable patience with the Middle East, despite continued Arab hostility. He was neither for nor against either side in the conflicts, except for whatever might enhance British interests. But, after another decade of continual riots and murders, he came to the conclusion that the Arabs were nothing more than 'barbaric hordes'.[2]

What most Western nations had not considered was that the peoples of the Middle East and North Africa did not want democracy or Western culture or European values of any kind, but preferred their own tribalism of patronage under a strict Muslim warlord who would protect them and their extended families. They resented a democratic Western nation planted in what they claimed was their own territory, which might encourage their own young generations –particularly their slaves and confined womenfolk – to seek freedoms and education that they had no intention of allowing.

On the other hand, although the Zionists praised Churchill, their nationalistic aspirations were a heavy burden that often conflicted with Britain's interests. Britain was still loyal to imperialism, but had nothing to do with conquest or self-aggrandisement in the Middle East.[3]

Winston's youthful experiences of empire, as a young soldier on the borders of Afghanistan, Pakistan and India, had focused his attention on pacification of mischief-makers and cost-effective administration. But, regardless of his intention of 'fair play', he was continually thwarted on all sides by lack of cooperation, rioting, destruction and massacres. Whether in Iraq, India, or Ireland, all sorts of troublemakers were always stirring up discontent.

Churchill was well aware that the British Empire had become a financial and political burden, but imperialism seemed to be the only way to pacify entire continents that would otherwise fall completely out of control, to their own detriment, and prevent progress. He was very conscious that without rational leadership of their own, some nations needed help from outside to protect them from themselves and their leaders, as well as from their enemies.

History described how the pragmatic Roman Empire had pacified nations with the brute force of their invincible legions. But it was no longer an option in the twentieth century. The alternative was a costly policing exercise for Britain, which pursued it with reluctance, but with firm resolve, as efficiently as it could. The Middle East had become Britain's responsibility. There was no choice, other than some form of independence, which would have led to the internal slaughter of millions by different religious, ethnic groups, and tribal passions. Better to gradually coax it towards a sensible acceptance of living peacefully together for the common good.

The socialist science fiction writer H.G. Wells offered an alternative to empire. His views on British imperialism were first published in the *Empire Review*. Churchill attacked it with one of his own articles, claiming that Wells was an unrealistic dreamer, of the type who is always gleeful at any setback to the British Empire.

Wells responded by dismissing Churchill's cant. The Empire in its present form, he wrote, was 'unstable and bound to undergo major changes in the future'. Then he became personally insulting by describing Churchill as his friend, and adding, 'There are times when the evil spirit comes upon him and when I can think of him only as a very intractable little boy, a mischievous, dangerous little boy, a knee-worthy little boy. Only by thinking of him in that way can one go on liking him.'[4]

Wells argued for a federal world government to act as a trustee in place of the British Empire. But there was no such thing, and no one else was interested in creating it. The British Empire would have to continue replacing the old *Pax Romana* or Roman Peace, however difficult and costly it was. It turned out that Churchill, and his friend Brendan Bracken, had persuaded Wells to write an article to help revive the failing *Empire Review*, and Wells had exploited the opportunity to air his own views.[5]

Churchill saw Wells's concept as sweeping away all the checks and balances and guard rails that Britain had managed to build up over time. 'British credit and currency would, for instance, be dissolved in world-federal credits and currency to which German insolvency, French extravagance, Russian rapacity, and Chinese indolence, would have loyally made their contributions.'

Churchill claimed that the British Empire was multifaceted with room for diversities of national, racial and ethnic segments and opinions. He provided examples of democratic communities in Australia, the progressiveness of Canada, the builders of the Irish Free State, the burghers of the Transvaal, the princes and populations of Hindustan, inhabitants of fifty tropical dependencies, and a thousand islanders, who willingly included themselves under the British Crown.

Another alternative to parliamentary democratic colonisation was to follow the more authoritarian forces of fascism, which was the preferred choice for many followers in Italy, Germany and Spain, and was on the rise all over Europe.

Masters of the Field

After continual street battles between Italian fascist youths and socialists in the latter half of the previous year, the fascists broke into socialist headquarters in Cremona and looted them, occupied municipal buildings, and attempted to burn down the apartment of the Deputy of the Liberal Party, which was the biggest political party in the Italian Parliament.

The populist journalist Benito Mussolini, who led the Fascist Party, joined in a provocative debate in Parliament on whether his party was constitutional, or whether it was a revolutionary one. If they were revolutionaries, he claimed, they would no longer be obligated to sit in Parliament. He warned that, 'The party had at its disposal large, well-disciplined and well-organised forces.'[6] They would have to be used to put down the chaos to the economy caused by inefficient and undisciplined liberals, socialists, and hysterical mobs that imagined they had rights. It would require force.

Mussolini possessed a bombastic but seductive personality that made his empty promises, both as a populist rabble-rouser and a womaniser, succeed. It had enabled him to amass a private army of black-shirted fascist hooligans, which was the trump card he held to reinforce his bluff with violence. His charisma won the battle to control the streets.

When the predominantly Liberal government, led by Luigi Facta, failed to deal with the fascist mobs in Cremona, Facta was forced to resign. As a result, King Victor Emanuel was obliged to endorse a new administration. Mussolini might have joined it, but the king ignored him.

In any case, Benito Mussolini was a seasoned and cynical politician who knew the power of insinuation and subtle threats to get his own way. He and his black-shirted thugs could make a threat far more effective than a mass demonstration.

He had come a long way politically by recognising that life consists of games of bluff. He was a gambler, eager to boast triumphantly whenever he won. He knew on this occasion that he could become more powerful by standing back and making provocative threats while he waited watchfully for a more advantageous opportunity to strike.

His moment arrived when a power vacuum was left by Facta, and Italy was without a government for twelve days. The king asked Luigi Facta to form a new government, but a socialist general strike erupted as soon as he was appointed. Then Mussolini warned the government it had only forty-eight hours to quell the strike before he moved in with his private army.

When the left-wing strikers persisted, the fascists took over all essential public services and ran them. It took only twenty-four hours for Mussolini to break the strike by a show of force. 'The fascists are masters of the field,' claimed a socialist newspaper.

Most Italians wanted law and order, and it had been achieved swiftly and smartly by force. It was a blow to traditional authority. Now, having demonstrated his power and discipline over disorder, Mussolini followed up by organising his army of Blackshirts for a march on Rome. He announced that violence could be a 'moral necessity' in resolving a cancerous political situation.

The Prefect of Milan admitted that the regular army could not be depended on to challenge a fascist militia that was 200,000 strong.

Mussolini now warned unruly hooligans at a fascist rally in Udine that violence was not a sport; it had to be organised and disciplined to be truly effective. He claimed that his aim was to destroy social democracy, which served Italy so badly, and replace it with the disciplined authority of fascism. Italy had a choice to make between discipline or disorder. Under fascism, the Italian State would oppose all who threatened its sovereignty, and people would do what they were told in future.

He ordered his militia to occupy Bolzano and Trent, and planned to seize Parma. When he spoke at Cremona on 11 October, his fascist supporters, buoyed up with success, chanted, 'To Rome! To Rome!'

Fascist commanders set up military headquarters at Perugia and brought three armed columns of troops within 30 miles of Rome. But Mussolini held back, still hoping to obtain sole power by constitutional means. At a Congress of the Fascist Party in Naples on 24 October, he claimed that the party was at a crossroads, where they could obtain power constitutionally or take it by force.

Then on 25 October, he announced an imminent march on Rome. It was planned for three days' time, but he kept the actual date a secret.

Luigi Facta considered whether to form a coalition government with Mussolini, or resign. His rival was Antonio Salandra, who had led Italy in 1915. Salandra invited Mussolini to Rome, with the implication that Mussolini could play a significant role in a new Salandra government. But Mussolini assessed his options carefully and wisely decided not to join Salandra. He didn't need him. He had his own army.

Facta resigned, explaining to the king that he did not have the resources to prevent the fascist plans. Mussolini's fascist militia took control of the main government buildings in Perugia on the same day. The fascists also seized power in other towns in Italy, and advised the king to proclaim a state of siege. But the king knew that a strong arm was needed to restore law and order, and he no longer trusted or respected Facta with his hesitations and incompetence.

He invited Mussolini to meet him in Rome on 28 October, ostensibly to join a new government led by Salandra. But Mussolini continued to bluff, by stating that it was not worthwhile mobilising the fascist army to cause a revolution, and killing people, just for the sake of a Salandra–Mussolini coalition. He would do so only if he were able to form the new government himself. Benito Mussolini would be Prime Minister or nothing.

Fascist leaders in Rome implored him to accept the king's offer in a Salandra government, fearing that if he marched on Rome instead, the insurrection would fail and they would all be arrested. But Mussolini had judged the situation correctly. When Salandra failed to form a new government, the king sent Mussolini a telegram as an invitation.

Mussolini took the earliest night train and stopped off at Civitavecchia to inspect his fascist militia. He was in Rome an hour later, and drove to meet the king. The king asked him officially to form a government. And Benito Mussolini became Prime Minister of Italy and Minister of the Interior at the age of thirty-nine.

As Prime Minister, Mussolini put before both houses of Italy's parliament his political programme on 16 November, recognising that he had only four fascists in his Cabinet of fourteen, and they had no experience of parliamentary democracy. It meant that Mussolini would have to abide by democratic rules to begin with. Even so, he treated the lower house with disdain. He asked the Chamber of Deputies to grant him full powers, and warned them that if they refused, he would take power anyway. Italy became a parliamentary dictatorship as a consequence of Mussolini's 275 votes to 90.

20

Chartwell

Winston continued to prepare Chartwell for Clementine's return from holiday in the south of France: 'All yesterday & today, we have been turfing & levelling the plateau. The motor mower acts as a roller, and we have done everything now except from the yew tree to the kitchen garden end.'

Churchill enjoyed the comfort and tranquility of living at Chartwell that summer. He liked using his hands in creative ways. It reflected his sense of harmony. He drained a lake below the house and built a dam. He had pulled in help from everyone, including the children, their chauffeur, and his detective. 'In the evenings we play the gramophone ...'

In July, Prime Minister Stanley Baldwin agreed that Winston could stand at the next election as a 'Constitutionalist' candidate with official Conservative support, with which he would be able to speak against MacDonald's loan to Soviet Russia and the perils of socialism. Winston told Clementine two weeks later that the Conservatives planned to obtain a constituency for him that they would not oppose.

The Enemy on the Left

What many, including Winston, saw as the perils of socialism was viewed very differently by many of the working classes and some public intellectuals as a golden opportunity for social equality and justice for the poor, and a more balanced distribution of wealth to narrow the huge income gap between wealthy property owners and the labouring classes. Young Churchill would also have known that the Fabian socialists' more gentle system of 'gradualism' towards communism had succeeded in persuading many to have faith in Karl Marx's theories about the way society should be organised in England. Their most vocal supporter was the much-admired playwright George Bernard Shaw, who lived in his own long-winded world of self-righteous left-wing preaching.

Part of the success of the first of the three heavy volumes in which Marx sought to describe the flaws in capitalism was probably due to its formidable length and density and weight. Few readers would have been dogged enough actually to study its theories. It would have been more likely to befuddle readers. Engels apparently thought so, since he had felt compelled to rework the second and third volumes, or at least attempt to give them some clarity or polish after his collaborator died.

The first volume was published in 1867. The second and third were published in 1885 and 1894, when Engels wrote, edited, or rewrote them.

Marx had spent much of his time in the circular reading room of the British Library in London, supported by funds from the wealthy Engels. As a penniless freelance journalist, Marx avoided actually investigating primary sources by interviewing small entrepreneurs or big factory owners, who would have first-hand experience and known far more about how capitalism worked in practice than he did. But they would not have agreed with his theories. And he could not tolerate anyone who disagreed with him. He was motivated more to establish his own stubborn opinions than search for the truth.

Marx possessed a rebelliously overwhelming personality of intellectual arrogance. He was a dictator who was convinced he knew better than anyone else, and denounced any opinions contrary to his own. 'He spoke only in the imperative, brooking no contradiction.' He rarely spoke at public meetings to avoid opposition. He was also 'prey to obsessive ideas such as that the British foreign minister, Lord Palmerston, was an agent of the Russian government'.[1]

His relentless denunciations of the comfortably off middle classes appeared to be based on envy at their success, while he continued to live with his wife and children in relative poverty. He scrambled for power, which he claimed the bourgeoisie possessed. Engels, on the other hand, worked at his father's mill in Manchester at the age of twenty-two, and in Salford, making sewing threads. He disliked his father and clashed with his parents' opinions. He would avenge himself against them by condemning all capitalist and well-off middle classes. Although a capitalist himself, he was strongly influenced by a fiery young Irish woman who worked in his father's factory, named Mary Burns, with whom he lived for twenty years.

To give Engels his due, he was evidently genuinely shocked at the misery in Manchester's slums, and had written an influential book in 1845 entitled, *The Conditions of the Working Class.* He and Marx followed it by publishing their Communist Manifesto as propaganda against capitalism three years later.

Marx was skilful at setting up a committee composed of less intelligent members he could intimidate, and establish it as the official power base of The Party – a principle that Stalin would follow to place and keep himself in power in Soviet Russia.

Marx wrote that, '*Socialism* cannot be brought into existence without *revolution.*' But he provided no evidence to support his claim. He insisted that industrial conditions were worsening and would continue to deteriorate until the workers exploded in rebellion. In reality, responsible inquiries showed that working conditions were improving constantly in accordance with the numerous Factory Acts, and as a result of continual improvements and innovations by industrialists.

As historian Paul Johnson wrote of Rousseau, Marx combined all the salient characteristics of an angry and rebellious modern prophet who demanded the power to turn the world upside-down, according to his own vision of what it should be like: 'the assertion of his right to reject the existing order in its entirety; confidence in his capacity to refashion it from the bottom in accordance with principles of his own devising; belief that this could be achieved by the political process; and, not least, recognition of the huge part instinct, intuition and impulse play in human conduct.'[2]

Envy

Mathematician Bertrand Russell was among several intellectuals who had approved of the idea of communism at first, but had just returned disillusioned from a visit to Russia where it was being implemented by Stalin. 'Unlike most members of the left, Russell had never been taken in by the Soviet regime. He had always rejected Marxism completely.' He was critical of Lenin and described Stalin as a monster.[3]

Others, like Bernard Shaw, who were motivated by wishful thinking, preferred to avert their eyes from the worst injustices and atrocities in the Soviet Union, in the hope that socialism would prove itself to be an ideal political system for Britain and everywhere else.

H.G. Wells had visited Tsarist Russia before the revolution and was convinced that socialism would form the ideal society. What he hoped for the future prevented him from admitting publicly to the failings of socialism. International Communism was, for him, linked to his own philosophical ideal of a federal world State. The difference between Wells's naive idealism and the reality of the human condition was viewed by Winston Churchill as mere daydreaming.

Wells's travelling companion to the USSR was another dreamer named Maurice Baring. He was an optimistic Utopian. At least he had the honesty to admit that his beliefs were 'inadequate, incomplete, and superficial'.[4] How could it be otherwise, when they had not travelled across the huge continent but seen only what Stalin had wanted them to see?

Socialism appealed in particular to the self-pitying classes who constantly complained at their misfortunes. Marx was not alone in possessing that characteristic of self-pity; so had Rousseau.

H.G. Wells was a novelist whose financial success had elevated him above the social class into which he had been born. His mother had been a domestic servant. It made him untypical of the average working-class intellectual. But Britain's class system thrived on social climbing. Her mobility had placed her in a more refined class than being a shop girl or a factory worker. Wells's father had gained similar advantages as a head gardener who was an outstanding cricketer. It had placed him too at an advantage in the social pecking order.

Working-class intellectuals tended to be neither one thing nor another, stuck as they were between the lower middle classes and the comfortably settled middle classes. Such individuals – mostly men – appeared in larger and larger numbers after the Education Acts of 1870. Their education isolated them. A problem arose of what to do with proletarian intellectuals who were trapped in their social class but felt themselves to be above it by virtue of what they had learned. Pride in personal achievement made them patronising towards others.

The result was a consciousness of the injustice of their own inadequacy, wrote a leading literary critic of the times; 'and envy of those who possess by right of birth the graces and freedoms he has had laboriously to acquire ... From working-class life as a whole, he turns with a shuddering revulsion.'[5]

Every other form of life respected its own pecking order, whereas education made some men socially ambitious. Working-class young men, and some women in post-war Britain, would claim that a glass ceiling limited their aspirations, while through it they could see seductive possibilities that they could not reach. It caused bitter envy of those who were more successful. Some bore a lingering grudge. They would become the so-called 'angry young men', who reached out in frustration for communism or socialism as an equalising weapon that might topple competitors from their pedestals.

Winston, when still young as Home Secretary in 1911, had discovered all of that for himself when he had to protect Britain against subversives of every political stripe. Six years later, at the eruption of revolution and civil war in Russia, he would be propelled by his new ministry into the thick of the communist conflict, which he would find difficult to leave behind as it would become the root cause of much of the insecurity across the world for years to come.

21

Social Reengineering

Churchill did his best to build a bridge between the Conservative Party and the Liberals that autumn, since they were the only barrier to a creeping socialism that promised equality by sacrificing anyone who stood out above the rest. He visited Lloyd George secretly at home at *Churt* on 31 August, and pressed him to support the Conservatives at the next General Election. Their common cause, he felt, was their revulsion at Ramsay MacDonald's loan to Soviet Russia.

Lloyd George agreed that the Labour Party 'had put their fingers in the cog wheels and would be drawn to their ruin'.[1]

Young Winston had already learned that history could provide a key to the future, and the farther back he went the more likely he would learn what might lay in store for him. New information could change an individual's entire perception of what was going on and where it was most likely to lead. He knew from Reade's observations that human nature had remained much the same and habitually repeated itself. It could even be found two and a half thousand years ago in the writing of Herodotus, the first dependable historian with deep insights. Herodotus wrote how dictatorships keep a people in slavish fear and subjugation.[2]

He related in *The Histories* how Periander, the ruler of Corinth, sent a messenger to one Thrasybulus. The messenger took him into a field where Thrasybulus's crops were growing. As they walked through the grain, Thrasybulus urged the messenger to explain what he had come to tell him. Instead of replying, each time the messenger saw an ear of grain standing higher than the rest, he broke it off and threw it away. He continued until he had destroyed the choicest, tallest stems in the crop.[3]

The message conveyed to Thrasybulus was that the ruler of Corinth advised him to kill all outstanding citizens in case they might want to compete with him. He took Periander's advice, and from then on treated his people with unremitting brutality by cutting them down to size. Winston had read similar stories by Winwood Reade, who wrote in the nineteenth century about how the same economic sterility had been imposed in China for at least a thousand years in yet another case of how history repeated itself:

> In the despotic lands of the East, the peasant who grows more corn than he requires is at once an object of attention by the police; he is reported to the governor, and a charge is laid against him, in order that his grain may be seized. He not only loses the fruit of his toil, but he also receives the bastinado. In the same manner if a merchant, by means of

his enterprise, industry, and talents, amasses a large fortune; he also is arrested and is put to death, that his estate may escheat to the Crown.[4]

That same envy took hold of intellectuals in the twentieth century, who chose a levelling process to re-engineer society by making everyone equally mediocre. It was evident how intellectuals who claimed to fight against oppression were often the first to use it.[5]

Historian Tony Judt would remark on how intellectuals like Sartre disappeared from the literary scene after the twentieth century. He described their 'propensity for self-aggrandisement, preening contentedly in the admiring mirror of an audience of like-minded fellow thinkers'. He quoted Camus, who wrote: 'Mistaken ideas always end in bloodshed, but in every case it is someone else's blood. That is why some of our thinkers feel free to say just about anything.'[6], *

Science Fiction

When Churchill accepted the nomination for a safe Conservative seat at Epping, he was drawn back into a party in which his former Conservative adversaries had treated him badly. But he returned to them because the Liberal Party had declined, and there was nowhere else to go.

The Scottish Conservatives in Edinburgh supported him because Conservatives and Liberals were convinced that the real threat was socialism. His chief supporters on the platform were Lord Carson, Sir Robert Horne, and Lord Balfour. He urged them to resist the Labour Party's desire for an Anglo–Soviet Treaty. International Communism meant helping Bolshevism to grow, and thereby giving aid to every foreign nation that supported extremists of the left.

His speech was publicised widely by the press, and his article was published in *Nash's Pall Mall* on 4 September, then reprinted and distributed as a pamphlet across the United States. It warned of the possibility of a huge bomb with the force of 1,000 tons of cordite, which had been forecast in the science fiction of H.G. Wells. Who might possess it?

Wells's futuristic science fiction books had stimulated thought in a number of modern scientific directions ever since the publication of *The Time Machine* in 1895 – from the possibility of aliens arriving on earth, or fighting in outer space, to limiting the world's growing populations by euthanasia – meaning killing off the less productive or so-called 'enemies of the people'.

'Could not explosives, even of the existing type,' Churchill wrote, 'be guided automatically in flying machines by wireless or other rays, without a human pilot, in ceaseless procession upon a hostile city, arsenal, camp, or dockyard?'

---

* That 'admiring mirror of an audience of like-minded thinkers', would reappear in the twenty-first century in the forms of social media.

To Churchill, the concept of nuclear war was not mere science fiction to be dismissed out of hand. He had been attracted to the scientific intellect of the Oxford Professor Frederick Lindemann, and sought his advice on the latest new technologies. They became firm friends. The 'Prof', as he began to be named at Chartwell, had been born to an American mother in Germany. He had studied in Berlin and Paris, then worked in the Royal Air Force Laboratory at Farnborough from 1915 to 1918, and learned to fly there, so as to investigate the aerodynamic effects of aircraft spin.[7]

Churchill frequently invited him to Chartwell for weekends, where he was encouraged to describe the most recent inventions and trends of scientific advances. Churchill's article in *Nash's Pall Mall* had been influenced by Lindemann's up-to-date scientific inputs. His aim was to use the article to warn of the dangers of International Communism, and of building up Soviet Russia to be a potent military threat to the rest of the world. It also described Germany's search for revenge for its defeat in 1918, and the dangerous clash between France, which hoped to preserve the Treaty to keep Germany weak, and Germany's constant demands to whittle the treaty away.

Germany, Churchill warned, was far stronger than France, 'and cannot be kept in permanent subjugation'.

With all the media publicity Churchill received, his criticism of Ramsay MacDonald's loan to Soviet Russia was cheered and applauded by his constituents. It helped him win the seat for the Conservatives at the General Election on 29 October, by a majority of over nine thousand votes. Now he was back again as a Member of Parliament.

Although he felt that he would not be offered a role in the government because they were in such a strong position with 419 seats compared with 151 for Labour, and the Liberal Party was left with only 40, evidently his contribution to the Conservative victory was recognised and Baldwin considered several different posts for him. Clementine's favourite choice was the Ministry of Health.

On 5 November, Baldwin asked Churchill to visit him. 'Will you be Chancellor?' he asked him. It was the office that Churchill had set his heart on. He had even kept his father's traditional robe as Chancellor of the Exchequer.

When he returned back home to Chartwell, he had considerable difficulty in persuading Clementine that he wasn't just teasing her. It was the second most senior job in the government. Not only would he be in charge of the nation's purse strings, but he would work and live at 11 Downing Street, next door to the Prime Minister at Number 10. And, depending on how long Stanley Baldwin might last before the public grew tired of him, Winston could be first choice to fill the most powerful office in the land. They were thrilled.

The Red Scare

'Red Scare' tactics had been used to defeat the Labour Party in the 1924 General Election. Churchill would not have been averse to using such tactics himself, since he believed that a Labour government was nothing but 'a socialist monstrosity ... corrupting the character of the British nation'. He described it as 'sham and humbug'.

The right-wing *Daily Mail* had published a forgery known as the 'Zinoviev Letter', which purported to demonstrate how Moscow gave secret instructions to British communists to stir up civil conflicts in Britain. It had helped to return the Conservatives to power. The object of their scorn was Labour Prime Minister Ramsey MacDonald, whom Churchill derisively called 'this futile Kerensky', after the former prime minister of imperial Russia whose indecisiveness at the most crucial moment in Russian history had lost the nation to the communists.

Lloyd George continued to criticise the Labour government for giving away hard-earned British tax revenues as a loan to Soviet Russia. The government was swept aside. Despite the forgery being exposed later on, accusations stuck to Britain's Labour Party for generations to come that it took its instructions from Moscow.

As for Churchill's unexpected appointment, according to Austen Chamberlain's diary entry of the time, Baldwin told him that he had decided to take Winston in at once, since 'He would be more under control inside than out.'

Churchill would have understood Baldwin's motivation perfectly, and probably grinned, as one of his most quoted remarks about appointing mavericks was, 'I'd rather have him in the tent pissing out than outside pissing in.'[8]

~ III ~
BAD NEWS FROM GERMANY

22

Hunting Down the Idle Rich
1924

Twenty-five days after accepting his new appointment as Chancellor of the Exchequer, Winston Churchill turned fifty. It was an exciting moment on 30 November 1924, when he addressed his first responsibilities at the Treasury. It had been two decades since he had been a member of the Conservative Party. Now he was MP for Conservative Epping. He worked and lived behind the dark brick façade of 11 Downing Street, with its white-painted lower level that distinguished it from the home of his closest neighbour, Prime Minister Stanley Baldwin, who lived next door in Number 10.

The heart of the British Empire beat quietly in that modest terraced townhouse, which was, nevertheless, situated in the most famous street in the borough of Westminster in London, surrounded as it was by the Admiralty, the War Office, the Department of Trade and Industry, Scotland Yard, and other government departments that obeyed the instructions of Britain's Prime Minister next door to Winston.

Unheeded most of the time by millions of inhabitants in the capital city, the invisible but finely tuned threads of power reached out all over the world from Number 10 to address the safety and security of Great Britain and its empire. Communications directed every British embassy and consulate in the world to ensure that, at the first signs of trouble, a battleship of the Royal Navy could swiftly transport a load of marines to topple upstart dictators, subdue vicious demonstrations, or pacify hysterical mobs bent on violence, theft, and destruction to British personnel and property and interests.

Whenever there had been a power vacuum at the top of the government, the first choice to fill it had often been the man from next door in Number 11. The Chancellor's job was to balance the Treasury books of the British Empire, and he would know, to a penny, which of Britain's functions were too costly and which were essential for peace and prosperity, and security.

Even before moving into Number 11, any ambitious politician would have rated the chances of the incumbent at Number 10 remaining in office much longer before the public grew tired of him. And, before that happened, he would be aware of every one of Britain's activities without being responsible for any of them, while positioned to advise what the country could afford and what it should not undertake. At that particular moment, it was a matter of creating and financing a considerable extension of the national health insurance scheme, which he had been instrumental in creating at the height of his Liberal career fifteen years previously. He had worked with Prime Minister Lloyd George then. Now he worked on it closely with Neville Chamberlain, who was the new Minister of Health.[1]

His other responsibilities were to limit the burden of income tax on professionals, businessmen, and small merchants, and intelligence workers of all types, and recommend pensions for widows and orphans, old age retirement insurance, and cheap housing for those who could not afford the market prices.

He had initiated and supported social reforms when in the Liberal government, and he intended to continue to do so in the present one. But he needed to raise taxes in order to be able to afford them. As he explained to Lord Salisbury, the son of a previous Prime Minister, it was a question of making a distinction between earned and unearned income.

He was against 'hunting down the idle rich,' since the longer they were idle the sooner they would no longer be rich. By and large, they were foolish and idle sons of the aristocracy.

'I think the rich,' Churchill explained, 'whether idle or not, are already taxed in this country to the very highest point compatible with the accumulation of capital for future production.' That phrase alone demonstrated how Churchill understood the uses of capital better than Karl Marx had. The capitalist system, Winston reminded Salisbury, is the foundation of civilisation. 'The creation of new wealth is beneficial to the whole community.'[2]

Unfair taxation meant that those who had accumulated wealth from speculating in business enterprises stopped investing and failed to compete with the United States, Germany, and Japan, which had already taken the lead in the global economy away from Great Britain.

He knew that without venture capital there would be unemployment. He would never change his view that, although capitalism suffered from many flaws, it and democracy was still the best system of all. Viewed in another light, as he liked to quip, it was 'the worst system except for all the others'. But he had a problem as far as the electorate was concerned, because Marx had managed to tarnish the capitalist system with his Communist Manifesto, simply by using the word 'Capital' on its cover.

> Churchill's concern for the underprivileged, for the plight of the working man was entirely genuine. But as it was coupled with swingeing attacks on Labour and the deadly menace of socialism, assaults that never ceased, indeed grew in intensity, this became too fine a distinction for the unemployed and poverty-stricken to make. His compassion masqueraded in the guise of a crusty old Tory diehard – or so it seemed. Also his aristocratic lifestyle and apparent disdain for the sensibilities of the lesser-favoured distanced him from those he sought to nourish.[3]

Debts and Loans

As Chancellor of the Exchequer, Churchill was now concerned with payments of all the international war debts, and struggled against stubborn resistance from Germany. At the beginning of the year and throughout the whole of 1923, Germany denounced the burden of reparation payments, and the German government attempted to postpone payments for another year.

The Cambridge economist Keynes had published an attack on the reparation clauses in the Versailles Treaty at the end of 1919, since he knew it was unworkable.[4] It had influenced America's Senate to reject the Treaty in 1920.

French Prime Minister Raymond Poincaré was already furious at the postponement of payments by Germany in the previous year, 1922, and threatened to seize a number of productive enterprises from Germany and exploit them until Germany fulfilled its obligations according to the Treaty of Versailles. French and Belgium troops descended on the Ruhr to take over factories on 10 January 1923. They entered Essen the next day. French soldiers who entered Krupp's factory in the occupation of the Ruhr used machine guns on workers who resisted. Britain chose not to join them, while Keynes claimed that making payments would destroy Germany. Krupp printed its own currency, which was the only reliable one in Germany.

German workers were ordered to continue production, but a movement of passive resistance spread, and it became obvious that France would not be able to obtain their payments by force. Yet France owed £1.3 billion herself. Where would it come from now? Poincaré declared that France intended to withdraw its payments in proportion to the amount of the instalments Germany owed. It took the rest of the year for Britain and the US to persuade the premier to wait for a committee to investigate the capacity of the German economy to pay its debts.

Reparations for the damage caused by the war had to be cancelled from Austria, Hungary and Turkey because of the post-war state of chaos in those countries. The same soon applied to Bulgaria. The main controversy and clash and anger were over Germany's debts, which France stubbornly insisted they must pay.

Britain's debt to the United States of £1 billion would be paid in instalments when it received proportionate payments simultaneously from France, Italy, Belgium, and Japan, which, together, were indebted to Britain for £2 billion. Churchill travelled to Paris on 6 January 1925 to negotiate, and secured a settlement. His scheme was also accepted by other debtors like Czechoslovakia, Romania, Serbia, and Brazil. It was described as a rare achievement.

But the effect of the French occupation of the Ruhr and Germany's refusal to pay its debts began to destroy the foundations of the Weimar Republic. The German government began printing more money to pay the 2 million workers who had put themselves and others out of work by undertaking passive resistance. It reduced the value of the German Mark still further.

By the beginning of April the value of the German Mark had fallen to one tenth of its previous buying power. Shortages of ready cash caused widespread looting.

Right-wing and left-wing political extremists exploited the situation, and so-called 'fighting unions' demonstrated. Powerful right-wing forces set themselves up in Munich, including Hitler's National Socialists, now known as the Nazi Party.

A March on Berlin

While Hitler's Brownshirts battled for control of the streets, so did the communist 'Proletarian Hundreds'. The Bavarian government suspended civil law and banned Nazi meetings. Bavaria's Prime Minister, Dr von Kahr, supported the monarchy and announced that he aimed to fight against Marxism. Hitler increased the size of his Brownshirt militia, and declared to a mass audience on 12 September, 'There are now only two alternatives before us, the swastika or the Soviet star, the world despotism of the Communist International or the Holy Empire of the Germanic nation.'

In the forefront of Hitler's mind was evidently his admiration for his hero Mussolini's successful threat to march on Rome, when he stated, 'The first act of redress must be a march on Berlin and the installation of a national dictatorship.'

While communist demonstrators in Leipzig retaliated by calling on citizens to arm and establish a Soviet regime, a Captain Erhardt escaped from prison and recruited a private right-wing army to help the Nazis. He had led a Putsch three years previously in Berlin, and been imprisoned for it. This was the so-called *völkisch*, or people's forces. A *völkisch* uprising erupted when 400 men broke into the fortress in Küstrin and took control of the town. The army forced them to surrender. But there were similar incidents in other towns. Troops were sent to put down several other rebellions or insurrections in the Rhineland, in Düsseldorf, in Saxony and some other areas.

When Chancellor Stresemann attempted to end the anarchy, he was confronted by hostility. Many of the right-wing militia wanted a rebellion to succeed in toppling the government.

Meanwhile, right and left-wing leaders, federal and provincial, issued orders to each other. When General von Seekt – who was Commander-in-Chief of the German army – ordered General von Lossow (the military leader of Bavaria) to resign, Lossow replied that he was not obliged to obey a government tainted by Marxists. Bavaria was ready to separate from Germany. But, when von Lossow ordered them to swear a personal oath to him and the Bavarian government, the Berlin government accused him of violating Germany's constitution.

Germany was split between stubborn forces that refused to yield to each other.

Von Kahr, who headed the Bavarian government, banned fourteen mass meetings planned by Hitler. Kahr's successful opposition to the Nazi Party was met with an angry reaction from Hitler, who had decided to emulate Mussolini's audacity by bluffing. He threatened to take power by force, not just in Munich or Bavaria, but across the entire nation, in what he called the 'renewal of Germany'.

CHURCHILL'S CHALLENGES, 1918–1940

By November 1923, the value of German currency had collapsed to such an extent that it now took a million times one million paper marks to equal the purchasing power of a single Mark back in 1914. Such unprecedented deflation was bound to have catastrophic repercussions for Germany's national debt. Who would foot the bill if they would not, or could not pay?

23

Churchill in the Roaring Twenties

A considerable amount of alcohol was consumed in the period after the First World War ended – thousands of barrels of it in the bootlegging era of Prohibition in the United States, known as the 'Roaring Twenties'. Biographers of Winston Churchill often remarked on how much alcohol he consumed. Perhaps it was then – at a time that some writers now see in retrospect as a Golden Age – that Churchill began to be depicted in fun as a good-humoured tubby individual full of *joie de vivre* and glasses of champagne.

No one wrote about Clementine's consumption in those biographies, or much about anyone else's. The image she managed to project to the media and the public was a masterpiece of self-possession from a young woman who had grown up in unfortunate circumstances. There was no doubt that she found living with such an energetic overachiever as her busy and demanding husband something of a strain, which she managed to overcome by taking holidays alone on the Mediterranean to relieve the pressure of his powerful personality. Did she drink too? It seems from all reports of that time that everyone did.

Yet, neither she nor Winston were social butterflies. She despised the artificiality of the Smart Set, while he preferred to invite interesting people to Chartwell, where they would stay up all night over long dinners to the early hours of the morning, deeply immersed in conversation and stoked by bottles of champagne. His friends drank much the same amount of alcohol as he did; according to reports, far more; but it seemed to have had no effect on him other than initiating imaginative ideas and lubricating his witty conversations. As he said himself, 'A single glass of champagne imparts a feeling of exhilaration. The nerves are braced, the imagination is agreeably stirred, the wits become more nimble.'[1]

Drinking cocktails and champagne at cocktail hour and well into the night was unexceptional, even typical of the times. Four o'clock tea dances with champagne became very popular in London from about 1910, and cocktails before dinner began in England in the 1920s, partly to unwind in a more leisurely Edwardian age, and partly because of the influence of America's speakeasies. It helped to overcome a permanent sense of insecurity that had replaced the Victorian age of certainty after the experience of masses of unimaginably gruesome deaths in No-Man's-Land in 1915.

When Winston and Clementine had married in 1908, the earlier part of their marriage took place in a New Age when strangers began to connect in dance

CHURCHILL'S CHALLENGES, 1918–1940

halls and at tea dances in more elegant hotels. The atmosphere of those times of self-indulgence was, perhaps, borrowed from the example of jolly King Edward gambling at cards and helping his pretty mistresses to innumerable bottles of champagne. The marriage of Winston and Clementine continued into the same post-war period as Prohibition and bootlegging began in the United States. When Winston had stood for re-election as a Liberal in 1908, the reason he lost to a Conservative was attributed to cartoons by 'Poy' that depicted him as a frivolous figure of fun.

Just as there had been temperance societies you could join to keep you dry in Victorian England, there were preachers from local churches in the United States who warned that drink caused all sorts of social evils. It was breaking up marriages everywhere. American blue-collar family men could not wait to splurge most of their wages on drink on pay days, if they were not married to a strong-willed wife who immediately took it from them to pay for food and rent.

Prohibition had seemed acceptable at first, because it was viewed as an act of patriotism during the war. It brought instant success to entrepreneurs who saw how to exploit the demand for alcohol by supplying what the public wanted when legal supplies were cut off. Quick-witted businessmen like Al Capone made huge profits and kept the public happy. His liquor business in Chicago made him a millionaire a hundred times over.[2]

Illegal bootlegging spurred the growth of organised crime in the United States.[3]

Once started on binge-drinking, Americans became hooked on it. It was a time of excess, when they were always thirsty. The opportunity to open speakeasies as an escape to alcoholic bliss was too good to be missed. It was a sign that most Americans were thoroughly enjoying the naughtiness of Prohibition in their own ways. Speakeasies welcomed women with open arms, as well as men addicted to alcohol.[4]

What had been a sordid business in Victorian England with gin a penny a glass and free straw to sleep it off on the floor, was now considered elegant, sophisticated, and even witty in American cities. A new night club society sprung up. Young women smoked cigarettes incessantly, were enchanted by jazz music, and danced in short skirts to new Negro rhythms with total strangers – shaking their limbs, flapping their arms like wings, and cavorting drunkenly. Women regulars at speakeasies were named 'flappers' or 'good-time girls'.

Among the regulars who were happy to allow themselves to be exploited by bootleggers was a young couple, frequently named in newspaper headlines and magazine articles. The popular novelist Scott Fitzgerald and his scatty and elegant wife, Zelda, became symbols representing the 'flapper' era. It was an empty phase, perhaps best defined by one of Fitzgerald's immortal characters, the shallow Daisy, in *The Great Gatsby*, who cries out plaintively; 'What'll we do with ourselves this afternoon, and the day after that, and the next thirty years?'[5]

None of it had any relevance to the real world. That was the point – drinking alcohol was an escape from the grim reality of the world outside into an illusion that you and everyone else were having fun.

The Golden Twenties

Winston Churchill was now a cheerful Edwardian. It seemed as if he had always been one, with his informal modern ways and lack of prejudices. Champagne was the tipple of choice for the so-called Smart Set, but he had been ahead of them.

In fact, Prohibition cut alcohol consumption down from its pre-war levels in America by half. Limiting the hours of consumption in pubs and clubs in the UK had the same effect.

But for young officers like Winston Churchill, who had experienced battle conditions at the front, and were unable to talk about it for some time afterwards, the shock of finding that most of his school friends had been killed in battle never left him. Foreign Secretary Anthony Eden, who later became Prime Minister, was haunted throughout his life by the cries of his men when German sappers ignited fuses beneath the trenches and blew them all up. Stewart Menzies was a young officer in the Life Guards in the First World War, who became Chief of Britain's Secret Intelligence Service in the Second World War. He could never forget the pain of seeing his fellow officers disappear forever when German shells buried them alive. A little alcohol helped to ease the pain of bereavement, and fill the gap they left behind.

Winston Churchill did not appear to have succumbed to the cocktail hour at the Waldorf Hotel or the Dorchester, but brandy or champagne would serve him very well at any time of the day. He thrived on champagne in particular. And yet, there were only half a dozen times in his entire life when it was recorded that friends remarked on his visible inebriation.

It is not easy to equate leisure and the cocktail hour in peacetime with waging a continuous war, as Winston did with political subversives and battalions of troops. But the two conditions were closely knitted, as anyone who spent time at the *Ritz* or the *Piccadilly Hotel* during the Second World War could confirm. Bars and pubs were continually invaded by soldiers and sailors of both sexes who depended on alcohol for their composure. Champagne and brandy, gin and tonics, or beer, were barricades between putting on a show of polite pretence and the grimness of the real warring world. Glasses of champagne kept violence at bay for a while, and held a special significance for Winston Churchill.

There was, for example, the twenty-six-year-old Winston, after the Siege of Ladysmith by Boer guerilla fighters in South Africa was finally relieved in 1900, before the British might be forced to starve from the blockade or capitulate: 'I dined with the Headquarters staff that night. Ian Hamilton, Rawlinson, Hadworth, Lambton, were warm in their welcome. Jealously preserved bottles of champagne were uncorked ... Our pallid and emaciated hosts showed subdued contentment ... I rejoiced to be in Ladysmith at last.'[6]

Another comradely recollection from him of a few years previously, at the age of twenty-four, was when he fought on horseback in the Battle of Omdurman in the Sudan. He had strolled with a group of other officers by the Nile, when he was recognised and hailed from one of the gunboats several feet from the shore.

It was Lieutenant Beatty in his white naval uniform, who tossed him a bottle of champagne. It fell into the Nile. Fortunately, the water turned out to be shallow: 'I nipped into the water up to my knees, and reaching down seized the precious gift, which I bore in triumph back to our mess.'[7]

Many of the words he wrote in 1929 as a memoir of his youth are tributes to old comrades. Henry Rawlinson would command his troops with distinction in the Battle of the Somme in 1916. Lieutenant Beatty would become First Sea Lord and Admiral of the Fleet in 1919. Sir Ian Hamilton would become probably the most decorated general of them all, as well as a lifelong friend. Winston would write a book about Lieutenant General Hamilton's exploits in the Boer War at Bloemfontein; 'Weary of war, but cheered by hopes of the peace, and quite determined to see the matter out.'

We can almost see their names lingering pleasurably in his mind as they slid easily from his pen on to his paper and into his memoir for all time. Champagne was the drink of winners. It gave them a sense of defiance and rewarded them with an uplifting feeling of celebration. It also distracted them from the grim fate of those who had failed to win. The long list of tragic failures included the courageous Admiral Kolchak, who had found himself on the losing side.

'I could not live without Champagne,' Churchill admitted in 1946. 'In victory I deserve it. In defeat I need it.'[8]

24

A Brilliant Creature

British governments had long been accustomed to a lack of reasonable cooperation from all kinds of foreign political or religious upstarts who emerged and were eager for power. Britain tended to turn its back on them unless its interests were endangered, recognising that Great Britain did not have sufficient resources to be involved in every catastrophe on the continent of Europe, or Africa, or the Middle East. They could no longer afford to be 'policemen of the world'.

Churchill had already experienced a lack of popular support for his resistance to the spread of communism, very likely because most communist supporters imagined it offered social equality. Now, he was Chancellor, Soviet Russia was no longer his affair, unless it was raised by the Prime Minister, the Admiralty, the War Office, or the Foreign Office.

Instead, he took the post of Chancellor of the Exchequer seriously because he was following in the political footsteps of his father, whom he admired. He urged substantial reductions in spending on plans for the Royal Navy, which he considered were far too grandiose and unnecessary. As he explained, inevitably there will be gaps in armaments during a long peace, and, 'Britain would have to choose only the essential elements of war power to fill those gaps quietly, gradually and unostentatiously, to avoid an arms race.'[1] But as the Admiralty feared a naval expansion by Japan, he reluctantly agreed to an extra £2 million to be available in an emergency.

Determined to encourage productive enterprises, he was unhappy with the decision to return to the Gold Standard, which was recommended to him by the Chamberlain–Bradbury Committee in 1925. Its aim was to restore the balance between the pound sterling and the US dollar. He believed that it would only favour special interest groups in the financial sector, instead of the interests of producers in industry – whereas the financial sector produced nothing.

He had learned a lot from the world-leading economist John Maynard Keynes, and gave a dinner for him with his own officials. But the pragmatic Prime Minister Baldwin urged him not to 'rock the boat', as the Bank of England was already committed to the Gold Standard.

While Winston was planning his first budget as Chancellor, Clementine was recovering from exhaustion in the south of France. He wrote her in March; 'Mary is flourishing. She comes & sits with me in the mornings & is sometimes most gracious. Diane is just back from school & we are all planning to go to see Randolph this afternoon.' He added, 'I feel far safer from worry and depression when you are with me & when I can confide in your sweet soul.'

He commiserated with her a week later on the death of her mother Lady Hozier at seventy-three.

A Brilliant Creature!

Churchill was propelled in his career by the purposefulness of the great cause of social reform. He was concerned about the hardships that fell on a family after prolonged unemployment, and in old age, sickness or death of the breadwinner when, in a matter of only a few months, 'the result of the years of thrift may be swept away, and the house broken up'.[2] Pensions should commence at sixty-five, not seventy, he told Neville Chamberlain. And widows should benefit immediately financially.

He spoke for two hours in the House when he introduced his first budget on 28 April. Clementine listened to him from the gallery with Randolph and Diana. Baldwin remarked to the King on Winston's ability as a Parliamentarian to describe his insurance and pension schemes with lucidity, rhetoric, levity and humour.

Churchill knew that similar schemes had already been instituted in Germany by Chancellor Bismarck, and they had worked to create stability. Bismarck's solution to most troubling situations had been to buy off people and nations with money. He'd had to threaten and bully the German government to get his way, whereas Churchill was required, instead, to use sweet, reasonable and convincing rhetoric to persuade Parliament to pass his own budget, even though his welfare schemes for the needy were designed with the best intentions.

Winston explained patiently to the affluent Members of Parliament – many of whom had never been near working-class homes or seen factory conditions at first-hand – that, when misfortune struck, whether from unemployment, or devastation at the loss by death of a breadwinner, 'it leaves this once happy family in the grip of the greatest calamity. Although the threat of adversity has been active all these years, no effective provision has been made by the great mass of the labouring classes for their widows and families in the event of death.'

He used a military metaphor for the situation, since few, if any in Parliament had experienced those dire circumstances: 'It is not the healthy and fit marching troops who require special indulgence or rewards, but the stragglers, the weak, the wounded, the veterans, the widows and orphans to whom the ambulances of State aid should be sent.'

He would remove restrictions from payments, such as inquiries and means tests, altogether. It would be nobody's business what they had or how they spent their time: it was more a matter of decency and dignity. In addition, the bottom income groups would have their taxes reduced by 10 per cent. The objective was to 'liberate the production of new wealth'.

A BRILLIANT CREATURE

Minister of Health Neville Chamberlain, who worked closely with Winston on the pension scheme, wrote in his diary on 1 May, 'I don't think we should have done it this year if he had not made it a part of his Budget scheme, and in my opinion he does deserve personal credit for his initiative and drive.'

Churchill's skills in conciliation were also observed when he took a general view of the chaos and lack of cooperation on the continent of Europe. On 11 March he persuaded senior ministers not to become involved in a separate treaty with France, since it would inevitably isolate and embitter Germany even further. Any arrangement should rather include Germany. It led to the Locarno Treaties, in which Britain, Germany, France and Italy guaranteed the security of their existing frontiers. He also advised the Polish ambassador to reach out for friendship with Germany. Otherwise, if Germany was obliged to seek Russia's support, Poland would be crushed between the two military powers like a walnut between the levers of a nutcracker.

'What a brilliant creature he is!' wrote Chamberlain to Prime Minister Baldwin, several weeks later. 'But there is somehow a great gulf fixed between him and me which I don't think I shall ever cross. I like him. I like his humour and vitality. I like his courage. I like the way he took that – to me – very unexpected line over the coal crisis in Cabinet. But not for all the joys of Paradise would I be a member of his staff! Mercurial! A much-abused word, but it is the literal description of his temperament.'[3]

The significance of Chamberlain's feelings and opinion of Churchill was that it showed the marked difference between their mindsets, their attitudes and skills, and values that separated them – certainly their priorities. Those differences would influence their future relationship when war clouds gathered threateningly over Europe.

Churchill appeared to Chamberlain to be mercurial because his military experience enabled him to be utterly ruthless as a negotiator, whereas he had to be diplomatic as a political conciliator. He had no problem with ambiguity, because he was conscious of being able to mould events, whereas Chamberlain saw everything as either black or white.

Historian Andrew Roberts would write of Churchill, 'He was a young man in a hurry who always broke the rules. It was a secret behind his greatness.'[4] Another biographer remarked that he could also be 'self-regarding, ruthless and inconsiderate'.[5] Both remarks were true, even if not easy to understand out of context.

> Here were the two most dominant personalities of Baldwin's government, brought together in a measure of teamwork that yielded immense benefits. Their association was replete with friction. But their political disagreements were more on points of emphasis than on broad lines of policy ... It was a promising partnership. But although they cooperated, they never harmonised. Temperamentally, they were poles apart. Chamberlain found reasoning with Churchill was 'like arguing

with a brass band'. He regarded Churchill as a kind of political magpie, flitting from one nest to another, making off with other birds' eggs, a highly amoral creature.[6]

Churchill could reflect grimly that he knew the world. He had served as an army officer in several wars, where he had seen what little value life possessed in combat, with thousands cut down in minutes by machine gun and cannon fire; whereas Chamberlain did not. Chamberlain had mixed only with his own kind of provincial gentlemen, who were friends and members of the same clubs. They shared feelings of goodwill and were always ready to compromise politely with each other when they sat down together on committees.

Neville Chamberlain, with his mindset and experience of the civil service, was primly intent on form, whereas Churchill was focused directly on achieving his goals. Chamberlain imagined that most people were the same as him and his friends. It would take him years of dull misunderstanding of the outside world before he realised with naivety, hurt pride and dismay, that he had been completely wrong.

It was only then that he may have reflected that part of the human tragedy is that people do not know all the facts before they take initiatives, or react to what they only imagine is happening – as would occur with him several years later in the Munich Crisis. Hitler knew what he did not.

25

Bad News from Germany

Bad news from Germany revealed the consequences of Hitler's ambition to divide the nation in order to seize power, as Mussolini had done in Italy. Like the Italian leader, Hitler knew how to exploit situations to his own advantage. He blamed the economic collapse on all of his enemies; the government in Berlin, Marxist subversives, and Jewish financiers. He persuaded embittered and poverty-stricken ex-servicemen and failed small businessmen in his audiences that those were the same enemies who had conspired in Germany's defeat in 1918. In reality, his so-called 'enemies' were myths he invented to spur on the miserable losers who wanted to believe they would have won the war if they had not been stabbed in the back by conspirators on the inside.

He had a useful ally in the previous Commander-in-Chief of the German Army, General Ludendorff, who was known and respected by every German soldier, since he had fought with them at the battlefronts, to the last bullet. He had been active since then with the *völkisch* groups in Munich. Now he had much to gain from Hitler's delusions, since he had been in command when the German Army was defeated by the Allies. He had also fought to the last man, disposing of tens of thousands of German soldiers with complete indifference. His goal had been German domination of Europe. That goal had justified the means in the eyes of Germany's Chief-of-Staff.

Ludendorff was a Prussian. He had worked on the flawed Schlieffen Plan with General von Moltke that was used to start the German war against the French. He had been appointed Chief-of-Staff by Field Marshal von Hindenburg. The two men had supreme military control in Germany by 1916. General Ludendorff's offensive against British and French troops had failed by 1918, when he had demanded an armistice. But he was determined to continue the war after spreading a conspiracy theory that blamed its failure on the Jews, Christianity and the Freemasons.

The reason for the First World War could be attributed more to Ludendorff than the Kaiser, who was happy to go along with it and then realised (too late) that it could be a catastrophe. In which case, Ludendorff could also be blamed for the criminal act of starting the war and the deaths of Allied and German troops, as well as for its failure.

Hitler was of little importance in the grand scheme of things without the support of such celebrities as Ludendorff and von Hindenburg, who were viewed by Germans as heroes. Hitler was still just a useful street corner rabble-rouser who increased recruits to the Nazi Party, but he had no political value unless he had deputies in the Reichstag. Mussolini had been *invited* to take power in Italy, whereas Hitler might easily be pushed aside by someone more politically useful. So neither von Kahr nor von Lossow invited him to join them in their proposed march on Berlin. Hitler decided to do it on his own.

> Hitler knew that he could rely on the amalgamated forces of the Fighting League. Six months had passed since their first attempt to seize power. They did not want to miss out now, or be overtaken by others, or to find that the government in Berlin was strong enough to reassert its authority over Bavaria, as it had done earlier over Saxony and Thuringia. On November 8, von Kahr and von Lossow attended a meeting of two thousand Munich citizens in the Bürgerbraü beer cellar. The heads of most Bavarian government departments were there, many industrial leaders, and the directors of various municipal and patriotic organisations. Before von Kahr and von Lessow could take the podium, however, Hitler burst in with his Brownshirts and fired a single shot into the ceiling to command attention, seized von Kahr and von Lessow at pistol point and pushed them into a side room.[1]

Having captured the attention of the entire audience by taking them by surprise, Hitler announced over the pandemonium, 'The national revolution has begun. The hall is surrounded by six hundred heavily armed men. No one may leave the premises. Unless quiet is restored immediately, I shall have a machine gun placed in the gallery. The Bavarian government and the national government have been overthrown, and a provisional national government is being formed. The barracks of the *Reichswehr* and the state police are already approaching under the swastika flag.'

He announced that a new government had been formed with him as its leader, and that the German army would march on Berlin behind Ludendorff as its Commander-in-Chief. He added that the entire might of Bavaria would be mustered for the march.

'The German people must be saved,' he declared. 'Are you in agreement with this solution of the German question? You can see what guides us is not self-interest, nor egotism. Rather, we wish to take up the cudgel for our German fatherland, at the eleventh hour. We want to rebuild Germany ...'

He had von Kahr and von Lessow brought back to the podium and offered them positions in the new government. They promised him their personal loyalty before slipping quietly away.

When Hitler learned next day that Kahr and Lessow were mobilising the Bavarian militia against him, he knew he would have to act fast to stop them. But he was in a state of panic, indecision and paralysis. He had taken them by surprise, but his bluff had been called, and he was no longer safe unless he could enlist their support and that of their military forces. Ludendorff came to his aid by lining up the forces of the Fighting League behind Hitler and the other Nazi leaders, heading a column of thousands of Brownshirts, who marched to one of Munich's city squares.

A line of police had already sealed off the route to the *Odeonsplatz*. They opened fire on the procession. Fourteen marchers were halted in their tracks and fell to the ground, while Ludendorff marched sternly on with determination. The others followed him. Hitler had been thrown to the ground too, but hurriedly got up and fled from the scene with a dislocated arm. The police arrested him two days later in a Munich suburb where he was hiding, and put him in a prison cell.

The Nazi putsch had failed. Hitler was accused of treason at his trial, and sentenced to nine months in prison. As a result, he was prevented from marching at the head of his militia to Berlin. Where the incident was given space in the newspaper columns, it was treated with contemptuous ridicule, as just another example of Nazi hooliganism.

The League of Impotent Nations

The League of Nations had been set up to provide arbitration between level-headed and reasonable leaders of nations and their bureaucracies, who were accustomed to work as Neville Chamberlain had done in his well-meaning committees dedicated to achieving satisfactory results by compromise. They might work like Winston Churchill, moving between coercion and conciliation. What they were not equipped to do was crush Nazi hooliganism, which had already spread across the border into Austria. Austrian Nazis disrupted the meetings of Social Democrats. And, at first, former Chancellor Dr Johannes Schober dismissed the interruptions and advised the Social Democrats to ignore them.

The League had been helpless during the French occupation of the Ruhr, since it had no army or police force to establish law and order. Now it was confronted by a new crisis resulting from the assassination on 27 August of three Italian members of a commission deciding on the exact border of Albania and Greece. Mussolini showed his strength by immediately sending a severe ultimatum to Greece. One of its seven points was that they must pay cash indemnity within five days.

As the Greeks had no evidence of who had committed the murders, they defiantly rejected some of the demands – at which the Italian navy bombarded Corfu.

When Italy was condemned for its action by the British delegate to the League, Mussolini responded by announcing that Italy would withdraw from the League. It had been formed only three years previously to 'deter war and punish aggression', but it had no teeth. It hastily backed down. Its reaction clearly showed it was incapable of fulfilling its responsibilities when threatened by one of its members. It was unworkable and unreliable, and only demonstrated how effective Mussolini was with his fascists taking immediate and determined action.

Mussolini withdrew his troops as soon as the indemnity was paid and the Greeks had apologised. Italians and other nations were impressed with his firmness and authority at a time of anarchy all over Europe. They were even more impressed when he signed the Pact of Rome on 27 January 1924, with Yugoslavia, which recognised Italy's sovereignty over the port city of Fiume. Yugoslavia received the Delta and Port Barros in exchange.

It was Mussolini's first year as Italy's dictator, and he had not scared anyone yet, except The League.

The Times wrote: 'People have become impressed by the fact that *Fascismo* is not merely the usual successful political revolution …' It had done away with the usual parliamentary games of chess. Its ability to take control 'provided Italy with internal security and national respect'.

Another blow to the League that showed its impotence was the overthrow of democracy in Spain in September 1923, only a year after Mussolini had obtained power in Italy. Spain's monarchy lost all power when General Marquis Primo de Rivera suspended the Spanish constitution and set up an army and navy Junta to control Spain. He exiled his opponents to one of the Canary Islands and crushed others who wanted a return of the Constitution. He also dealt with Catalonian separatists who had been demanding autonomy. Ruthless firmness by fascist institutions appeared to be the answer to all those who created chaos.

Anarchy and Order

The separatist movement revived in Spain. And an uprising of the Rif in Spanish Morocco spread. It resulted in the deaths of four thousand Spanish troops who attempted to quell the tribal rebellion against colonial forces in North Africa.

As the instability in Spain was attributed to communist and Soviet Russian pressures, it was suggested that Mussolini and British Prime Minister Stanley Baldwin should organise an anti-Bolshevik conference, with Spain playing a leading role. Baldwin declined.

According to the *Edinburgh Review*, it was the strong hand of de Rivera that had settled the lawlessness and violence of previous years. 'No one ever attempted to do what had been done with impunity under the old regime. Murders and general strikes ceased. Banks were no longer held up, and courts, when they acted, began to give judgment according to the evidence.'

Fascismo seemed to be the answer to keep people and institutions honest in Spain as well as in Italy and Germany.

At the same time, the anarchy and banditry in China that Churchill had drawn attention to in 1922, increased in 1923, with fragments of armies led by warlords plundering the country for food and loot, and resorting to kidnapping prominent citizens for ransom. The *Kuomingtang* Nationalist Party attempted to seize important customs revenues in Canton. The Chinese government in Peking continued to refuse to pay its wartime debts. European currencies became problematic with the intense inflation in Germany and fears that it would diminish the value of what instalments were paid – if they ever were.

BAD NEWS FROM GERMANY

At the same time, the United States turned its back on all the trouble spots and plunged into isolationism. Foreigners were not admired, not even celebrities, who became tainted with the illegal actions of their nation. Whereas the British were wary of foreigners from unpleasant past experiences, dislike of foreigners was mutual. Germans either envied or hated the British. The French, who felt they had invented and owned civilisation after the Enlightenment, hated the Germans for their barbarism and arrogance. And Hitler hated the French above all: they were and always had been the enemy.

Most surprising to Winston, who loved France and French culture, the French hated the English. 'They envied, disliked, and despised the Anglo-Saxons. Their best young novelist, François Mauriac, would write in 1937: "I do not understand and I do not like the English except when they are dead."'

But the main grievance of the US against the world outside their borders was the debts owed to them by other governments who considered that America's concern for repayment was mean and greedy. At least Britain had negotiated a successful debt repayment plan, due to Churchill's persistence and efficiency.[2]

President Harding was delighted at Britain's commitment: it had kept faith with its pledge. Ethical standards were still being met. But even in England there was considerable anti-American sentiment, since the British had leapt forward eagerly to protect the free world from tyranny, banditry, and oppression, and suffered massively as a consequence.

Racial and religious hatreds could not be blamed solely on the unprecedented violence of the war, since they had already existed in abundance throughout Austria-Hungary, the Russian Empire, Germany, the Ottoman Empire, and France. That legacy from pre-war times would continue, and even increase to grotesque proportions throughout the entire twentieth century, causing not only divisiveness but violent hatreds that would result in genocide.

26

Collective Security
1925

Lenin never recovered from the attempt on his life several years earlier by an idealistic young woman who felt he had betrayed them all. He suffered from a number of strokes and died at the beginning of the previous year. By that time he had transformed Russia from a tyrannical empire ruled by terror into a communist dictatorship, in which even worse horrors were applied by secret police chief Felix Dzerzhinsky and his murderous organisation known as the CHEKA.*

The battle to become Lenin's successor culminated in a choice between Leon Trotsky, one of the main initiators of the 1917 October Revolution and founder and leader of the Red Army, and Joseph Stalin, who was General Secretary of the Communist Party. Trotsky was an icy intellectual, while the other was a street fighter. Stalin had already become the most powerful figure in Soviet Russia, although Lenin had warned in his last will of Stalin's dangerous character. But Joseph Stalin had successfully marginalised Lenin after his first serious stroke. There was little difference between them in their cold and inhuman ruthlessness and their determined will to power. Lenin had come from a wealthy middle-class family in Perm, and was chilly by nature, whereas Marshal Stalin had made his way to the top by cunning. He too had no interest in human beings except as stepping stones to power. And he knew how to achieve it.

They and the nation they created would become Churchill's antagonists from the left. Meanwhile, he was not responsible for foreign affairs in 1925, but still happy to employ his skills as Chancellor of the Exchequer at 11 Downing Street, and continue to pursue his policy of free trade. The Under-Secretary at the Foreign Office from December was Anthony Eden. So far, Eden was more concerned with finalising the frontier boundaries between Iraq and Turkey. A year later, he urged the League of Nations to admit Germany as a member.

Stalin had become Chairman of the Communist Party by the mid-1920s and had destroyed all opposition in Soviet Russia from his political left. After which he began to eliminate those on the political right who had previously helped him to

---

* It would be changed to the OGPU a few years later under Menzhinsky, as each successive police chief who knew too much was murdered or forced to commit suicide.

crush competitors like Trotsky, Kamenev, and Zinoviev. Now he warned Bukharin, Ryakov and Tomsky of disloyalty to the Party and of dangerous political deviations, and accused them of being traitors.

Treachery was unforgivable, and Stalin was steely. He possessed an even temperament that allowed him to take cold revenge at the most expedient time – whereas when Hitler obtained power, he would go into a mad and abnormal fit of rage at the smallest sign of treachery. He possessed an uncontrollable German hot anger called *Wut* that required taking the most brutal revenge immediately.[1]

Stalin's remedy was simply to deprive Tomsky and Ryakov of their power, and then show his disdain for them by inviting his discredited left wing to return to the Party. In that way, he managed to keep everyone uncertain and on edge, disarmed by anxiety about their fate, and in constant fear of offending their leader.

The Soviet Communist Party, which had begun with the eager support of ideologues, dreamers and romantics who genuinely wished to improve the lives of Russia's industrial workers and peasants, had become cynical and self-serving. It provided opportunities for power by ambitious leaders. But now, both the left and right opposition, who had been brought back into the party, began to seek better economic conditions for the peasants by recommending an end to Stalin's enforced collectivisation programme. Party member Frumkin, for example, demanded that they should be invited to join the Administration, and also that the pace of industrialisation should be slowed and no longer centralised. Apparently, even by then, they had little idea of the meaning or purpose of communism, which was based on one powerful warlord and centralised planning.

Stalin instantly denounced Frumkin and his associates by accusing them of attempting to restore capitalist elements in Russia. At which the Executive Committee of the Central Committee declared that all land belonged, not to individual farmers who worked it, but to the community. The most successful and prosperous of the peasant farmers, known as Kulaks, would not be allowed to serve on any committees, since they were enemies of agricultural socialism. Once that stand was taken, it marked the development of a political campaign against all Kulaks. It would be described as one of the cruellest persecutions of the twentieth century.[2]

As soon as Lenin was dead, Stalin launched a drive to eliminate the educated and politicised middle classes in Russia, whom he viewed as a threat. Like Karl Marx, who did not want intellectuals on his committees, so that he could dominate semi-literate working-class members, nor did Stalin. Neither would tolerate opposition of any kind.

Children of the middle classes were denied any right to attend high school or university. Middle-class property owners were denied the right to vote on the housing committees that determined who should live where. The consequence was that they ended up living in one room while the remaining rooms were allotted to strangers. Stalin's primary aim was to degrade and destroy the middle classes, since they were educated and might pose a threat to his leadership. When families were forced to share a room with other families, it became known as 'living in a corner'.

The first countries that Stalin decided to restore relations with were Britain, Italy and France. Yugoslavia refused to recognise or trade with Soviet Russia, and created an anti-Bolshevik League with Bulgaria and Romania. Russia played a prominent role in fermenting Bolshevik uprisings anywhere. As soon as the British government discovered that Soviet Russia had been financing British trade union activities, it broke off relations with Stalin.

Prelude to War

In Spanish Morocco, when General Primo de Rivera decided it would be better to walk away from the problems of the Colonial Protectorate, the monarchist Colonel Franco, who was head of the Spanish Legion, challenged his decision by declaring in his presence at the dinner table, 'Where we tread is Spanish soil, because it has been bought at the highest price and with the most precious coin – the Spanish blood which was shed there.'

When de Rivera began to defend his decision, he was greeted by hissing from a number of officers. Even so, Spanish forces began to withdraw from Morocco, but were immediately attacked as soon as those troops became small enough to be defeated by Abd el-Krim's Moorish forces of wild Berbers and Rifs. The Spanish Legion with an army of 123,000 men, repelled 12,000 of them, supported by 150 aircraft. It was the prelude to the Spanish Civil War.

Although it took place in Europe when Churchill's attention was absorbed by the Treasury, he was acutely aware of what was taking place all over Europe. While its most powerful nations prepared for war, the League of Nations in Geneva finalised what was called the 'Geneva Protocol', which enabled members to reduce their armaments as a first stage to abolishing wars. It would be achieved through Arbitration, Security, and Disarmament. The League would have the right to challenge any aggressor collectively. That would be possible only if member nations were willing to entrust their security to an international body that could use its collective bargaining powers whenever there was a threat of aggression.

The theory was that abolition of the right of nations to make war would create security. In future, war would be a collective enterprise against the aggression of a single rogue state. The League would not commence with actual physical hostilities, but use economic and financial sanctions. Nations that made war on their own were warned that they would be isolated and challenged.

Seventeen governments signed the Protocol. It was an international response to the horrors of trench warfare in the First World War and a pledge that the previous war was intended to end all wars. The Protocol resolved small border disputes. It also agreed to raise finance required by Greece, which had accepted a million Greek-speaking refugees from Anatolia and Thrace. The Bank of England provided the initial loan.

Conflicts that created turmoil in Europe and its colonies were largely over rights and privileges. The League enabled them to use reason instead of emotions, and hope against power.

COLLECTIVE SECURITY

Collective security already existed internally in Britain through arbitration by trade unions. Churchill was at his most effective as a conciliator in the government's efforts to persuade mine owners to think again concerning the notices of dismissal they had handed out to workers in their mines. It was the age-old problem that had come to prominence after the growth of the Industrial Revolution, when crippling overhead costs had left mine owners with unsatisfactory profit margins. Landowners continued to blame coal miners, over whom they considered they had a right, while miners felt they were being crushed to extract more profits from the mines.

Caught between two powerful forces that he knew could destroy Britain's economy, Churchill saw that both sides were right about the injustices but wrong about the way they attempted to remove them. Both sides were fired up by a belief in their rights, and neither was prepared to be reasonable. Coal miners were invigorated by a belief in their overwhelming numbers to threaten the landlords. On the other hand, the mine owners with their capital were just as arrogant in their determination to intimidate their workers, knowing that barely one of them had enough pocket money to put food on their family table for more than a day or two. They could be threatened with being starved.

Churchill, with his knowledge of how history unrolls beneath the feet of peasant hordes, and his fear of the spread of communism and revolution, must have been in awe at their determined obstinacy to destroy themselves and everyone around them. That was the reality of industrial poverty and strife in England and Wales in 1925.

Churchill was persuasive in establishing a middle way by using government to subsidise the mining industry, so that payrolls would not have to be cut. He pointed out in the House that the miners had certain rights. He warned Parliament that if they wanted a struggle, there would be a complete stoppage in the mines, and the railways would be paralysed and put a halt to the entire industry of Great Britain. Trade would slow down and social reform would be put back. It would close the door on progress towards better living conditions for everyone.

He cautioned that Britain's economy could shrink, but he was prepared to examine every possible alternative first. Otherwise this government would spend the rest of its time in office working back in an attempt to reach the better position it had formerly occupied. There would be no chance of improving the economy and no hope of expansion.

He thought little of either side in the disputes, but had to conciliate both. He would have regarded the conflict between classes at home as little different from the situation in the larger territory of Europe, which was intent on tearing itself apart through fear, anxiety, and hatred in the battle to survive. Meanwhile, he used his reasoned arguments again in the autumn to negotiate an agreement for France to pay its war debt to Britain by sixty-two annual payments of £12.5 million. France would be allowed to reconsider the conditions if Germany defaulted on payments of its own debt to France. The problem of who should pay the bill for reparations had still not gone away.

Conciliating Germany

Churchill had just turned fifty-one when Baldwin asked him, on 30 November, to mediate between the Irish Free State and Ulster. There were fears in Ireland of possible border changes between north and south, and they were also reluctant to pay their debt to Britain of £155 million. Churchill developed an acceptable formula after only three days, in which no borders would be changed and the debts of the Free State would be paid by instalments over sixty years.

Next in line was a settlement of Italy's war debts to Britain. When he reached agreement with Italy, Churchill remarked with irony on the fairness of the equation by pointing out that the compromise satisfied neither party, but at least it was a victory of reason over wild emotions.

By the end of January 1926, Clementine had left for a long holiday in the south of France, while Churchill remained at Chartwell, where he entertained political friends. He wrote to her to say that fruit trees were being planted every quarter of an hour. He took friends and colleagues around the estate to inspect the property. Among them was Sir Samuel Hoare, who remarked to friends on how happy Churchill was while supervising the work of creating a series of ponds in the valley.

The Churchill children continually entertained themselves in their new home by discovering 'hidden corners and rolling fields'. While continuing to work at home on his second budget, Winston wrote to Clementine in Rome, 'All is well here. Mary breakfasted & Sarah dined with me. Diana talked quite intelligently about politics & seemed to have a lot of information derived from the newspapers. They are all very sweet & it is a joy to have them down here.'

Diana was already seventeen, Sarah was eleven, and Mary was three. Randolph, age fourteen, was away as a boarder at Eton.

Outside of the tranquility of the Churchills' country house at Chartwell, the League of Nations congratulated itself at the signing of the Geneva Protocol, while Winston carried on with his hectic work schedules at home. They included the hustle and bustle of builders and workmen improving the estate under Churchill's shouted instructions. Clementine returned home and argued to prevent him from spending more money on the estate. It added to the bustle of his secretary and researchers asking him continual questions about the current draft of his book, the chatter of domestic servants who were with them at all times, and their children happily playing underfoot.

Overseas, the French were still anxious about Germany's ability to make war, and sceptical about peace in Europe. They preferred to seek an alliance with Britain. Churchill believed that it would send the wrong message to Germany and deepen the fear and suspicion between Germany and France. French President Gaston Doumerge took the opposite view, that it was essential to form a powerful front that Germany would understand was 'unbreakable'.

Churchill insisted that France should try to come to good terms with Germany by settling their grievances. 'The only security against a renewal of war would be a complete agreement between England, France, and Germany.'

COLLECTIVE SECURITY

Instead, the antagonisms between France and Germany were left unappeased, and Churchill felt sure that Germany would find ways to regain the territories they had lost in 1918.

Britain's Foreign Secretary – now Austen Chamberlain – preferred an Anglo–French Alliance. But Churchill pointed out that such alliances were exactly what the League of Nations was set up to avoid. The world had already been broken up several times because Germany and France were at each other's throats. An alliance between France and Britain would trigger the same thing again. He wrote to his colleagues that, despite the Versailles Treaty, Germany would, sooner or later, be armed. And France might pre-empt a German military strike by attacking first. He insisted that if Britain had an alliance with France, 'we would be drawn in to support the French against Germany'.

His argument to conciliate Germany was successful, and negotiations opened in Paris that March between Britain and France, which included Germany. The Treaty of Locarno was signed on 16 October, according to which the frontiers of Western Europe were established and accepted as they were after Germany's defeat in 1918, and even protected against aggression.[3]

As Germany was not a member of the League of Nations, the Locarno Treaty could not come into force until it was. Perhaps that was why the Treaty was not negotiated by the League. Its wording simply stated that its aims were 'within the framework of the Covenant' of the League. Austen Chamberlain declared it was a regional pact that would link up with other such regional agreements into a system of world security. Wishful thinking though it may have been, 'world security' was at least a serious and a reasonable goal.

27

A Liberal at Heart

In between all the discussions and arguments, the Churchills took a Mediterranean holiday in the sunshine of the south of France, which Clementine didn't really like. Despite the conviviality of friends, she was impatient with the self-indulgent lifestyle of the rich, which she found unnecessary and artificial. She was still a Liberal at heart, although she had to put on a welcoming face for Winston's new Conservative friends. But she suffered from the typically English Calvinist sense of guilt at spending money. It seemed so wasteful when she had grown up having to guard every penny. Conspicuous shows of wealth sickened her by reminding her of her childhood poverty.

Clementine complained endlessly of the cost to keep up their country home, Chartwell, which she considered was an absurdly large manor house and estate that Winston had bought for the family, and which he considered essential for a man of destiny; particularly one who was determined to match his reputation with his famous ancestor, John Churchill, the 1st Duke of Marlborough.

Winston would keep interrupting their holidays to rush back to London at every opportunity to deal with business and supervise the work on his estate, and check the status of his new book. He made another £20,000 from serialisation rights to pay into the money pit of Chartwell that Clementine so feared would drain away all their funds. He had already spent three times the price he'd paid for Chartwell on improvements. As far as he was concerned, it was their home that they would never leave, and which would be passed on to their heirs.

In spite of Clementine's mixed feelings about the Riviera, it was at least an escape from the hectic life with Winston that she often felt compelled to run away from. His moods went up and down and he was too demanding, then became petulant when disappointed. And he was unhappy when she was displeased. At this stage in their marriage, she needed to get away from him, while he needed her to be supportive. She felt stifled by his dependency on her, and they spent longer and longer periods apart.

Furthermore, 'both Churchills were exceedingly demanding, Winston in particular insisted on a rigid if eccentric regime and Clementine ensured the staff complied with it fully. It was no easy task. Her nephew Peregrine recalled that for everyone except Winston, "life at Chartwell was continual chaos".'[1]

An Age of Conflict

When Churchill announced his second budget as Chancellor of the Exchequer on 27 April 1926, Randolph heard his father's speech from the Gallery of the House of Commons. The theme for the coming year was to be conservative fiscal responsibility with thrift and economy. Luxuries, including betting, would be taxed. He informed the House that the economic picture was not black, but there were dark patches. Even so, they were less prominent than in the previous year. And he warned that the crisis in the coal industry could result in a need for substantial new taxes.

Mine owners still received a subsidy to prevent them from cutting miners' wages in order to compete in a tight overseas market. Next day after his budget speech, he told Prime Minister Baldwin that the mines were losing money, and a wage cut was essential, or overseas customers would buy coal cheaper from elsewhere. The miners refused to accept a cut. As a result, the owners shut out the entire labour force from the mines. The Trade Union Congress immediately announced a General Strike in support of the miners. It was scheduled for a minute to midnight on 3 May.

Negotiations continued between the government and the TUC right through 2 May when, just after eleven o'clock that night, the Cabinet heard that unionised printers at the *Daily Mail* had suppressed the edition 'because it did not like its leading article'. The attempt to silence the press halted further negotiations.

A Cabinet strike-breaking committee was organised on 3 May under the Home Secretary. Churchill was not a member of the Cabinet, but was asked to prepare a government news sheet explaining to the public what was going on, in order to relieve their minds. It would focus on the possibility of injury to trade and Britain's reputation.

He also spoke in the House that afternoon, praising the moderation of the speeches by Labour MPs, including Ramsay MacDonald. And he welcomed the cooperation of trade union negotiators, who had done their best to ward off any possible disaster to national life. But the government could not avoid its responsibility for maintaining essential services and public order. Once strike notices were withdrawn, negotiations could be renewed. Churchill insisted that it was their duty to parley.

The night when the General Strike began, Churchill supervised the printing of the government news sheet at the presses of the *Morning Post*, with Samuel Hoare, who suggested it should be called the *British Gazette*.

Students and other volunteers drove copies of the *Gazette* to towns through the Home Counties and the south of England. Lindemann sent fourteen Oxford undergraduates to the Treasury to collect their copies for distribution. Hoare instructed aircraft to fly the *Gazette* to the north of England. More than 230,000 had been printed by 5 May. Each issue was protected for security reasons. The War

Office sent troops to the paper mill that supplied the newsprint. The Admiralty sent a naval guard to escort the barge carrying the paper up the Thames. At the same time, the editor of the *Morning Post*, who was an old Conservative enemy of Churchill's, attempted to keep him out of the building.

Churchill, at the Treasury, made a point of avoiding alarming the public by not mentioning the serious shortages of flour and sugar, and the stoning and overturning of trams, and looting, in which police used their truncheons to clear looters from the streets.

In Cabinet on 6 May, he pressed for the maximum protection of food being transported to London from the docks. On 7 May Baldwin supported his proposal to incorporate volunteers from the Territorial Army into the volunteer police forces. They would have armbands instead of uniforms, and truncheons instead of rifles. When the Home Secretary asked who would pay for this, Churchill replied, 'The Exchequer will pay. If we start arguing about petty details, we will have a tired-out police force, a dissipated army and bloody revolution.'[2]

A Nation Divided

In a BBC broadcast on 8 May, the Prime Minister appealed for an end to the General Strike, using Churchill's theme of five days earlier: 'No door is closed.' More than a million copies of the *British Gazette* were distributed three days later. Then, on 12 May, the General Council of the Trade Union Congress decided not to support the miners any longer. TUC leaders called on Stanley Baldwin at 10 Downing Street to announce that the General Strike was over. It had lasted for only nine days, but it had divided the country.

Eight days later, Baldwin asked Churchill to take over negotiations between the government and the miners, because of Winston's ability to understand the problems of each side and build a bridge between them. When the mine owners still insisted on a reduction in coal miners' wages, he proposed that any such reduction should be met by a reduction in their profits. He insisted on social grounds that there was a limit below which miners ought not to work. It was a repetition of his argument five years previously that the owners could have stopped the strike at less cost if they had done so sooner with a realistic understanding of the miners' needs of minimum wages for survival.

Churchill invited the socialist leader Ramsay MacDonald to Chartwell to help mediate. After friendly discussions, MacDonald offered to ask the miners' leaders for a national settlement on the basis of a minimum wage. Then Churchill worked out an acceptable formula with them, which could not be undercut by individual mine owners.

But the owners' attitude was uncooperative and unreasonable. Now Churchill sought to have the principle of a minimum wage incorporated in a Government Bill. But the Cabinet refused to put pressure on the owners. That encouraged the owners to refuse even to consider a minimum wage. In a last effort to resolve the conflict, Churchill offered to set up an independent National Tribunal to examine the situation and secure a fair settlement in each region. But the miners were inflamed by the owners' refusal to accept a national minimum wage, and refused his offer.

'These people think themselves stronger than the State,' he remarked of the miners. 'But that is a mistake. There is a similar attitude among the owners.' In the end, he was obliged to leave the miners and owners to their own devices, and return to writing the third volume of his war memoirs.

Morocco

The tribes of the Rif, who had caused such damage to Spain's colonial rule during the previous year or two, now became the burden of the French when the rebel leader Abd el-Krim prepared for war against France in the spring in order to obtain autonomy for the Moroccans. France sent military reinforcements with the intention of crushing the rebellion immediately. The Spaniards, who had withdrawn with pessimism, were now encouraged by France's firmer attitude, and took a new initiative. Primo de Rivera left Madrid to take personal command of Spanish forces. He built a line of fortified blockhouses from the Mediterranean to the border of French Morocco. The line held, in spite of continual attacks by the rebels.

The Rifs (or Riffs) were Arabic-speaking Muslim Berber peoples of northeastern Morocco, a region known as the Rif.

Abd el-Krim persuaded the Rif tribes to declare a *Jihad*, or Holy War, against the French and Spanish. In his drive for supreme power, he had already captured his main rival, who had (typically) 'died in captivity'. It was a euphemism meaning tortured or starved to death in chains. Abd el-Krim had attacked any tribes friendly to France and destroyed their villages. But in the struggles that ensued, his forces were pushed further and further back into the interior by French troops, culminating in a major attack headed by General Pétain, the hero of Verdun.

The first Spanish troops ashore were led by Colonel Franco. French troops amounted to 75,000, while 160,000 Spanish troops disembarked by August, before the joint offensive began.

France, supported by Spain, demanded unconditional surrender. But people in Britain generally sympathised with Abd el-Krim's fight for independence. He was viewed as a hero fighting for freedom against Spanish and French colonial forces.

Similar popular sympathy in the United States inspired an operetta called *The Desert Song*, loosely set against the Riff uprising. It included 'The Riff Song', which many English-speaking people found catchy.[3] The avenging romantic lead was named 'The Shadow'. And the desert wastes of North Africa began to appear in romanticised form in short stories, books and films in the West. Fiction transformed reality so that no one knew anymore what was true and what was invention.

As the military offensive against Abd el-Krim gathered in momentum and success, what led to his defeat was the failure of the harvest and the spread of a typhus epidemic. He surrendered, and was sent into exile on the French island of Réunion in the Indian Ocean. The Spanish Colonel Franco became the hero of the landing on Morocco and was promoted to general at the youthful age of only thirty-three, becoming one of the youngest generals in the world.

28

Winston, a Star Turn
1925–26

The reason for Churchill's appointment to the office of Chancellor of the Exchequer by Prime Minister Baldwin was often debated. It was explained very much later by another minister – possibly Leo Amery.[1] According to him, Baldwin's dominant motive had been fear that Lloyd George was courting Winston.[2]

In reality, David Lloyd George and the Liberal Party still appeared to be in decline, and Churchill thought Lloyd George was no longer as closely in touch with current politics as he had been. But the Welsh Wizard had been a great leader in wartime, and most people still viewed him with respect. Evidently the respect of a few friends was not enough to obtain sufficient seats in order to assume his old mantle of power.

Stanley Baldwin loathed Lloyd George and was hugely suspicious of his influence on Churchill and Churchill's close friends. Apparently Baldwin still harboured suspicions of a Liberal revival in opposition to him, so he did his best to separate Winston from Lloyd George's influence. Shortly after Baldwin had formed his Cabinet, he had remarked to his confidant Thomas Jones that it would now be up to Churchill to be loyal, 'if he is capable of loyalty'.[3]

Another reason for his appointment was said to be that, 'Baldwin was a quiet, pipe-smoking person who needed a "strongman" at his elbow. Others said that Baldwin was a wily old fox who, committed to a return to the gold standard, to satisfy the bankers, wanted somebody to take the blame when this policy led to unemployment …'[4] As expected, it received scathing criticism.

Winston's pushiness and his instinct for publicity were not appreciated in a society that still believed in modesty to a point of self-effacement, particularly in the civil service. According to Robert Boothby, who was Churchill's Personal and Private Secretary at the time, 'When Churchill joined the Conservative Party and Baldwin's government, he and Lloyd George inevitably drifted apart.'[5]

Winston was keen for Lloyd George's support for his first budget with its extension of social insurance, in which he praised Lloyd George's previous work with him on pensions in the former Liberal-led government.[6]

Despite the lack of enthusiasm for the Liberal Party, David Lloyd George and Winston Churchill were still the dominant figures in Parliament. Or, as H.A.L. Fisher put it, they were 'the only men who can fill the House of Commons'.[7]

But Lloyd George was increasingly distrusted.[8] Churchill predicted early in 1926 that his old mentor and rival would move steadily to the political left. Surprisingly, several leading politicians did so before switching to the extreme right.[9]

In July 1925, the government avoided a showdown with the mining industry 'by announcing a nine-month subsidy to maintain existing wages while a Royal Commission investigated the problems of the industry', It was an attempt by the government to buy time while it constructed an emergency framework necessary to keep the country running in the event of a strike. Lloyd George presented it as retreat in the face of a threat from sectional interests.

'Quite frankly,' he told the Commons, 'the Government were afraid of facing cold steel.' At the end of his speech he rubbed salt into the wound with a quotation from Lord Randolph Churchill, whom he had admired: 'You call yourself a Government. Whom do you govern?'[10]

Baldwin thought the remark poisonous, but trusted Churchill to answer it. And he did – making the case for patience, restraint, and delay. The breathing space he brought about lasted until the spring of 1926, when negotiations came to nothing and the General Strike erupted. After it was over, Churchill remarked, 'When the General Strike was let loose upon us the Public, we had uncommonly little help from him!'[11]

It was a critical point of leadership over the 'rebellious masses'. But, when it was all over, the strike was portrayed by the press as typical of the good-natured British way of conducting politics, with chit-chat about football matches between strikers and police sent to prevent them from breaking the law. Some violence was inevitable when passionate crowds gathered to protest their case and knew how hard-up they were for cash to survive for another twenty-four hours. Despite those hardships, they were all for fair play – even with the possibility of their families going hungry; even with the police, who were from the same working-class neighbourhoods, and sympathised with them. But they were public servants required to do their duty in an impossible situation.

Not so for the mine owners, who had first begun 'harvesting' coal on their estates at the beginning of the English Industrial Revolution, when it was lying on the surface. Now the miners had to dig deeper and deeper to find it, which cost the land owners more and more for equipment and labour to dig it out. The strike ran out of steam in November and the miners went back underground on the owners' terms.

John Maynard Keynes

One of Lloyd George's assets during the General Strike was his partnership with Keynes, the most admired economist of the twentieth century. Keynes was committed to Liberalism and supported Lloyd George. He became an important member of the Liberal Industrial Inquiry, which was founded at the end of 1926, and was Chair of the Industrial and Financial Organisation subcommittee. Another of its experts was social economist Seebohm Rowntree. Rowntree was the social researcher whose statistics had startled Churchill when he had discovered to his astonishment that nearly half of Britain's population lived below the poverty line. Winston had left the Conservative Party in order to create and implement social reforms through the Liberals.

The Liberals deliberated during the following years on how to solve the problem of Britain's continually high rate of unemployment that never dropped below a million jobless from 1921 onward. They published their 'Liberal Yellow Book' in explanation. But Churchill was unimpressed with its answers, which were little more than a list of existing proposals. Its major theme was borrowing funds to undertake infrastructure programmes, like building more roads, clearing the slums, and electrification. It favoured interference by the state, regardless of the free market orthodoxy of the times.

Churchill continually urged the government to intervene even more in the economy. But one question continued to surface. How could internal job creation programmes alter the fact that Britain's export markets were in a state of chaos and conflict, when former customers were no longer buying British goods? The Conservatives aimed at conserving whatever Britain already enjoyed, but there were no new or practical or imaginative ideas for economic growth arising from the other political parties.

The Weimar Republic

The Weimar Republic in Germany had, so far, survived all attempts by the political far-right and far-left to seize power, and continued to stabilise their position at the centre, where political parties were committed to parliamentary democracy and republicanism. They still managed to consolidate their position and held the balance of power when Gustav Stresemann was Foreign Minister.

Then, two months after Hitler was released from prison, he held a meeting on 27 February 1925 in the *Bürgerbräu* beer cellar in Munich, with the intention of refounding the Nazi Party. He had been successful in denouncing the government for not challenging the Treaty of Versailles. Now he had achieved notoriety, he drew an audience of three thousand, which jammed into the cellar with its wooden tables and vaulted ceiling, and even spread outside into the streets. He told the admiring throng that only the Nazi Party opposed Marxism in Germany. 'Either the enemy goes over our dead bodies, or we go over his.'

Ebert, the first President of the German Republic, died the following day. He had differed from much of the aristocratic nature of pre-war politics by coming from a working-class background. As a respected socialist editor of a newspaper, he ensured that German politics maintained a moderate middle path that carefully avoided the autocratic excesses of Marxism or fascism.

The problem with finding a suitable successor was to ensure the candidate was dedicated to republicanism and the parliamentary system. One of the candidates was General Ludendorff, who had led Hitler's failed Putsch two years earlier. Another was the German Communist leader Ernst Thaelmann. The Weimar coalition chose Wilhelm Marx as their candidate. He was the Prime Minister of Prussia. The Nationalists preferred Field Marshal Hindenburg, the hero of the war, whom they hoped would restore the monarchy. But he was now seventy-seven and failing in health.

Hindenburg had been hoping to withdraw from public life to enjoy retirement as a country gentleman. He announced on 6 April that he would not stand as a candidate – but he was persuaded to do so. His reputation as an old warrior from the Franco–Prussian War was decisive in electing him President by 48.3 per cent of the votes. Wilhelm Marx was close with 45.4 per cent. The creation of a 'Red Scare' ensured that communist candidate Thaelmann took only 6.3 per cent of the vote. Most Germans felt that the Weimar Republic was in safe, traditional, and dedicated hands. But Hindenburg's mental grasp declined. 'He had become increasingly prejudiced, arbitrary, and senile.'[12]

Hitler's Troubles

Another problem with the government's optimistic outlook arose from a book that had been published on 18 July, but had barely even been noticed by most reviewers at the time. It was the first volume of *Mein Kampf*, which Hitler had written while in prison, with some help from his close friend Rudolf Hess.

Hitler's book explained his philosophy. He claimed that there was not just one peril facing Germany, but two – Marxism and Judaism. He invented both as threats to raise a conspiracy theory that they were out to destroy Germany's so-called 'Aryan' society – which was another myth. To back his claim of a conspiracy, he sought elaborately to give the word 'Aryan' a new meaning. What was merely linguist terminology, he managed to turn into false science by inventing a concept of an Aryan race of people that was superior to all others and of which the 'pure blood' of the Germanic tribes played a leading role.

It was all invented to convince his followers that they were superior to so-called 'Semites', despite the fact that both semantic terms were unscientific. He knew his constituents were partly illiterate and not given to deep thought. He expressed contempt for their idleness in private. So Hitler invented his own so-called 'science' based on mythology from a science fiction book that had planted the ideas in his head five years previously. It was believed to be called *The Names of Germania's Tribes*. Its authors named some three hundred.

Lenin had died little more than a year previously. 'In a rare moment of frankness, he had once said that only a country like Russia could have been captured as easily as he took it. Germany was a different proposition. It could not be raped – it had to be seduced.'[13]

Hitler was well aware of it. In his preface to the first edition of *Mein Kampf*, he explained that the German people 'had to be gulled to be led'.[14] He would make sure to delete that give-away remark in the next edition. And so he had carefully woven a seductive tapestry of deceitful fiction in which he appeared as a godlike figure ready to save the German people and lead them to their long-sought destiny to rule Europe, and then the world.

Most importantly for his political ambitions, the mythology provided him with propaganda to claim a so-called 'racial purity' of the Germanic-speaking peoples in a self-indulgent fantasy. He knew how to give his constituents what they sought. What might be considered bizarre to more knowledgeable voters would satisfy the gullibility of the less sophisticated segment of the German population.

'Hitler, like Lenin, had nothing but contempt for parliamentary democracy or any other aspect of liberalism.'[15] But he would have to use political means to seduce the electorate, as opposed to using the overwhelming violence of Lenin in Soviet Russia. He designed his populist political platform to appeal largely to society's 'losers'; the not very bright, the uncompetitive and envious, the marginalised, discontented, forgotten, and alienated, in German society. Plenty had been left economically and emotionally broken after the war. About one third was working class, one third lower middle class, and the rest were minor officials, clerks, and small shopkeepers and businessmen.

It would be surprising if Hitler had not read Reade's book *The Martyrdom of Man*, since its publication ran into twenty-four editions. Cecil Rhodes claimed to have been motivated by it: 'That book made me what I am.'[16] The explorer and colonial administrator Sir Harry Johnston had been influenced by it. So had author H.G. Wells, who wrote his own *Outline of History* afterwards and acknowledged Reade's influence. It triggered George Orwell's thinking; also psychologist Susan Isaacs and others, as well as Winston Churchill.[17]

Evidently it inspired powerful emotions. Rhodes saw it as an invitation to conquer and possess Africa: 'Africa is still lying ready for us – it is our duty to take it.'[18] His ambition was echoed in Hitler's inspiration to conquer the vast plains of Russia and colonise them and the Middle East with Germans who would use the huge existing populations as slave labour, until they died from overwork and disease. It would be a monumental land-grab.

The more level-headed young Winston had evidently learned something different from *The Martyrdom of Man*. The breadth and depth of its history provided him with the consolation of the long view from Reade's contemplation of the enormous time span in which human beings had endured and survived. It had evidently instilled humility and courage in Winston to hope of overcoming each crisis that came along.

Part of Hitler's fiction was based on his myth of a race of blond, blue-eyed *Aryans* 'whose physical and intellectual superiority enabled them to spread out from somewhere in northern Europe, conquering as they went …' His fraudulent theory, which was no more than science fiction, would be embroidered by Nazi propagandists in Germany, and become a Nazi delusion that would result in the Second World War.[19]

29

The Enemy on the Right

Winston Churchill described Adolf Hitler as 'the little corporal... who had been temporarily blinded by mustard gas in a British attack'.

Despite Hitler's delusions and the hovering war debt, the society of the Weimar Republic was remarkably vibrant. It was headed by a respected old soldier with middle-of-the-road world views and without any disruptive political ambitions of his own. And it produced a number of creative people in the arts whose work was notable for its originality and vitality. According to journalist Arthur Koester, who worked in the German capital at that time, 'Berlin in the 'twenties was the most cosmopolitan capital in Europe, throbbing with life and excitement.'[1]

The surge in inflation had evaporated and employment had begun to rise. Germany was offered equal participation in European diplomacy for the first time since its defeat.[2]

The Weimar Republic looked solid at last. And it would have been, but for Germany's unemployed and marginalised citizens whom Hitler managed to stir up with his discontents and his myths.

Psychologist Carl Jung wrote an essay to explain the rise of the Nazis. He described the phenomenon by stating that one man had infected the whole of Germany because he was 'possessed'. Modern man had placed himself at the mercy of the psychic underworld of Wotan. Jung viewed Hitler as a primitive medicine man transformed into the archetypal figure of the German god of battles, with his psychic forces of destruction. Those forces were *Evgriftenheit* (the state of being possessed). The condition involved an individual who seizes others in his grip, and those who are willing, even eager, to be seized. Jung could see no other explanation for the German phenomenon and its powerful energies that spread so widely, so fast.[3]

To summarise historian Stephen Kotkin's political explanation of the strategic situation; the Treaty of Versailles could not last since it was imposed on Germany without involving Russia when both nations were in no position to resist Britain and France – it was they who had won the war and could force it through. France had suffered the greatest destruction from the German war. But what would happen when Germany's and Russia's economies grew? Hitler would defy the treaty in 1933 by building up Germany's fighting forces. And Russia's motivation was to encourage a war against the two imperialist/capitalist nations so that Russia would come out on top through a socialist revolution in Germany (and possibly France).

Hitler's motivation was the same as Chamberlain's in the UK, which was to recruit Hitler to his side.[4]

On the other hand, the German communist intellectual Bertolt Brecht viewed Hitler simply as a gangster.

Novelist Thomas Mann wrote of the phenomenon in a more self-indulgent literary style: 'This fantastic state of mind, of a humanity that has outrun its ideas, is matched by a political scene in the grotesque style, with Salvation Army methods, hallelujahs and bell ringing and Dervishlike repetition of monotonous catchwords, until everybody foams at the mouth. Fanaticism turns into a means of salvation, enthusiasm into epileptic ecstasy, politics becomes an opiate for the masses, a proletarian eschatology; and reason veils her face.'[5]

That was how Germany became conditioned for another war through uncontrolled emotions. Regardless of whose version was the correct one, Hitler merged his personal sense of failure with that of the German people so that they would identify with him. He had suffered from hysterical blindness in a military hospital named Pasewalk in 1918, and dreamed incessantly of avenging the shame of defeat in the Great War.

> One of the doctors at Pasewalk was a Dutch psychiatrist, Edmund Forster. His methods were not subtle and he would usually bully shell-shocked soldiers into returning to active duty. He dismissed most of his patients as malingerers, but Hitler seemed very different. Hitler did not want to be declared unfit for duty and was eager to get back to the front line. Forster observed Hitler for a week and became certain he had not gone blind out of cowardice. That made Hitler interesting. Forster was familiar with Freud's work and often used hypnosis. He reasoned that Hitler's unconscious had made him blind and that it had done so because Hitler could not bear to see what he would inevitably see, the destruction of Germany.[6]

'Shining before him,' Winston Churchill imagined as he wrote, 'he saw his duty, to save Germany from these plagues, to avenge her wrongs. And lead the master race to its long-decreed destiny.'[7]

The Root of an Idea

An important element in the mixture of bizarre ideas that created the foundation for Nazism was the connection between Hitler's intention to dominate Europe and the 'superman' (*Übermensch*) philosophy of Nietzsche, which he borrowed. At the heart of that philosophy was Nietzsche's contempt for the slave mentality caused by Christianity, which wanted its followers to be meek and mild. It was a defeatist attitude that encouraged mediocrity by focusing on an imaginary next life, instead of on this one: the real one, not an imaginary one.

Nietzsche claimed that life should be above merely existing from one day to the next like mindless cattle. He believed that human beings should be superior to the herd by self-improvement to become supermen.[8] Hitler was so impressed with the theory that he was drawn to visit Nietzsche's home, which had become a shrine managed by Nietzsche's sister, who appears to have been a fanatical fascist.

The much-misunderstood Nietzsche had expressed support for the mystical Ancient Greek cult of Dionysus, whose followers delighted in physical excesses that incited ecstatic and bloodthirsty mob hysteria. The idea of creating mass hysteria suited Hitler's purpose. Now he had the ideological backing from Nietzsche's claims that meek and mild mankind who followed Judeo-Christian ethics should be challenged by 'supermen'. But, in order to obtain enough support to turn a society upside down, tradition demanded a more reasonable pretext for Hitler's heated emotional solution.

> It is important to give it the rank of a universal imperative or of a divine commandment. The range of choices is not great: either it is that we must defend ourselves, or that we have an obligation to help others, or that we are fulfilling heaven's will. The optimum pretext would link all three of these motives. The attackers should appear in the glory of the anointed, in the role of those who have found favour in his chosen god's eye.[9]

Historical Fiction

The Nietzsche justification lent reason to Hitler's delusion from reading the myth of the so-called 'City of Atlantis', from which there was supposed to be a lost race who had escaped before the island sank into the sea, forcing the islanders to migrate and found some of the leading cultures of the ancient world. But, 'The description of Atlantis given by Plato appears to be implausible ... there is no geological evidence that such islands even existed.[10]

Nevertheless, most people become enchanted by mysteries to the point of obsession, and the legend fitted neatly into Hitler's delusion that, whereas post-war Germans were reviled as war criminals and losers in the Great War, they were really a race of supermen who were born to conquer the world. It was sheer wishful thinking by an unbalanced mind. But some cultures have a high regard for the delusions of so-called 'Holy Fools' who find ways out of seemingly impenetrable dilemmas.

Despite proven histories of Europe and Africa, there were still plenty of question marks with only little dots for lost civilisations and newly discovered areas by explorers like Winwood Reade.[11]

The dots, which could have represented facts or fiction, that Hitler wished to join were the German-speaking tribes. He knew from his meetings in Munich's beer cellars that unemployed and bitter ex-servicemen and the marginalised millions of German society wanted their dignity restored and their guilt and shame swept aside by a fantasy from a demagogue or a mystical prophet, even a science fiction writer, all rolled into one possible saviour. They wanted someone who could provide jobs and give them a sense of purpose. Hitler knew what he was doing for superstitious and impressionable audiences when he interspersed his paragraphs in *Mein Kampf* with apocalyptic imagery. It had worked when evangelical preachers used it to prepare the gullible for the end of the world. Although it gave an eerie quality to his narrative, it was intended to unleash superstitious and violent people in his constituency who were drawn to *Sturm und Drang* (Storm and Stress) and *Gotterdammerung* (Catastrophic Violence and Disorder).

He warned readers that the alternative to supporting him would be an unpopulated planet orbiting through the ether, as it had been millions of years ago. His conduct, he claimed, was 'in accordance with the will of the Almighty Creator'. He even claimed that he was 'defending the handiwork of the Lord'.[12]

The publisher he approached believed there was no market for the book, and decided not to publish it. Its author's stubborn nature made him persist in quoting extracts whenever he spoke in public, so that his views and intentions became known to others than the 100,000 Nazi Party members who already knew his claims; and 'they were also known to the 850,000 Germans who had voted for him'.[13]

Six months after the election, he began arguing in his speeches that the half a million Jewish citizens who lived in Germany should be driven out. That was how Germany became conditioned for another world war.

30

Balancing the Budget
1925–26

At the same time as Hitler was complaining about his personal failures in *Mein Kampf*, Winston Churchill presented his third budget as Chancellor on 11 April 1927, and Prime Minister Baldwin was happy to report to the King that Mr Churchill was a star turn with the power to attract attention that no one in the House of Commons could excel.

More people were buying motor cars, but they were still a luxury that most people could not afford. So he raised taxes on imported motor car tyres and imported wines, and increased existing taxes on tobacco and matches. Who could possibly argue with taxing inessentials? Even his old enemies were impressed. The Conservative MP Lord Winterton wrote to a friend that Churchill as Chancellor had suddenly acquired tact, patience, good humour and banter – now he was friendly and accessible to everyone, both in the House and in the lobbies – he had become what he never was before the war, 'very popular in the House generally'.

He was cartooned as 'Winsome Winston' and 'the Smiling Chancellor'. Baldwin even regaled the King with Churchill's 'cheerful and buoyant optimism', adding, 'His enemies will say that this year's budget is a mischievous piece of manipulation and juggling with the country's finances, but his friends will say that it is a masterpiece of ingenuity.'

In the meantime, Winston was working on a scheme to abolish local rates, in order to relieve British industry and Britain's farmers of the burden, at a time of increasing unemployment and falling revenues from shrinking trade. He intended to balance the budget figures by taxing petrol and profits: he required £50 million. But he needed to stimulate industry and agriculture, to 'lift us above the ruck of current affairs', as he explained to Baldwin on 6 June.

Churchill was sufficiently encouraged to develop more plans throughout the summer at Chartwell, his old Elizabethan manor house on 80 acres that had already served him so well as a meeting place for leaders of industry and nations. He continued to build brick walls there as part of his reconstruction scheme, organising the landscaping with dams and ponds. He relaxed occasionally by painting watercolours. He also began to write an autobiography of his early years as a young army officer and an ambitious young Member of Parliament, feeling confident that a ready audience would want to know about his early life of twenty-five years ago, since when so much had already changed.

If he seemed unconcerned at any possibility of rising dangers from across the Channel, he would not have been the first Chancellor to discover that when a nation focused exclusively on the welfare of its own people at home, it generally failed to notice storm clouds gathering from over the border or across the Channel. It was rare for a nation's budget to stretch to preparing for war as well as footing the bills for its citizens' welfare in peacetime.

Clementine was knocked over by a bus in London during the summer and left 'badly shaken'. She spent six weeks in Venice to recuperate, while he dictated paragraphs of his memoir at Chartwell. In between bouts of working, he and his brother Jack listened to music on the wireless, which was still a novelty. He was very fond of his younger brother, who kept modestly in the background. Winston fished for salmon and hunted in Scotland with the Duke of Westminster, then joined Clementine in Venice in October, where he painted and carried on writing his memoir.

A letter that the successful entrepreneur of Britain's pottery industry, Josiah Wedgwood, wrote to a friend, showed that Prime Minister Baldwin relied more and more on Winston because he was exhausted and probably ill, and may retire before the next election, 'and advise the King to send for Churchill'.

Winston left Clementine in Venice to return to Chartwell to develop his derating plan. So far, he had been unable to find the funds he needed to pay for it. He had hoped to make cutbacks at the Admiralty, but Neville Chamberlain opposed the cuts, while Treasury officials warned him that money could not be taken from the amounts required to pay down the national debt. Nevertheless, he was optimistic about 'the growing strength of the country'. He tried out his plan first on Baldwin, then on Chamberlain, who reminded him that a tax on motorists 'would antagonise a growing slice of the electorate'. Nevertheless, the funds had to come from somewhere if he reduced rates and taxes.

The following January, an undergraduate at Oxford was among the guests at Chartwell. He later described how, after dinner was over, Churchill entertained them all for two hours with a demonstration on the dining table, with the tablecloth removed, of how the Battle of Jutland had been fought in the last war. They were all fascinated when Winston became as excited as a schoolboy, by barking for the gunfire and providing gun smoke with his cigar.

The following morning he was hard at work again, dictating his memoir as he paced back and forth across the room. He fished in the lake with his waders in the afternoon.

A Modest Sense of Achievement

Germany signed the Locarno Treaty on 16 October 1925, to become an equal partner with Britain, France, Belgium and Italy, with its borders guaranteed, just as were the frontiers of Western Europe. Germany, France and Belgium undertook not to attack or invade each other's territory or make war against each other. It was three months after *Mein Kampf* was published in German without causing a stir.[1]

CHURCHILL'S CHALLENGES, 1918–1940

Unresolved disputes would be arbitrated by the Council of the League of Nations. In the event of a breach of the pledge, each of the other nations undertook immediately to come to the aid of the other one, against whom belligerence had been directed, just as soon as that nation was satisfied that the violation was an unprovoked act of aggression, and that immediate action was necessary by reason of crossing a frontier or engaging in hostilities, or the assembly of armed forces in a demilitarised zone.[2]

Those undertakings – together with the Geneva Protocol outlawing war – at last offered security for a world hoping to return to the tranquility and joy, and the levity of the Edwardian Era. Similar treaties were linked with the security of the borders of Poland and Czechoslovakia.

That there appeared to be more and more conflicts between conservative forces and reformists, or rebels, came as no surprise, since that was why such treaties were thought necessary; particularly in South American and Central American countries. On a more sinister note, it was alleged that Soviet Russia had a base just over the border from the United States, in Mexico.

Women were now seen to participate more in national life. The first woman mayor was appointed in Belgium, and the first woman state governor in the United States. In Britain, the statue of Eros was erected in the middle of London's Piccadilly Circus to become a national monument to love.

An important milestone in the United States, with its inheritance of racism, was the popularity of Paul Robeson when he gave his first public recital of Negro spirituals. Motor cars had now become a necessity in North America, with its extensive rural areas and rambling roads of dust between farmland. Deaths from motor car accidents in the United States had now become commonplace, with 17,671 Americans killed in road accidents in one year alone. The increasing numbers of drivers and their passengers created a need for motels near some of the busier highways. But Britain was much smaller, and its extensive transport systems made private cars less essential.

Those symptoms of increasing economic growth and personal wealth resulted in a peaceful pause in life, in which some nations enjoyed a moment of relaxation to rejoice in the rising standard of post-war living. Even so, there were the usual conflicts between unhappy individuals and self-righteous activist groups and nations, which continued unabated.

'What an enormous waste and loss two months' coal strike must mean,' wrote Gertrude Bell from Baghdad to her mother on 30 June. 'It is amazing that the world seems to go on just the same – Ascot and parties are what I read of in *The Times*.'

There was no sense that this moment of bliss might be just another interval between wars, which history showed were normal events of life.

Winston Churchill had grown up in just such an optimistic cultural environment, as the prosperous and dignified Victorian era had merged gently into the more relaxed and leisurely Edwardian England, where the sun always seemed to be shining on tinkling teaspoons and gleaming cups and saucers scattered on garden tables on the rear lawn, with fingers of toast and honey attracting the gently buzzing bees from the flowerbeds. Such idyllic visions had been woven into nostalgic words by the romantic war poet Rupert Brook, who had died young in the last war.

Churchill would certainly have known of the frustrations of the scholarly philosopher-emperor Marcus Aurelius, who had been forced to battle continuously against envious neighbours who wanted to steal parts of the Roman Empire. Nevertheless, it would have been easy to conclude that Britain had reached a reasonable plateau in its lifestyle in 1925, on which Britons could one day reflect with a modest sense of achievement. It was not exactly a Golden Age in the pre-war Edwardian sense, but at least the political and economic formulas of Lloyd George and Winston Churchill had seemed reasonable enough to most people, who easily dismissed the uneasiness emanating from Germany and the continent of Europe on the far side of the English Channel with a casual flip of the hand. Now, for a moment at least, it was time to enjoy the ordinary pleasures of daily life.

31

Living Space
1925–26

Churchill always moved with the times, and was frequently ahead of them. He enjoyed change and welcomed modernity. He also understood the need for mass entertainment, and would use the BBC later on for broadcasting his speeches and extolling the virtues of English democracy. But what *were* the times he moved in? For one thing, much of the wealth being created in Britain and the United States was initiated by immigrants who had arrived at Britain's docks at the end of the past century with nothing more than their energy and new ideas, or specialised skills, and their ingenuity and determination to succeed. They saw plenty of opportunities, and were eager to take initiatives.

Most people in pre-war England had limited themselves to traditional and fairly narrow routine, mixing only with their own social class, with whom they shared the same values, customs and familiarity. Being thrown into a large-scale war in 1914–18 had changed that. It had once been commonplace for children to be told, 'Don't speak unless you are spoken to.' It had contributed to the typical English reserve. Now new technologies suddenly emerged – like affordable motor cars, gramophones, wireless and telephones and motorised public transport. The opening of new cinemas, cafés, hotels and dance halls, loosened social customs even more by drawing people closer together in a spirit of polite intimacy. Popular novelist E.M. Forster, who wrote about class distinctions and their hypocrisies, advised, 'Only connect …'

More and more people had become accustomed to greater leisure time. Railways and the handiness of telephones reduced distances by keeping friends, family, and lovers, more closely in touch; even though they kept conversations short and to the point, because they had been accustomed to respect people's time and privacy. Telephones were unfamiliar new instruments from which people preferred to distance themselves from such intimacy with others. Despite that, each new technology drew people closer together.

New entertainments helped to lift the grief over the war, which still hovered in the atmosphere. They raised people's spirits. Telephones began to be installed in more homes, with 12 million in service in Britain by 1925. Those without a phone connection could use bright red public telephone kiosks, which had begun to be installed in country areas and near busy traffic intersections from 1921, with automatic coin boxes for payment.

The British Broadcasting Company had been established three years previously, and had already achieved a reputation for the dependability of its news broadcasts. Dance music and dance halls were 'all the rage'. The year 1925 welcomed people to a modern age of self-indulgence; to tea dances between four in the afternoon and seven o'clock at tea rooms; to restaurants and hotels with palm court orchestras. Part of a new social agenda included Pernod cocktails and pink gins for those who could afford them. Popular Lyons Corner House restaurants served food on several floors late into the night in prime West End locations, where busy waitresses wriggled in between tables that bustled with the excited voices of regular customers and strangers.

Good times brought population explosions to life in the West. The first popular ballroom dance halls had already opened in Britain in 1919. Some 11,000 dance halls and night clubs opened in Britain between then and 1926. Their dance floors were packed with the swirling bodies of strangers connecting with each other. Cinemas and dance halls were the two most popular forms of entertainment. All it required to participate was the modest price of a ticket.

Cinemas became the most influential innovation of all at this time, because audiences began to imitate Hollywood's stars. The talkies were almost ready to herald a new age of impulsive conversation and quick wit. Winston Churchill would become an ardent movie fan, and even think of writing for the cinema when the industry burgeoned. It provided a window on American values and customs that brought the United States closer to the British Isles than ever before. Its influence on British attitudes and lifestyles was transforming.

Britain was not slow to develop its own small film-making industry. And Churchill was not slow in becoming associated with the Hungarian Korda brothers, who would become one of the leading British film-makers later on. Film director and producer Alexander Korda was in Hollywood in 1926, while Alfred Hitchcock directed his first film in England in 1925, to show that he was a master of suspense. Oscar Deutsche, a second-generation Jewish immigrant from Hungary, chose film distribution instead of film-making, by planning to open his first cinema in the Midlands; then founded a chain of 258 Odeon Cinema throughout Great Britain. Three thousand cinemas would soon operate throughout the British Isles.

Like the normalcy that seemed to have returned in Germany's Weimar Republic, Britain too seemed to be returning to something approaching a leisurely way of life with more opportunities and more exciting entertainment than had existed ever before.

Hitler's Grievances

The sights and sounds of the British public enjoying a resurgence in the economy and a comfortable socialising lifestyle by 1926, should have lasted longer, had it not been for a book written by an embittered German rebel who had been locked up in Landsberg Prison, west of Munich. *Mein Kampf* had been published quietly the previous year in Germany. So far its readership was too small to impress or influence anyone. But it was like a time bomb waiting to detonate.

The German economy had stabilised while Hitler was still out of circulation. He was favoured with plenty of fawning guests who visited him in prison to show their support. It was difficult to know what was happening in Germany. But if Britain was blessed with an increasing population due to its enhanced living standards, Germany was cursed with a burgeoning population that Hitler claimed required more *Lebensraum* (Living room). Novelist and poet D.H. Lawrence would soon write home from Germany about what he saw. He had been influential enough socially to be invited to join the Cosmic Circle of intellectual German friends, including the knowledgeable feminist Frieda von Richthofen, and sociologist Max Weber, who discussed heatedly what was happening in the Weimar Republic. They argued about patriarchy, feminism, Prussian militarism, the centralisation of power, and much more.[1]

Lawrence wrote that life there appeared to have 'retreated eastward ... As if the Germanic life were slowly ebbing away from contact with Western Europe, ebbing to the deserts of the east ...' It was still too soon to know exactly what he meant.

> The moment you are in Germany, you know. It feels empty, and, somehow, menacing. A fear of the invisible natives ... The positivity of our civilisation has broken. And there is no work – consequently no money. Nobody buys anything, except absolute necessities. The shopkeepers are in despair. And there is less and less work. Up to the Annaberg, the suburb, the lines are rusty, no trams ever go. The people can't afford the ten Pfennig for the fare. Ten Pfennigs is an important sum now: one penny ...[2]

He depicted a bleak, empty and menacing future. Germany was now looking east with acquisitive longing and thieving eyes, to the empty spaces on the map of Russia. It was likely that Lawrence had already read *Mein Kampf,* in which Hitler wrote in his fourth chapter, 'We ... turn our gaze towards the land in the east. At long last we break off the colonial and commercial policies of the pre-War period and shift to the soil policy of the future.'[3]

By 'soil policy' he meant his demands for more living space for Germany's fast-expanding population, who wanted to seize the entire territory of Soviet Russia, not by a benign method, but by slaughtering the entire population of Slav peasants after using them as slave labour, and annexing their land.

32

Consolidating Power
1926–27

The return to gold in Britain while Churchill was Chancellor may have contributed to inflation and unemployment, which devastated the coal industry in particular.[1] Nevertheless, he continued in office as Chancellor to present five budgets in all. He managed to reduce the age for the start of pensions from seventy to sixty-five, and provide widows pensions immediately they were needed. He reduced income taxes and imposed taxes on luxury items.[2] He also reduced military expenses, and planned to establish a legal minimum wage.[3]

The situation looked altogether rosy for Britain's middle and upper classes, with plenty of their newfound wealth making its way into the hands of other classes, particularly in the service sector with far more jobs created for women typists and shop assistants, and in the growing numbers of hotels and restaurants as a result of the growing economy. J. Lyons and Company alone provided thousands of jobs, as the leader in the catering industry, and also by producing its own canned and packaged branded goods.

It was not the case in other European nations. Poland was in its usual indecisive state of disorganisation with the appearance of another dictator – a familiar and benevolent one who had led his troops against Russia in the Great War and remained unscathed after being a prisoner of war. It was the former socialist Josef Piłsudski, a battle-hardened general who had only contempt for the leaders of the Polish government because, as he told them bluntly, they behaved like children.

Poland needed a strong leader against the land-hungry Germans over one border, and the territorial Russians who pressed against their frontier. Piłsudski was still unharmed after battling with Polish parliamentary forces in which 300 Poles were killed, before he returned to Warsaw and formed a new government. After rejecting the position he was offered as president, which, he said, did not provide enough powers, he appointed himself minister of war, then transformed himself into Poland's prime minister five months later.

Stalin emerged as the General Secretary of the Communist Party in January 1926. He had won the struggle for power after Lenin's death. As awareness of his tight control of Party affairs spread, opposition leaders met secretly to plan how to get rid of him. But Stalin – like Piłsudski –had always survived by being a step ahead of his enemies. He countered their move in the old-fashioned way, by having all his critics discredited as enemies of the State.

Trotsky was the main speaker at a Moscow factory on 1 October, where Zinoviev attacked Stalin for having betrayed the revolution. Stalin acted at once by warning opposition leaders to toe the Party line. He had Trotsky expelled from the Politburo and Kamenev struck off the list of possible future members, then summoned them to speak at the Fifteenth Congress of the Communist Party of the USSR, where the majority overwhelmingly supported Stalin. By the beginning of 1927, members of the Bolshevik old guard who had opposed Stalin had lost their positions and influence.

Despite opposition, Trotsky openly criticised the Comintern policy set by Stalin for not pressing for a world revolution. Stalin retaliated by removing him from the only remaining Soviet committee of which he was an executive member. He failed to recognise that his days were numbered under Stalin's ever-watchful and unblinking gaze.

Dissent within the Party was examined and discussed by the Central Committee on 28 July. It brought competitors for power into the open, so that they could be more easily destroyed. Opposition by eighty-three Communist Party members was set out in a formal declaration and supported by Trotsky. Stalin hesitated to expel them all, because of their wide support. Nevertheless, expulsions from the Party began in October when he denounced Trotskyism as an 'anti-Soviet' force. Twenty people were shot without trial that winter as an example that Stalin would not tolerate opposition.

Italian Posturing

Mussolini, too, was busy consolidating his power. Nation and nationalism were words he repeated in his speeches for some time. He made striking illegal. Italy's negative trade balance ensured that his fascist regime imposed economies and tightened the fascist fist. From now on the state would control associations of workers and of employers, and any labour disputes. There would be far less spending on luxuries. No new licences would be issued for cafés, dance halls, or restaurants. Luxury housing would be replaced by mass construction of tract housing for lower and middle classes. Italians would be instructed to buy local products rather than imported goods. Meanwhile, the amount of Lira currency in circulation would be reduced to strengthen its buying power.

A great deal of publicity was made of Mussolini's continued successful attempts to increase the harvest. The annual yield was already much greater than before.[4] The 'Battle for Grain' was intended to make Italy self-sufficient, so that it could reduce imports.

Churchill met Mussolini in Rome in the early part of 1927 and praised his stand against communism. Since neither Mussolini nor Hitler had revealed the trump cards up their sleeves, Churchill had no reason to believe that they were not genuine patriots doing their best to stabilise their countries.[5]

Even Churchill could be taken in at that stage of the rise to total power of the two dictators, by giving them the benefit of any doubts when writing about them: 'Although no subsequent political action can condone wrong deeds, history is replete with examples of men who have risen to power by employing stern, grim, and even frightful methods, but who, nevertheless, when their life is revealed as a whole, have been regarded as great figures whose lives have enriched the story of mankind. So may it be with Hitler.'[6]

There was speedy Italianisation of territories in the South Tyrol that Austria had lost to Italy in the war. Mussolini also made haste to sign a treaty of friendship with Spain, with regard to 'mutual defence in Africa', meaning that both military forces still faced tribal uprisings among Arabic-speaking peoples in Italian Libya and Spanish Morocco. He signed a treaty with Yemen in September to challenge Britain's influence in Aden.[7] He signed other treaties with Romania, Greece, Albania, and Germany, since his anti-communist stance enabled those who might otherwise have been repelled by his fascist regime to turn a blind eye to it. The Catholic Church was particularly upset by the suppression of religious worship in Soviet Russia, and at the constantly repeated denunciation by Marx that religion was the 'opium of the people'.[8]

Mussolini strengthened his power by suppressing all opposition newspapers. He placed 522 political opponents under preventative detention. Democratic elections were abolished, including the system for electing mayors. In future, a list of candidates would be submitted to the government, which would make its own choices.

Britain and the United States

On 26 January 1926, a shy and withdrawn inventor named John Logie Baird undertook an experiment in secret to transmit his new invention, which would be known as 'television'. But when his television sets were commercialised, they turned out to be too expensive for most customers. But every year of Queen Victoria's past reign had involved more and more people who shared in Britain's wealth.[9]

In spite of all kinds of improvements to Britain's economy, the population was still divided into two nations. Although living standards in Britain had been poor in the earlier part of the Queen's reign, they had been far better than in most other European countries. Comfort provided a feeling of cheerful inclusiveness. Coal miners were still the exception.

Britain had once produced half of Europe's coal and a fifth of the world's coal needs. It had exported over 34 per cent of its production.[10] And it had all been done by brawn, with no more sophisticated technologies than picks and shovels. The continuing problem was based on the owners' desperate need to compete with the more mechanised coal industry in the United States. Britain had been selling all it could export when demand for coal had risen all over the industrialised world, so it had not bothered to install new technologies for digging it out of the mines. Employment had more than doubled then from 439,000 to 910,000. Profits had nearly trebled to £28 million in 1913.'[11]

That was the conundrum: why invest in costly new technologies and modern management, and pay good money for disruptive reorganisation of the pits? Now the United States had become the biggest supplier in the world, it was too late. Productivity in Britain had fallen from 403 tons per miner per year in 1881, to 309 tons in 1911.[12] It left mine owners and coal miners alike feeling scared about the future.

After years of exploitation, the miners' attitude was to dig in their heels and fight for their rights.[13] But human rights and justice had nothing to do with the realities of the marketplace.

In the United States, on the other hand, 1926 had been a bumper year for the collection of wartime debts. America had become a new-rich nation. Profits and productivity in the US economy had reached record heights. They were even criticised in Europe, particularly in France, where 20,000 war veterans, many blind or crippled, or both, paraded through Paris to protest. Clemenceau, still a 'Tiger' at eighty-five, wrote an open letter to President Coolidge, criticising America's 'hardness'. He was answered in America by Senator Borah, Chairman of the Senate Foreign Relations Committee, who remarked sarcastically that if France wanted to cancel debts, they should cancel reparations from Germany as well.

The Americas

The United States signed a treaty with Panama to secure control of the Panama Canal. Where the United States scored in particular was with its involvement in the sphere of science, with more than seven hundred graduates of the Massachusetts Institute of Technology (MIT). In the same year that German scientists were experimenting with chemical warfare in Soviet Russia, American scientists of the US Naval Department launched a wireless-controlled aeroplane that could blow up a target with explosives from a distance of 35 miles.

President Coolidge – no doubt inflated by American successes – retorted to snide remarks about America's new-rich status by saying that there was more hope for the progress of true ideals in the modern world from a new-rich nation than from chronically poor ones. 'I see no need to apologise for it. Honest poverty is one thing,' he said, 'but lack of industry and character is quite another.'

'They tell me we are not liked in Europe,' he added. 'Such reports are undoubtedly exaggerated and can be given altogether too much importance. We are a creditor nation. We are more prosperous than some. This means that our interests have come within the European circle where distrust and suspicion, if nothing more, have been altogether too common.'[14]

Class conflicts inside the United States persisted, and were far more passionate and violent than in Britain. As well as from striking workers, it came even more violently from its large organised criminal element, which had continually disrupted normal life since Prohibition had been established.

On 30 May 1927, a thousand so-called 'knights' of the Ku Klux Klan, and 400 women members of the Klavana, paraded through New York City in their white masks and caps and gowns. The crowd of onlookers was hostile to them all along the 4 miles of streets. Police clashed with the Klan throughout the day and battled with members who refused to leave afterwards.

The first show of violence had come when two Italian members of the fascist movement on their way to join 400 other black-shirted fascists in the Memorial Day parade were attacked by anti-fascist groups and murdered. According to the *New York Times*, 'the "Black Shirts" are in direct communication with their leader in Rome, and are, in this country, opposed to Americanism.'[15]

The previous custom of lynching innocent black men continued in the South where sixteen blacks were lynched. Police prevented further lynching in forty-two other heated situations.

Captain Charles Lindbergh made a record flight across the United States in 1927. Eight days later he flew non-stop from New York to Paris. It was the first solo flight across the Atlantic. He was twenty-four years old, and became an overnight American hero. Although it was eight years after the famous flight by the English pilots Alcock and Brown, from Newfoundland to Ireland, its significance was that it came a month after America's first television transmission. It was also a time when commercial flights were being considered seriously, and established the idea that aircraft were safe for civilian passengers.

China Exploited

Most people in England and America were unaware of the struggle for Chinese independence from foreign occupation. There was fighting everywhere on the continent of China, and the war between north and south had intensified in the past year. A number of provincial warlords and the Nationalist Party in Canton gained more territory, while pro-Japanese forces in Peking were driven out by the combined tactical forces of bombing by air and infantry advances by Manchurian troops led by Marshal Chang. At the end of 1923, Stalin had sent an emissary from Moscow to bind the *Kuomintang*, with its leader, Sun Yat-sen, to the Soviet communists, who would provide Soviet military instructors in exchange.

China had been exploited by European governments and Japan. Now all the different Chinese military factions were determined to take control of their own country away from foreign nations. But there was confusion on all sides by different forces with different aims – to drive out the Japanese; or to set up a nationalist government; or remove all foreigners; or to impose a Chinese communist government; or to ally with Soviet Russia; or simply to obtain power as an independent warlord. After the Nationalist General Chiang Kai-shek's troops had captured Changsa in August, he announced, 'If we want our revolution to succeed, we must unite with Russia to overthrow imperialism.'

He was scornful and distrustful of the Chinese communist leader, Mao Zedong.

Anti-foreigner riots continued to erupt again and again in China in 1927 – mostly against the British who attacked its treaty ports, like Hankow and Kiukiang. Six British traders were murdered in Nanking. A division of British troops was sent to the Far East to retaliate, and foreign warships on the Yangtse River fired on the city. American, French, Italian and Japanese governments sent naval reinforcements. But Chiang Kai-shek established his own government in Nanking and negotiated with the foreign governments to keep them at bay.

In spite of all the military and political activities taking place outside the British Isles, of which most Britons were unaware, Churchill, in his official position as Chancellor was engaged mostly with home affairs. Even they did not include any part in Stanley Baldwin's negotiations with the coal miners or owners that led to the 1926 General Strike, although he wrote to Baldwin with advice for a final settlement.[16] His responsibility was still to take care of Britain's Treasury.

33

A Clash of Cultures

"We are lucky to be German," wrote economist Franz Oppenheimer to his wife when visiting the backward coal mining region of Galicia in Austria. Germany seemed more civilized and orderly than most other nations in Central and Eastern Europe, despite all its shortcomings. It was said that 5,000 Galician Jews starved to death annually.[1]

Heartfelt remarks of that kind from German-Jews were not unusual before and soon after the First World War, although difficult to credit now with historic hindsight of what was about to happen. Reasons for that genuine sentiment were twofold. In the first place, they knew from experience what hall-holes existed elsewhere in Europe, and what twisted beliefs and cruelties still remained in most other countries where medieval customs and superstitions were still rife. On the other hand, Jews had been successful in establishing careers and making their homes in burgeoning and exciting cities like Berlin, Munich, and Vienna, that vibrated with intelligent conversation and purposefulness.

Despite all the signs of economic chaos in Germany's postwar Weimar Republic, corruption in government, a politicized police force that sided with criminals, and open gangsterism and assassinations in the streets, it was perfectly reasonable to recognise that there were even worse places. Surprisingly - despite its Prussian customs of giving and taking orders instantly without question, while snapping to attention and clicking the heels - each of the three major Central European cities had become reservoirs of a more literary, musical and artistic nature. Such culture was met with raised eyebrows by less appreciative military types who found the postwar changes to modernization incomprehensible. They read little or nothing, and sneered at Jewish culture.

The vitality and industry of the Weimar Republic came about from a clash of two very different cultures: one productive, the other destructive. Weimar bubbled over with imagination and creativity. The source of most of the energy injected in the economy emanated largely from the Jewish community.

> When we think of Weimar, we think of modernity in art, literature, and thought; we think of the rebellion of sons against fathers, Dadaists against art, Berliners against beefy philistinism, libertines against old-fashioned moralists; we think of *The Threepenny Opera, The Cabinet of Dr. Caligari, The Magic Mountain,* the *Bauhaus,* and the New Woman

exemplified in the saucy Marlene Dietrich. Above all, we think of the exiles who exported Weimar culture all over the world.[2]

Compared with all that deep thought and literary culture, the Prussians had increased their territory and power for centuries – since the days of the armoured Teutonic Knights – by means of a policy of "blood and iron" against their neighbours, in a firm belief that the weak were the natural victims of the strong. Set against that rigid attitude which persisted in the twentieth century, were the deep-seated ethics of the Jews, which were based on human rights, justice for all, and awe for life.

The German Democratic Party was founded in November 1918 by an outstanding group with brilliant minds. Many were Jews. They included the scientist Albert Einstein, Walther Rathenau, historian Hans Delbruck, lawyer Hugo Preuss, and sociologist Max Weber, in Theodor Wolff's office. Wolff edited the *Berliner Tageblatt* newspaper. Few made the deadly mistake of entering politics after Rathenau was assassinated in the streets in an open vehicle. But, when Germany's Jews were still supposed to be equal citizens in the Weimar Republic, Otto Landsberg was Minister of Justice and Hugo Preuss was Minister of the Interior in the first Cabinet. In that streak of postwar optimism Jews were no longer outsiders - in theory, at least. As far as they were concerned, their so-called Jewishness, whatever that wa, had been erased from their minds and sensibilities. They were Germans first and foremost, and felt it far more important to be responsible and proud citizens of the fatherland. It was thought that class barriers and the hurdles of ethnicity and religion no longer applied after the collapse of rigid and old-fashioned empires in 1918. Rathenau's assassination by a paramilitary group would change that attitude.

Foreign Minister Walther Rathenau was murdered in the streets on June 24, 1922, when his open car was overtaken by another open vehicle on the *Königsalle,* from which several pistol shots were fired. The bullets entered his chin and spinal cord. He died before a doctor could arrive.

Rathenau was only one of 354 victims of political assassinations by right-wing extremists after the war.[3]

The Golden Age of the Weimar Republic had been initiated very largely by German-Jews who possessed a sense of belonging and pride in being German citizens. Germany was where Albert Einstein created his theory of relativity, where German universities were enriched by the minds and skills of Jewish students eager for education, and in the sphere of music, like Schoenberg's compositions. The theatre was galvanized by Max Reinhardt. They were enthusiastic German patriots helping to develop a progressive society and enrich the culture of the world. Walter Rathenau had felt puzzled by his family's traditional but vague Jewish past and never thought of it as a problem. He felt honoured to accept an invitation to become Foreign Minister.

> For a time, Germans created a highly liberal political order with very substantial social welfare programs. The lives of so many ordinary people improved greatly: the working day was reduced to more humane

eight hours, at least in the first year of the republic, and unemployment insurance seemed to herald a new era that would protect workers from the vagaries of the business cycle. New public housing offered better-off workers and white-collar employees the chance to move out of old tenements into modern, clean apartments with indoor plumbing, gas stoves, and electricity. Women won the right to vote, and Germany had a lively free press.[4]

Another type of culture was created in energetic Berlin, which represented the essence of capitalism that energized Germany's economy. It too was led by German-Jews.

"Many of the publishing houses were located in Berlin and the biggest of these, Ullstein and Mosse, were owned by Jewish families. So were such distinguished publishing houses as Samuel Fischer's. Many of the journalists who wrote for their newspapers, many of the editors who edited their magazines, many of the authors who wrote their books, were Jews as well."

So were the drama critics and book reviewers, writers of editorials and sports columns. And so were the owners of the great Berlin department stores, like *Kaufhaus des Westens, Tietz, Wertheim*. Jews could be identified in such visible professions as bankers, lawyers, doctors, dentists, the garment and tailoring industries, salesmen and peddlers.[5]

Several new industries like "chemical factories, metal works, electrical, smelting, and printing plants, and mills" were started up by Jewish entrepreneurs. "They established the first German aircraft factory and department store chains and were among the first to introduce American production methods."[6]

The Prussian Military Tradition

German-Jews felt they were right to be optimistic about the postwar Weimar Republic. But the Prussian military cult was not dead. It was only in disarray. The military were still in charge, even if only obliquely. General Ludendorff, who had lost the war for Germany and run away after a failed attempt at revolution, apparently thought he was still fighting the war, despite the armistice. He returned to Germany and claimed that "the Jewish prince" – meaning Rathenau - had sabotaged the war effort. Rioters had cheered him by yelling their enthusiastic support.

Ludendorff claimed that "the Jewish prince" had sabotaged the war effort by accepting the peace terms from the Allies. Rathenau's assassination had been loyally carried out by his followers, the young and mindless sons of Junkers. Since the police, the judiciary, and state bureaucracy were on Ludendorff's side, little action was taken to prevent his terrorist activities. As for Germany's young men, the universities were virtually controlled by the anti-Semitic student fraternities and

Aryan dueling societies that had their own rigid rules and regulations to separate Jews from gentiles.

Rathenau had made the mistake of being conciliatory towards the Allies to enable Germany to obtain a better deal when it came to paying war reparations, whereas Ludendorff claimed that Germany had not lost the war and would not pay a cent. As far as he was concerned, any agreement with the Treaty of Versailles would be viewed as an admission of Germany's war-guilt, for which Germany would be made to pay reparations.

German students showed their barbaric and uncouth nature with its closed Prussian mind by rioting while Einstein was giving a lecture, and shouting "*Juden raus!* Jews out!"

Although the Minister of Culture immediately apologized to Einstein and his wife, who were known as a charming and modest couple, anti-Semitism was a signal that criminality was in the air. The atmosphere was toxic, and was bound to spread like any other lethal military virus.

Most Jews took considerable pride at serving in the Prussian army, although only converts to Christianity were allowed to hold commissions as officers. According to the *Frankfurter Zeitung* in 1909, 20,000 – 30,000 were qualified by their education to become commissioned officers since 1880, but only 300 were.[7]

The organization and power of the German army diehards had not vanished after their defeat in the war. Its military structure had been kept intact. And it continually denied it had lost. According to the generals, they had simply run out of military resources, including young men. It was true. They insisted they had been betrayed by a mysterious array of forces at home – which was false - and appeared to be preparing to fight the war all over again. General Ludendorf, who had lost the war, rebelled at the conditions imposed on Germany by the victorious Allies that prevented him from carrying on fighting a war that the German General Staff and the Kaiser had begun. Although the Kaiser had since fled, the former Chiefs of Staff remained.

Most Jews had become accustomed to the sullen and rebellious nature and crudity of the German rabble, and took little notice while they got on with their lives. Einstein was one of the few who realized that it was impossible to continue living in such an uncivilized country, and left. His departure for America would be an example of how mediocrities rose to fill the gaps left by elites who chose to take their skills to other countries that appreciated them. The result was an overall lowering of standards.

Several days after Rathenau's murder, Maximilian Harden - the editor of *Die Zukunft* - was almost beaten to death with iron bars when attacked in the street. He was one of many who had opposed the political far-right. Both of the Bavarian political activists who attacked him had been paid in cash by Nazi organizers.[8]

There was nothing new in religious, racial and ethnic persecution. All were part of a long history of the jostling of tribes for survival and dominance over thousands of years. Protestants had been terrorized in many Catholic countries to force them out. Catholics had been persecuted in Protestant countries to encourage them to leave. Christians and Jews had been attacked on a multitude of occasions over the centuries in the Middle East, to force them to flee. It had always worked. German-Jews had plenty of warning that they were not wanted in the Weimar Republic, or anywhere else in Germany or Ausreia, but continued to remain because they preferred to be German citizens while failing to understand the rigidness of the Teutonic mind. Part of the reason was that they lived in secure areas never mixed with the trouble-making rabble. Their neighbours were better behaved than the semi-literate mobs and violent antisocial criminals who caused trouble for others in a society in which law and order had broken down.

According to one of the most reliable reports at the time, whatever the residual pockets of anti-Semitism amounted to, and however persistent anti-Jewish prejudices were, in business and society, assimilation had appeared to be proceeding and Jewishness was receding.[9] The initial feeling of postwar optimism among Germany's Jews had still not evaporated and it was a challenge for them to contribute towards improving society in accordance with their sense of progress and German patriotism.

It would eventually prove to have been wishful thinking on his and their part, because of an inability of most Jews to see themselves through the eyes of a huge and hostile class of people who envied Jewish successes in finance, the arts, academia, law, science, and medicine. Professional people struggled to compete with them, while the working classes were jealous of their skills and successes. Such was the incomprehension of the masses – and even most of middle-class Germans – that they seemed unaware that Jewish employers provided millions of jobs, and much of the finance that inflated Germany's economy. In the naïve desire of German-Jews to please, they failed to understand the pettiness and spitefulness of Germans who felt, not only challenged, but diminished and threatened by the success that German-Jews made of their careers and their lives.

When Hitler had been a poor teenager in Vienna, he had been made acutely aware that Austria's leading politicians depended for their success largely on victimizing minorities, because their constituents hated them. There were more Czech migrants than any others. But there were also Slavs and Poles, Italians and Jews. Each of those minorities would be targeted by Hitler in order to rise to political and military power in Germany.

Churchill's Enemies
will be published later in the year.
It describes what led to World War 2
and the Holocaust.

Notes

Preface

1. The author's book on the Arab Rising named *The Passionate Spies* provides a detailed account. (Cune Press, Seattle, 2022).
2. According to historian Andrew Roberts.
3. Otto Rank, *The Myth of the Birth of the Hero*, 1909.

Introduction

1. Winston S. Churchill. The World Crisis. Scribner NY.
2. John Lukacs, *The Duel.* (Tickner, NY, 1991), p.15, p.22.
3. Ibid., p.25.
4. Winston S. Churchill, *Marlborough: His Life and Times* (Scribner, NY, 1933), introduction by Henry Steele Commager, p.xx.
5. Churchill's Private Secretary Montague Browne.
6. Winston S. Churchill. 'Consistency in Politics.'
7. Benjamin Disraeli: 'In those days England was for the few – and for the very few.'
8. Sigmund Freud.
9. Winston. S. Churchill, *The World Crisis 1911–1918* (Free Press, NY, 2005), p.5.
10. Ibid., p.6.
11. Ibid., p.24.
12. In 1913.
13. Winston S. Churchill, *The World Crisis* (Free Press, NY, 2005), pp.251–2.
14. Erica Brenner, *Be like the Fox: Machiavelli's Lifelong Quest for Freedom* (Lane, London, 2017), p.10.
15. Winston S. Churchill, 'The Creed of the Devil:' Churchill between the Two Totalitarianisms. (1917–1945), p.3.
16. Winston. S. Churchill, *The World Crisis* (Free Press, NY, 2005), p.253.
17. Ibid., p.60.
18. Winston S. Churchill, *The World Crisis* (Scribner, NY, 1931), p.xvii.

NOTES

19. Barbara W. Tuchman, *A Distant Mirror* (Knopf, NY, 1978), pp.xiii–xiv.
20. W.S. Churchill, *Marlborough*, introduction by Henry Steele Commager, pp.xxvii–xxviii.
21. Ibid., p.xxviii.
22. Tony Judt & Timothy Snyder, *Thinking the Twentieth Century* (Penguin, UK, 2012), p.146.
23. A list composed by twentieth-century historian Tony Judt includes the French Prime Minister Léon Blum, Rosa Luxemburg, Luigi Einaudi, William Beveridge, Clement Attlee and John Maynard Keynes.

1. Clementine

1. Christopher Hassall. *Edward Marsh, Patron of the Arts* (Longmans London, 1959), p.130.
2. Sonia Purnell, *Clementine, the Life of Mrs Winston Churchill* (Viking NY, 2015), p.11.
3. www.history.com/news/meet-the-woman-behind-winston-churchill
4. Ibid. Sonia Purnell.
5. Ibid. Purnell.
6. Nel, *Mr. Churchill's Secretary*, p.187.
7. Purnell, p.3.
8. Ibid.

2. Pressures of Events

1. As economist John Maynard Keynes described it.
2. Martin Gilbert, *The First World War: A Complete History* (Holt, NY, 1994).
3. Mark Mazower, *Dark Continent: Europe's Twentieth Century* (Knopf, NY, 1998), p.116.
4. *The World Crisis 1911–1918*, p.4.
5. Karl Kantsky, *Outbreak of the World War* (1924), pp.348–350. Translated from the German by Carnegie Endowment for International Peace.
6. Margaret Macmillan, *Paris 1919: Six Months that Changed the World* (Random House, NY, 2003), p.182.
7. Ibid., p.182.
8. Gaston Monnerville, *Clemenceau* (Encyclopaedia Britannica, Paris, 2016).
9. Ibid.
10. Ibid.
11. *Paris 1919*, p.182.
12. War Cabinet minutes, 10 Nov. 1918. WSC CV IV. Part 1, p.412.
13. Public Record Office, Cabinet Papers, CAB 29/28 British empire delegation minutes, 34.
14. *Paris 1919*, p.188.

3. The World Crisis

1. Norman Rose, *Churchill: An Unruly Life* (S&S, London, 1998), p.157.
2. Tony Judt, *Reappraisals: Reflections on the Forgotten Twentieth Century* (Penguin, London, 2008), pp.66–67.
3. Franklin & Shepard, *The Emergence of Rus* (Longman, London, 1996), p.45.

4. The Bolshevik Power-Grab

1. Anthony Cave Brown, *'C:' The Secret Life of Sir Stewart Menzies, Spymaster to Winston Churchill* (Macmillan, NY, 1987), p.142.
2. *Paris 1919*, p.180.
3. *Paris 1919*, foreword by Richard Holbrooke, p.vii.
4. Eric Rauchway, *The Money Makers* (Basic, NY, 2015), p.1.
5. Robin Bruce Lockhart, *Ace of Spies* (Hodder, London, 1967), pp.16–17.
6. Winston S. Churchill, *The World Crisis* Vol. 2 (Scribner, NY, 1923), p.51.
7. Michael Kettle, *Sidney Reilly* (St Martin's Press, NY, 1983), p.11.
8. Winston S. Churchill. *Great Contemporaries* (Butterworth, NY, 1937).
9. W.S. Churchill, *The World Crisis* (Scribner's, NY, 1923–1931). In 5 Volumes.
10. According to the Fabian Socialist Webbs.

5. The Russian Civil War

1. Mikhail Bakunin, 1847. 'Russia is everywhere a synonym for brutal oppression and slavery.'
2. 1897 Russian Imperial Census.
3. But only after 1886. 'The New Colossus' was a poem by American Emma Lazarus (1883).
4. The *Okhrana* (sometimes anglicised in spelling as Ochrana) was a special corps of police formed to investigate all movements organised against the state, and their destruction. Forerunner of the CHEKA, the OGPU, the NKVD and the KGB.
5. Canadian historian Margaret MacMillan in a 2008 online interview.
6. The US also failed to notice Japan's victorious tactic in 1904 of a pre-emptive strike that destroyed Russia's imperial fleet at anchor in Manchuria – a tactic Japan would use again against the US Fleet in December 1941 that took the United States by surprise.
7. Russian Imperial Census (1897).
8. Except for the intelligent and brilliant Empress Catherine the Great who ruled from 1762 to 1796.
9. John Lukacs, *George Keenan: A Study of Character* (Yale, New Haven, 2007). Footnote on p.69.

6. The Warlords

1. Alexander Kazbegi, *Patricide*, 1882.
2. Martin Gilbert, *Winston Churchill; the Wilderness Years* (Macmillan, London, 1981), p.9.
3. Christopher Hassall, *Edward Marsh: Patron of the Arts* Attributed to Conrad Russell: "If I were making a list of sayings that have influenced me." (Longmans London, 1959), p.118.

7. Justice For All

1. Martin Gilbert, *Churchill and the Jews* (Holt, NY, 2007), p.31.
2. Ibid., p.30.
3. Dimitri Pisarev, *The Russian Word* (1862).
4. Joseph Frank, *Dostoevsky* Books III & IV (Princeton, NJ, 1996). Also *Dostoevsky The Prophet,* 2002.
5. Arthur Koestler, *Arrow in the Blue* (Macmillan, NY, 1952), p.165.
6. Dramatised as an opera by Tchaikovsky.
7. Isaak Babel, *Red Cavalry* (1920).
8. *The Brothers Karamazov* (1878–1911).

8. The Soul of Nations

1. Part of Churchill's 1920 speech against The Aliens Registration Act passed in Britain in 1919; Geoffrey Best, *A Study in Greatness* (Oxford University Press, 2002), pp.262–3.
2. *Churchill and the Jews*, p.32.
3. Letter of 9 October 1919: Churchill papers, 16/18.
4. *Sidney Reilly*, p.11.
5. Sir John Graham at the British Foreign Office, *Sidney Reilly*, p.11.
6. *Sidney Reilly*, p.79.
7. Ibid., p.82.
8. Sir Martin Gilbert, *A History of the Twentieth Century* (Morrow, NY, 2002), p.564.

9. Churchill's Obsession

1. Letter of 15 October 1919: War Office papers, 32/5732.
2. Cabinet memorandum, 14 October 1919. Churchill papers, 16/18.
3. For a detailed account read John Harte, *The Greatest Spy* (Cune Press, Seattle, 2022).
4. Hankey diary, 14 Sept. 1919, Hankey Papers. 1/5

5. Richard Toye, *Lloyd George and Churchill* (Macmillan, London, 2007), p.206.
6. *Churchill and the Jews*. Ibid. P. 38.
7. J.M. McEwen, *The Riddell Diaries, 1908–1923* (Athlone, London, 1986), p.267.
8. Richard Toye, *Churchill's Empire* (Macmillan, London, 2010), p.137.
9. *Michael Collins: A Life* (Mainstream, Edinburgh, 1996), p.226.
10. Henry Wilson diary, 23 January 1921, p.1319.

10. The Middle East Upheaval

1. Winston S. Churchill, *Great Contemporaries* (Butterworth, London, 1937), pp.99–100.
2. Michael Korda, *Hero: The Life and Legend of Lawrence of Arabia* (Harper, NY, 2010), p.509.
3. Ibid., p.510.
4. Winston S. Churchill, *Great Contemporaries*, p.97.
5. Ibid., p.98.
6. Ibid. p.99.
7. Michael Korda. *Hero: The Life and Legend of Lawrence of Arabia*. (HarperCollins NY, 2010).
8. Gertrude Bell, Ed. Georgina Howell, *A Woman in Arabia* (Penguin NY, 2015), p.3.
9. Ibid., p.xiii.

11. The Kingmakers

1. Walter Thompson, *Churchill's Bodyguard* (Hodder Headline, London, 2005), p.9.
2. Ibid., p.10.
3. David Fromkin, *A Peace to End All Peace: The Fall of the Ottoman Empire and the Creation of the Modern Middle East* (Holt, NY, 1989), p.25.
4. Kamal S. Salibi, *A Modern History of Jordan* (1993), p.91.
5. Bell, *A Woman in Arabia*, p.207.
6. Ibid., p.209.
7. Colonial Office papers, 935/1/1. And T.E. Lawrence papers.
8. Korda, p.520.
9. The San Remo Conference of former wartime Allies.
10. H. St. John Philby, *Sa'udi Arabia* (Benn, London, 1855), pp.40, 60, 80, 96, 111, 118, 139, 141, 162, 167, 170, 171, 173, 193, 194, 199, 202, 203, 226, 252, 290, 304, 352, 358.
11. Churchill papers, 16/71. T.E. Lawrence letter.
12. *Churchill and the Jews*, p. 46.
13. Ibid., p.47.
14. Gertrude Bell, *A Woman in Arabia*, pp.205–6.

NOTES

15. Scott Anderson, *Lawrence in Arabia* (McClelland Canada, 2013), pp.155–6.
16. Ibid, p.156.
17. Ibid.

12. Feisal's Reward

1. T.E. Lawrence, *The Seven Pillars of Wisdom*, The Battle of Awali (numerous editions).
2. Jewish Virtual Library.
3. Bell, *A Woman in Arabia*, p.217.
4. Korda, p.157.
5. Avi Shlaim. *Three Worlds: Memoir of an Arab-Jew*. (Oneworld London, 2024)
6. David Semple. Ibid.
7. Richard Rhodes. The Making of the Atomic Bomb. (S&S NY, 1986). P. 89.
8. Ibid. pp. 89-90.
9. B.H. Liddell Hart, *Lawrence of Arabia* (Da Capo, NY, 1935), p.372.
10. A quotation from James Elroy Flecker's play called *Hassan*. The sentence ends, 'where even lovers find their peace at last'.
11. Korda, pp.518–9.
12. Winston S. Churchill, *Great Contemporaries*, pp.97–105.
13. *Marlborough*, introduction by Henry Steele Commager, p.xxiii.

13. Gertrude of Arabia

1. Georgina Howell (Ed.), *Gertrude Bell: A Woman of Arabia* (Penguin NY, 2015), p.63.
2. Ibid., p.67.
3. Bell, *The Desert and the Sown* (Dutton, NY, 1907).
4. Bell, *A Woman in Arabia*, p.xi.
5. Ibid., pp.xxv–xxvi.
6. Korda, *Hero*, p.517.
7. Bell, *A Woman in Arabia*, description on frontispiece.
8. Ibid.
9. Bell, p.83.
10. Ibid., p.63.
11. Ibid., p.xvii.
12. By Lawrence, Shuckburgh, and Major Hubert Young, his three senior Middle East Department advisers.
13. *Churchill and the Jews*, p.48.
14. James Barr, *A Line in the Sand*: Britain, France and the Struggle that Shaped the Middle East (Simon & Schuster, London, 2011).
15. Ibid., p.1.
16. Winston Churchill was Colonial Secretary from 16 February 1921 to 19 October 1922.

17. Barr, p.166.
18. Ibid., p.128.
19. Ibid., p.131.
20. Ibid., p.149.
21. DLG to WSC, 22 Sept. 1919, p.868.

14. Churchill's Middle East Ambition

1. Churchill papers, 9/64.
2. *Churchill and the Jews*, p.64.
3. Ibid., p.66.
4. Winwood Reade, *The Martyrdom of Man*, Chapter 1: Egypt (London, 1872), pp.2–3.
5. *Encyclopaedia Britannica*.
6. *Hansard*, Parliamentary Debates, 14 June 1921.
7. WSC to DLG, 23 Sept, 1921, Lloyd George Papers, HLRO, LG F/9/3/87.

15. The Enemy on the Left

1. Winston S. Churchill, *The World Crisis* Vol. 5 (Scribner, NY, 1929), p.181.
2. Ibid., p.259.
3. Historian Peter Fleming.
4. Margaret MacMillan, *Peacemaker: The Paris Conference of 1919 and Its Attempts to End War* (Murray, London, 2001, p.91.
5. Sir Martin Gilbert, *Churchill: A Life* (Holt, NY, 1991), pp.420–1.
6. Philipp Blom, *Fracture* (Penguin, NY, 2015), p.81.
7. Ibid., p.81.
8. Ibid., p.31.
9. Ibid., pp.80–1.
10. Gilbert, *Churchill: A Life*, p.422.
11. Gilbert, *A History of the Twentieth Century*, p.599.
12. Tom Hickman, *Churchill's Bodyguard* (Hodder, London, 2005), p.36.
13. Field Marshal Sir Henry Wilson and Lieutenant General Sir Hugh Tudor. Irish Constabulary bulletin.
14. Source: Irish Constabulary.
15. Thomas Jones, Keith Middlemas (ed.), *Whitehall Diary, Ireland 1918–1925* Vol. III (Oxford Press, London 1971).
16. *Lloyd George and Churchill*, p.223.
17. Hickman, p.30.
18. James Mackay, *Michael Collins: A Life* (Mainstream, Edinburgh, 1996), p.226.

16. Realities and Illusions

1. Gilbert, *Churchill: A Life*, p.459.
2. Hickman, p.41.
3. Martin Gilbert, *Introduction to The World Crisis: 1911–1918* (Free Press edition, NY, 1959), pp.xv–xvi.
4. Hickman, p.41.
5. Ibid., p.66.
6. Ibid., p.44.
7. Ibid., p.45.

17. Political Rivals

1. WSC to DLG, 21 Feb. 1919, p.538.
2. Thelma Cazalet-Keir, *From the Wings* (Bodley, London, 1967), pp.62–64.
3. H.W. Wilson to Lord Northcliffe, 3 April 1919, Northcliffe Papers, British Library, Add. 62201, f.89.
4. Arthur Schopenhauer, translated by T. Bailey Saunders, *Studies in Pessimism* (Lightening Source, UK), p.4.
5. Ford Madox Ford, *The Good Soldier* (Lane, London, 1915).
6. Henry Wilson diary, 20 Jan. 1919, WSC CV IV, Part 1, p.471.
7. Frances Stevenson, A.J.P. Taylor (Ed.), *Lloyd George: A Diary*, p.241 (Entry for 3 Feb. 1922).
8. Sassoon to Esher, 6 March 1922, WSC CV IV, Part 3, p.1794.
9. Richard Toye, *Lloyd George & Churchill* (Macmillan London, 2008), p.228.
10. WSC to DLG, 20 Feb. 1922, WSC CV IV, Part 3, p.1783.
11. Toye, p.157.

18. The Most Terrible Event

1. Hickman, p.39.
2. Gilbert, *A History of the Twentieth Century*, pp.434–5.
3. Ibid., p.628.
4. Ibid., p.629.
5. Ibid., p.630.

19. Troublemakers

1. Toye, p.148.
2. Malcolm MacDonald, *Titans & Others* (Collins, London, 1972), pp.91–2.
3. WSC, memorandum, 25 Oct. 1919, p.939.

4. H.G. Wells, 'Winston', 10 Nov. 1923, in *A Year of Prophesying (Westminster Gazette)*. And (Unwin, London, 1924), pp.52–6.
5. David C. Smith, 'Winston Churchill and H.G. Wells: Edwardians in the Twentieth Century', (1989), pp. 93–116, at 104.
6. Gilbert, *A History of the Twentieth Century*, p.633.

20. Chartwell

1. Russian writer Pavel Amekov who observed Marx in debate in 1846, *Encyclopaedia Britannica*, Britannica.com
2. Paul Johnson, *Intellectuals* (Harper, NY, 1988), p.2.
3. Ibid., pp.204–5.
4. Maurice Baring, *The Mainsprings of Russia* (1914).
5. Walter Allen, *The English Novel* (Penguin, London, 1958), p.290.

21. Social Reengineering

1. Gilbert, *Churchill: A Life*, p.463.
2. Ryszard Kapuscinski, translator: Klara Clowczewska, *Travels with Herodotus* (Vintage, NY, 2007), p.6.
3. Herodotus, *The Histories*, 440 BC.
4. Reade, p.249.
5. Roger Scruton, *Fools, Frauds and Firebrands: Thinkers of the New Left* (Bloomsbury, London, 2015), p.94.
6. Tony Judt, *Reappraisals* (Penguin, London, 2008), p.12.
7. Gilbert, *Churchill: A Life*, p.464.
8. Austen Chamberlain was Neville Chamberlain's half-brother.

22. Hunting Down the Idle Rich

1. Gilbert, *Churchill: A Life*, p.467.
2. Ibid., p.468.
3. Rose, *Churchill: An Unruly Life*, p.175.
4. J.M. Keynes, *The Economic Consequences of the Peace* (Harcourt, NY, 1919).

23. Churchill in the Roaring Twenties

1. Winston Churchill in New York in 1931.
2. Andrew Sinclair, *Prohibition, the Era of Excess* (Little, Brown, Boston, 1963), pp.220–226.
3. Blom, *Fracture*, p.63.

4. Ibid., p.63.
5. Scott Fitzgerald, *The Great Gatsby* (Scribner, NY, 1925).
6. Winston S. Churchill, *My Early Life*, p.326.
7. Ibid., p.179.
8. Andrew Roberts, *Churchill: Walking with Destiny* (Penguin, London, 2019), p.859.

24. A Brilliant Creature

1. Gilbert, *Churchill: A Life*, p.469.
2. Ibid., p.470.
3. Gilbert, *Churchill: A Life*, p.472.
4. Reviewing Celia Sandys new book about her grandfather, Winston Churchill, *Churchill: Wanted Dead or Alive.*
5. Geoffrey Best, *Churchill and War* (Bloomsbury, London, 2005), p.30.
6. Rose, *Churchill: An Unruly Life*, p.181.

25. Bad News from Germany

1. Gilbert, *A History of the Twentieth Century*, p.657.
2. Ibid., p.666.

26. Collective Security

1. Derived from the High German Wuot. Old English word means 'mad, raging, enraged, insane, senseless, and blasphemous'.
2. Gilbert, *A History of the Twentieth Century*, p.434.
3. Ibid., p.687.

27. A Liberal at Heart

1. J. Pearson, *Citadel of the Heart: Winston and the Churchill Dynasty* (Macmillan London, 1903), p.205.
2. Gilbert, *Churchill: A Life*, p.476.
3. Operetta by Sigmund Romberg and Oscar Hammerstein.

28. Winston, a Star Turn

1. Individual unidentified in Thomas Jones, *A Diary with Letters* (OUP, London, 1954), p.xxxii. Corresponding with Amery's diary, 27 March 1952. Amery Papers, Churchill College Cambridge.

2. *Lloyd George & Churchill*, p.253.
3. *Whitehall Diary*, Middlemass, vol. 1, p.303 (entry for 8 Nov. 1924).
4. Hickman, p.47.
5. Lord Boothby, *Recollections of a Rebel* (Hutchinson, London, 1978), p.51.
6. Diana Mosley, *A Life of Contrasts* (Hamish Hamilton, London, 1977), p.40
7. To J.H. Lewis, 16 Feb. 1926. J.H. Lewis Papers, National Library of Wales. A1/293.
8. *Lloyd George & Churchill*, p.257.
9. Strachey, Mosley, and LG.
10. Parliamentary Debates, House of Commons, 5th Series, vol. 187, 6 Aug. 1925, cols. 1610, 1613.
11. Draft Press Statement, 14 Nov. 1927, WSC CV V, Part 1, p.1104.
12. W.S. Churchill, *The Gathering Storm* (Houghton Mifflin, Boston, 1948), p.58.
13. Paul Johnson, *Modern Times* (Harper, NY, 1983), p.132.
14. A.L. Rowse, *The Poet Auden* (Methuen, London, 1987).
15. Johnson, *Modern Times*, p.132.
16. Catherine Radziwill, *Cecil Rhodes: Man and Empire Maker*, p.126.
17. Reade, pp.31–32.
18. From his notes in Oxford in 1877.
19. *Quest for the Unknown Mysteries of the Ancients*, p.26.

29. The Enemy on the Right

1. Koestler, *Arrow in the Blue*, p.176.
2. Gilbert, *A History of the Twentieth Century*, p.695.
3. David Cohen, *The Escape of Sigmund Freud* (Overlook, NY, 2012), pp.149–50.
4. Stephen Kotkin online interview by Peter Robinson about his book, *Joseph Stalin: Waiting for Hitler*, The Hoover Institution, 2019.
5. David Cohen, *The Escape of Sigmund Freud*, p.88.
6. Ibid., p.87. Forster was believed to have been assassinated by the Gestapo after the Nazis rose to power, to conceal Hitler's mental condition and Goering's morphine addiction, which Forster treated.
7. W.S. Churchill, *The Gathering Storm* (Houghton Mifflin, Boston, 1948), p.48.
8. Frederick Nietzsche, *Thus Said Zarathustra* (Ernst Schmeiester, 1883–1891).
9. Kapuscinski, *Travels with Herodotus*, p.137.
10. Richard Williams, *Quest for the Unknown Mysteries of the Ancients* (DK, USA, 1993), p.122.
11. Winwood Reade was sponsored on his trips to Africa by the Royal Geographical Society and kept returning there – on one last occasion as the correspondent for *The Times* to report on the Ashanti Wars.
12. *Mein Kampf*.
13. Gilbert, *A History of the Twentieth Century*, p.445.

NOTES

30. Balancing the Budget

1. Ibid., p.695.
2. Ibid., pp.695–6.

31. Living Space

1. Martin Green, *The Richthofen Sisters* (Basic, NY, 1974), p.7.
2. D.H. Lawrence, 'A Letter from Germany' (1928).
3. Adolf Hitler, *Mein Kampf*, p.654; Paul Johnson, *Modern Times*, p.136.

32. Consolidating Power

1. Roy Jenkins, *Churchill: A Biography* (Farrar Straus, NY, 2001), p.404.
2. Martin Gilbert, *The First World War: A Complete History* (Holt NY, 1994), pp.468–489.
3. Ibid., pp.477–479.
4. Gilbert, *A History of the Twentieth Century*, p.704.
5. Gilbert, *The First World War*, p.480.
6. Winston S. Churchill, *Great Contemporaries* (Butterworth, London, 1937), p.165. Written in 1935.
7. Gilbert, *A History of the Twentieth Century*, p.704.
8. Ibid., p.722.
9. Winston S. Churchill, *The World Crisis*, p.5.
10. Michael P. Jackson, *The Price of Coal* (Croom Helm, London, 1974), p.5.
11. Ibid.
12. Ibid.
13. Correlli Barnett, *The Audit of War* (Macmillan, London, 1983), p.69.
14. Gilbert, *A History of the Twentieth Century*, p.710.
15. *New York Times*.
16. Source: International Churchill Society.

Chapter 33. A Clash of Cultures

1. The Genesis Prize Foundation online, May 2022. Ibid. P. 252.
2. Peter Gay. *Weimar Culture*. (Harper, NY 1970). P. xiii.
3. Amos Elon, *The Pity of It all: A Portrait of the German-Jewish Epoch 1743-1933*. (Holt NY, 2022) P. 370.

4. Eric D. Weitz. *Weimar Germany: Promise and Tragedy*. (Princeton University Press, 2018). P. 2.
5. Ibid. (Holt, NY 2002).
6. Amos Elon. Ibid. P. 265.
7. Amos Elon. Ibid. P. 248.
8. Amos Elon. Ibid. P. 372.
9. Peter Gay. *Freud, Jews and Other Germans*. (Oxford, 1978). P. 169.

Index

A

Abdullah, viii, 45, 53–56, 59–60, 72, 76, 77
Admiralty, xx–xxii, 7, 29, 30, 62, 75, 92, 101, 120, 129, 146, 159
Alexander, xi, 24, 26, 27, 34, 75, 163, 179
Al-Husseini, Amin, 60, 61, 78
Allied shipping, 20
Allenby, General, 14, 40, 43, 46, 59, 63, 78
Alsace-Lorraine, 5, 7
Ambition, v, xii, 4, 22, 29, 44, 49, 56, 61, 71, 76, 96, 98, 102, 133, 153, 154, 182
Anarchists, xx, 93
Ancient Greece, xiv
Anti–Semitism, 16, 33, 34, 104, 174, 175
Anti–Semites, 16
Arab Bureau, 67, 68
Arab Revolt, 46, 49, 55, 56, 58
Archangel, 84
Aristotle, xiv
Arms race, xix, 24, 129
Asquith, Herbert, 2, 29, 75, 90, 91
Asquith, Margaret, 101
Asquith, Violet, vii, 4, 35, 91
Attlee, xvii, 177
Austria, 7–10, 13, 15–18, 95, 122, 135, 137, 167, 171, 175
Austrian Emperor, 7
Austro-Hungarian Empire, xix, 9, 15, 17, 25

B

Babel, Isaac, 33, 34, 179
Bagge, Picton, 37
Baldwin, Stanley, xviii, 72, 90–91, 110, 116–117, 120, 129–131, 136, 142, 145–146, 149–150, 158–159, 170
Balfour, Lord, 69, 115
Balfour Declaration, 40, 42, 54, 71, 78
Banditry, 136, 13
Bank of England, 129, 140
Bavaria, 123, 134, 174
Blood and Iron, 172
Baring, Maurice, 112, 184
Barr, James, 70, 181
Beatty, Admiral, xxii, 128
Bedouin, 45, 55, 57, 67, 78
Battleships, xix, xxii, 101
Bell, Gertrude, v, 50–51, 53, 59–60, 66–69, 160, 180
Bell, Sir Hugh, 50
Berlin, 18, 41, 103, 116, 123, 133–135, 154, 171–173
Biblical Palestine, 54
Black and Tans, 88
Blake, William, 95
Blenheim Palace, xv, 4, 52, 74, 98
Bloody Sunday, 88
Bolshevik Revolution, 15, 19, 31, 43, 92, 94
Bolshevik Russia, 20, 31, 35, 37, 42, 87, 91
Bolsheviks, xx, 13, 27, 31–34, 36, 39, 41–43, 74, 78, 84, 86–87, 96–97

Bolshevism, 12–13, 22, 26–28, 34, 36, 41–44, 86, 94, 98, 115
Boothby, Robert, 149
Bootlegging, 125–126
Bracken, Brendan, 91, 106
British Empire, xiii, xvii, xviii, 15, 28, 31, 43–44, 88, 97, 105–106, 120,
British Intelligence, xx, 20, 67, 85
Brownshirts, 123, 134–135
Brownshirt militia, 123
Buckingham Palace, 99
Budapest, 18
Burke, Edmund, xvii
Byzantine Church, 31

C

Capability Brown, 4
Caporetto, Battle of, 16
Carlyle, xxiv
Chamberlain, Neville, 121, 130–132, 135, 159, 184
Champagne, 125, 126, 127, 128
Chancellor of the Exchequer, 15, 71, 75, 81, 116, 120, 122, 129, 138, 145, 149
Chartwell, v, 101, 110, 116, 125, 142, 144, 146, 158, 159, 184
CHEKA, viii, 41, 87, 138, 178
Chief of Staff, xxi, 9, 10
Christians, 56–5, 67–69, 77, 175
Christianity, 133, 155, 174
Churchill, Clementine, vii, xxvii, 3–5, 22, 52, 75, 77, 80, 91–92, 100–101, 110, 116, 125–126, 129–130, 142, 144, 159, 177
Churchill, Diana, 88, 130, 142
Churchill, John, xiv, xv, 29, 64, 144
Churchill, Mary, 100, 129
Churchill, Lady Randolph, 3, 5, 22, 79
Churchill, Lord Randolph, xiv, xv, xvi, 64, 74, 79, 150
Churchill, Randolph, 88, 129–130, 142, 145
Churchill, Sarah, 142

Churchill, Winston, vi–xxvii, 2–8, 11–15, 20, 22, 24–25, 29–30, 33–34, 37, 40–42, 44–47, 49–54, 60, 62–65, 67–69, 71–72, 74–80, 84–86, 88–91 93–98, 100, 105, 110, 112–114, 116–117, 120–121, 125–128, 131, 135, 137, 142, 144, 146, 149, 151, 153–155, 158–161, 163
Churchill's Enemies, vi, viii, 175
Cinemas, 162, 163
Civil service, 63, 132, 149
Civil War, v, vii, viii, xiv, xxvii, 11, 19, 21, 23, 28, 31, 34–37, 39, 73, 85, 87, 94, 113, 140, 178
Clausewitz, von, xv
Clayton, Sir Gilbert, 50
Clemenceau, 11–12, 19, 39, 47–48, 85, 168, 177
Coalition government, viii, xvii, 46, 75, 91–92, 98–100, 108, 152
Coal mines, 22, 141, 145, 168
Collective security, vi, 13, 138, 141, 185
Collins, Michael, 88–89, 189
Colonial Office, xxv, 2, 42, 44–46, 49, 55, 62, 93
Colonial Secretary, vii, xxvii, 14, 60, 71–72, 94, 181
Communists, vii, 13, 21, 23, 28, 33, 44, 67, 85, 87, 92–95, 98, 101, 111, 113, 121, 123, 129, 136, 138–139, 152, 155, 165–167, 169–170
Communist Manifesto, 93, 111, 121,
Communist Party of Great Britain, 92
Conciliation, 44, 79, 131, 135
Conservative Party, xvi, xvii, xxvi, 14, 30, 75, 90–91, 100, 114, 120, 149, 151
Conspiracy theory, 10, 21, 44, 102, 133
Constantinople, 7, 55, 57, 100
Cossacks, 37–38, 84, 87
Cossack troops, 37, 87
Cox, Sir Percy, 53–54, 59

INDEX

Cremona, 107–108
Cromie, Captain Francis, 41

D

Damascus, 47–49, 51, 55–56, 70, 72
Dance halls, 162–163, 166
Dardanelles, 7, 30, 86, 91, 100–101
Dardanelles Commission, 101
Darwin, Charles, xxv, 97–98,
Deception, xx, 63
Deedes, General Wyndham, 40
Denikin, General, 31, 35, 37–39, 74, 84, 86–87
Democracy, xvii, xviii, 11–12, 24, 94, 105, 108–109, 121, 136, 151, 153, 162
Depression, 20, 95, 130
De Valera, Eamon, 89
Dostoevsky, Feodor, 32–34,
Dreadnought battleships, xxii Dreyfus, Alfred, 12
Dundee, 4, 22, 100
Dzerzhinsky, Felix, viii, 138

E

Eastern Front, 22, 28
Eden, Anthony, 127, 138
Edwardians, xxvi
Egypt, 44–45, 52–53, 77, 79
Einstein, Albert, 172, 174
Engels, Frederick, viii, xxi, 9–94, 110–111
English Industrial Revolution, xviii, 24, 93, 150
Ewing, Alfred, xx

F

Fabian Socialists, 28, 110
Facta, Luigi, 107–108
Fascist Party, 107–108
Fascists, viii, 107–109, 135, 169
Feisal, Emir, viii, 45–51, 53, 55–56, 59–61, 72
Feisal-Weizmann Agreement, 61

First Lord of the Admiralty, xx, 7, 29–30, 75, 101
First World War, xi, xii, xxii, 7, 19, 22, 62, 92, 101, 125, 127, 133, 140, 171
Fitzgerald, Scott, 126
Flapper era, 126
Foreign Office, 37, 41, 45–46, 50, 54, 66, 129, 138
Franco, Colonel, 140, 147–148
Franz Josef, Emperor, 7
Free Trade, 30, 90, 100, 138
French Revolution, 11, 26, 70
Freud, Sigmund, 16–18, 33, 155

G

Gaida, General, 84
Galicia, 18, 39, 171
Gaza, 76
General Election, 4, 22, 90, 114, 116
General Strike, 107, 136, 145–146, 150, 170
Geneva Protocol, 140, 142, 160
German High Command, 8 German–Jews, 171–173, 175
Graham, Sir Ronald, 38
Gibbon, xiv,
Gold Standard, 129, 149
Golden Age, 125, 161, 172
Great Britain, vii, xii, xiii, xv, xvi, xviii, xix, 31, 44, 47, 62, 76, 90, 92, 94, 120–121, 141, 163
Great War, xix, xxi, xxiii, 27, 29, 31, 49, 56, 71, 87, 155–156, 165
Gulags, 28, 102

H

Habsburg Empire, 7–8, 15
Haifa, 76–77
Hamilton, General Sir Ian, xvi, 25, 127–128
Hardy, Thomas, xii, 95
Hashemite dynasty, 53, 55, 60
Hayyil, 51

Hebrew University, 77
Herodotus, xxv, 114
Hindenburg, 133, 152
Hitler, Adolf, ix, xiii, xv, xvii, xxiii, 16, 20, 77, 79, 102, 123, 132–135, 137, 139, 151–158, 163–164, 166–167, 175
Hohenzollern dynasty, 15
Holocaust, vi, 175
Home Secretary, vii, xiii, xx, 20, 29–30, 61, 75, 113, 145–146,
Hozier, Clementine, vii, xxvii, 3, 75
Hozier, Colonel Henry, vii, 3,
Hozier, Lady Blanche, 3, 130
Hussein, Sharif, 53, 55–57, 60, 67–68, 79

I

Ibn Saud, King, viii, 50–51, 59–60
Indemnity, 99, 135
Individualism, 90
Industrial Revolution, xvii, xviii, 22, 24, 93, 141, 150
Inflation, 136, 154, 165
Intellectuals, xxvi, 24, 26, 28, 110, 112–113, 115, 139
Iqhwan, 60
IRA, ix, xx, 88–89
Iranians, 67
Iraq, viii, 8, 40, 45–46, 50–51, 53–55, 58–61, 67–70, 77, 80, 97, 105, 138
Ireland, viii, 23, 42, 44, 57, 77, 80, 87–89, 92, 97, 99, 101, 105, 142, 169
Irish Constabulary, 87–88
Irish Fenians, 20
Islam, 69, 79
Islamists, viii
Isonzo, Battles, 16

J

Japan, xviii, 24–25, 28, 51, 84–85, 101, 121–122, 129, 169–170
Jennie, vii, xiv, 2, 4–5, 22, 79–80, 97
Jerusalem, 53, 60–61, 69, 76–79

Jewish National Home, 8, 34, 40–41, 43, 54–55, 69–70, 80
Jewish people, 31, 34, 38, 40, 43, 69–70, 87, 97
Jews, 16, 18, 31–35, 43, 45, 50, 57, 60–62, 67–69, 75, 77–79, 133, 171–175
Jordan River, 55
Judt, Tony, 115
Jung, Carl, 93, 154

K

Kahr, von, 123, 134
The Kaiser (Wilhelm), xviii, xx, xxii, 8–10, 13, 15, 20–21, 99, 103, 133, 174
Kamenev, 28, 139, 166
Kerensky, Alexander, 24–26
Keynes, John Maynard, 10–11, 20, 122, 129, 150
Kibbutz, 52
Kiel Canal, xx, xxii
Kiev, 39, 87
Kitchener, General, 57, 92
Knox, Colonel, 20, 85,
Koestler, Arthur, 33
Kolchak, Admiral, 36–38, 74, 84–86, 128
Kotkin, Stephen, 154
Krasnov, 84
Kremlin, 28
Krupp, xix, 25, 122
Ku Klux Klan, 169
Kurds, 61, 67–69
Kurdish people, 68

L

Bonar Law, 100
Lawrence of Arabia, T. E., 45–47, 49–50, 52–55, 59–65, 67–68, 72, 164
League of Nations, viii, 13, 40, 60, 70, 135, 138, 140, 142–143, 160
Lebanon, 8, 57–58, 68, 70–72, 79

INDEX

Lenin, viii, 15, 19, 21, 23–24, 26–28, 37–39, 41, 43–44, 73–74, 86–87, 94, 112, 138–139, 152–153, 165
Liberal government, xvi, 107, 121
Liberalism, xvii, 24, 90, 150, 153
Liberals, 30, 32–33, 90–91, 107, 114–115
Liberty, xvii, xviii, 23, 42, 49
Lindemann, Professor, 116, 145
Living room, 164
Lloyd George, David, viii, 12, 13–16, 21–22, 29–30, 35–36, 39–42, 44–46, 49, 54, 59, 62, 69, 74–77, 81, 85–87, 89, 96–100, 114, 117, 121, 149–150, 161
Locarno Treaty, 131, 143, 159
Lossow, General von, 123, 134
Lukacs, John, ix, xiii,

M

Macauley, xiv, xxv, 97–98
MacDonald, Ramsay, xviii, 91, 110, 114, 116–117, 145–146
MacMillan, Margaret, 20, 86
Magyar, 16
Malthus, xxv, 97
Manchuria, 24
Mandate, viii, 8, 40, 42, 48, 54, 60–61, 67, 70, 78
Mann, Thomas, 155
Marlborough, Duke of, xi, xiv, xv, xxv, 4, 29, 64–65, 144
Marigold, 22, 80–81
Martyrdom of Man, The, xiv, xxv, 95, 97, 153
Marx, Karl, viii, xxi, 27, 94, 110–112, 121, 123, 139, 167,
Marxists, Marxism, viii, xxvi, 28, 93–94, 112, 123, 133, 151–152
Mein Kampf, 152, 157–159, 164
Meinerzhagen, 50, 54, 63
Member of Parliament, vii, xii, xxvii, 30, 57, 74, 92, 116, 158
Menzies, Stewart, 19, 127

Mesopotamia, 15, 45, 53, 67–68
Middle East, vii, viii, xxvii, 7, 13–14, 20, 40, 43, 45–46, 48–51, 53–55, 57–59, 67–68, 70–71, 77, 79
Migrants, 69, 76, 78, 94, 162, 175
Milner, 14
Moltke, General von, 9, 153
Monte Carlo, 92
Moscow, 32, 37–39, 43, 85, 96, 101, 102, 117, 166, 169
Mosque of Omar, 77
Mosul, 54, 68
Mufti of Jerusalem, 61, 77, 79
Munich, 75, 123, 132–135, 156, 164, 171
Minister of Munitions, 7, 11, 29, 62, 75
Muslims, viii, 16, 25, 41, 56, 67, 69, 72, 77, 79, 100
Muslim warlords, 14
Mussolini, xviii, 107–109, 123, 133–136, 166–167

N

Napoleon, xi, 9
National debt, 124, 159
Nationalism, 25, 71, 77, 104, 166
Nationalists, viii, ix, 42– 43, 59
National Socialists, 123
Naval Intelligence, xx
Nazi\s, vii, ix, xxiii, 16, 77, 123, 135, 154–155
Nebi Musa Riots, 61, 78
Nelson, xix
New wealth, 121, 130
Nietzsche, 155–156
Nineteen Eighty-four, ix
North Sea, xx, xxi, xxii

O

October Revolution, 23–24, 94, 138
Okhrana, xx, 24, 28
Origin of Species, The, xxv, 97
Orlando, Premier, 85
Orwell, George, ix, 153

Ottoman Empire, 40, 43–44, 53, 57–58, 68, 137
Out of office, vii, xxvii, 11, 29, 72, 92

P

Palestine, 8, 40–41, 43, 45–47, 52–55, 57–58, 60–62, 68–71, 76–80
Palestinian Arabs, 77
Parliament, vii, xii, xvii, xviii, xxvii, 24, 29–30, 35, 53, 56–57, 74–75, 77, 89, 91–92, 100, 106–107, 109, 116, 130, 136, 141, 149, 151–153, 158, 165
Paris Peace Conference, 19–21, 40, 47, 59, 61, 68, 78
Pasewalk Hospital, 155
Pensions, 121, 130, 149, 165
Pension schemes, 130–131
Pershing, General John, xxiii, 10, 19
Petrashevsky Circle, 32
Petrograd, (St, Petersburg), xx, 32, 37–39, 41
Philby, St. John, 51, 180
Pilsudski, General, 21
Plato, xiv, xxv, 97, 156
Poincaré, 7, 122
Poison gas, 9, 16
Post Traumatic Stress Disorder, 17
PTSD, 17
Protectionism, 90
Prussians, xix, 133, 152, 164, 171–174
Putsch, 123, 135, 152

Q

Queen Victoria, xi, xvii, 74, 167

R

Rank, Otto, ix, 176
Rathenau, Walter, 103, 172–174
Red Army, viii, 19, 21, 28, 36–39, 41, 44, 67, 73–74, 85, 87, 138
Red Scare, 116, 152
Reade, Winwood, xxv, 78, 97, 114, 156, 182

Reich, Wilhelm, 17
Reilly, Sidney, 20–21, 25, 37–38, 92
Reparations, 9, 11, 13, 19–20, 40, 102–103, 122, 141, 168, 174
Revolution, vii, xvii, xvii, xxi, xxiv, xxvii, 8, 11, 15, 17, 19–22, 23–28, 31–32, 35, 41–44, 60, 67, 70, 84–85, 87, 92–95, 98, 101, 107–108, 111–113, 134, 136, 138, 141, 146, 150, 154, 166, 170, 173
Rif, 136, 140, 147
Rivera, Primo, 136, 140, 147
Riviera, 144
Roman Empire, xiv, xviii, 69–70, 106, 161
Roman virtues, xxv
Ruhr, The, 11, 122, 135
Russell, Betrand, 112
Russian Orthodox Church, 31
Russian Revolution, xxiv, xxvii, 21, 44, 95
Russo-Japanese War, 24
Rusta, Ibn, 18

S

Salandra, 108
Salonji, 85
Samuel, Sir Herbert, 52, 61, 79,
Sartre, Jean-Paul, 115
Saud, Ibn, viii, 50–51, 59–60, 67–68, 79
Saudi Arabia, viii, 59, 68, 79, 97
Savinkov, Boris, 21
Savrola, xvi, 64–65
Scapegoats, 8, 10, 12
Schopenhauer, xxv, 97
Scotland Yard, ix, 52, 63, 120
Second World War, x, xii, xvi, xxiii, 19–20, 79, 127, 153
Secret Intelligence Service, viii, xx, 19, 50, 66–67, 127
Secretary of State for War, xxvii, 8, 13, 29, 32, 40, 46–4, 75
Serbia, 7–9, 13, 15–16, 122

INDEX

Seven Pillars of Wisdom, The, 64
Shaw, Bernard, 110, 112
Shia, (Shi'ah), 54, 67,
Shockburgh, 50, 55
Schlieffen Plan, 9, 133
Shell-shock, 16, 155
Show trials, 102
Siberia, 28, 33, 37–38, 84–86, 102
Sinclair, Archibald, 53
Sinn Fein, 44, 80, 87–88
Slave labour, 28, 102, 153, 164
Slavs, 16, 175
Smith, Adam, xxv, 97
Social Darwinism, xxv,
Socialism, xxvi, 90, 92–93, 110–115, 121, 139
Soil policy, 164
Soviet Russia, vii, viii, xviii, 26, 43–44, 71, 77–78, 86, 94, 97, 101–102, 110–111, 114, 116–117, 129, 136, 138, 140, 153, 160, 164, 167–169
Solzhenitsyn, 26
Spanish flu, 22
Speakeasies, 125–126
Spanish Morocco, 136, 140, 167
Spring of Nations, 23
Spymaster, 51
Stalin, xviii, 26, 28, 41, 86, 101–102, 111–112, 138–140, 165–166, 169
Statue of Liberty, 23
Stresemann, Chancellor, 123, 151
Submarine warfare, xxi, 41, 84, 120
Suez Canal, 46
Sunni, 54, 60, 67–68, 79
Superman, 155
Sykes, Mark, 56, 58
Sykes–Picot Agreement, 47, 56, 58, 71
Syria, 8, 23, 40, 45, 47–48, 50, 55–61, 64, 67–72, 77

T
Teutonic, 16, 19, 172, 175
Thompson, Walter, 52, 79, 88, 93
Totalitarian regimes, xxiv, xxvii

Trade Union Congress, 145–146
Transjordan, viii, 53–55, 59, 70, 72, 76, 78
Treasury, xix, 19, 80, 120, 140, 145–146, 159, 170
Treaty of Versailles, 12, 19–20, 74, 122, 151, 154, 174
Trotsky, viii, xxiv, 19, 21, 28, 37–39, 41–44, 93, 138–139, 166
The Tsar, 15, 19, 24–25, 27–28, 31–32, 35, 42, 87, 101, 112
Tuchman, Barbara W., xxiv, 177
Tudor, General, 87, 88
Turgenev, 32
Turkey, 2, 13, 51, 75, 100, 122, 138
Turkish Empire, viii, 15, 41, 45, 71, 78

U
U–boats, 7
Ukraine, 31, 37, 38, 73, 87
Ukrainian regiments, 37
Undersecretary for the Colonies, xvi, 29
Utopian, 112

V
Versailles Treaty, 12, 19–20, 74, 122, 151, 154, 174
Victoria, Queen, xi, xvii, 74, 167
Vienna, 17–18, 171, 175
Viennese, 17–18

W
Wahhabi sect, 60, 67, 79
War Cabinet, xxiii, 13, 38
War debts, 122, 142
Warlords, v, 14, 21, 27, 136, 169
War reparations, 9, 19, 40, 102–103, 174
War, Secretary for, vii, viii
Wellington, Duke of, xi
White Russian Army, 31, 84
White Russians, 21
Wilson, Admiral Sir Arthur, xxi
Wilson, Sir Henry, 29, 44, 74, 86, 88, 93, 98

195

Wilson, President Woodrow, 11–13
Wealth of Nations, The, xxv, 97
Wedgwood, Josiah, 159
Weimar Republic, 8, 71, 103, 122, 151–154, 163–164, 171–173, 175
Wells, H. G., 106, 112, 115, 153
Western Front, xxiii, 7, 10–11, 16, 22, 29, 35, 49, 62, 75, 80
World Crisis, The, vii, viii, xvi, xvii, xviii, xxvii, 15, 20, 22, 84, 92, 101
World Government, 106
World security, 106
World War 1, vi, xi, xii, xvii, xxiv, 7, 19, 22, 28–29, 62, 92, 101, 125, 127, 133, 140, 171
World War 2, vi, x, xii, xvi, xxiii, xxiv, 19–20, 79, 127, 153, 175
Wrangel, General, 39, 87

Y

Yudenich, General, 37–39,

Z

Zinoviev, 28, 139, 166
Zinoviev Letter, 92, 117
Zionism, 34, 40–41, 43, 69, 77
Zionist, 34, 40–41, 50, 54, 57, 60–61, 69–71, 76–77, 79, 105
Zola, Emile, 12